Discola's fabulously rich and compellin
forgiving the unforgiveable: the murder o
beyond speculation based on normative
and emotional transformations of those who have lived through this trauma.
Drawing on symbolic interactionist theories, she meticulously unwinds the
strands of affect, identity, language, and group interactions to describe the process
of how people arrive at forgiveness—or not. Combining exceptionally readable
text and the deeply interesting personal stories of those mourning a homicide
loss, this book would make an excellent contribution to any course on social
psychology, emotions, victimology, qualitative methods, or other related courses.

Dr. Linda Francis
Associate Professor and Interim Chair
Department of Criminology, Anthropology, and Sociology
Cleveland State University

This book uncovers important discoveries about the realities that people who
have lost loved ones to homicide face after their lives are touched by tragedy.
With these findings, we will be better able to serve those who have suffered in
this way. Discola's insights initiate a truly open, non-judgmental conversation
that is needed in our community. Having personally experienced the loss of a
loved one to murder, I can speak to the need for such work from a unique, first-
hand perspective. I can also speak as an advocate and confidant of many other
individuals who have lost loved ones to murder. It is important that people be
heard in "their language" and that we seek to understand as fully as possible the
experiences of different people. This book allows us to do just that.

Marie Verzulli
Founder of Family & Friends of Homicide Victims; victim advocate

Discola does an incredible job taking something as complex as forgiveness and
making comprehension effortless. Students will not want to put this book down,
and it will leave them with a completely different outlook on what it means to
forgive.

A great insight into the process to forgiving the unforgivable. Through
extensive interviews with those who have lost loved ones to homicide, Discola
initiates the conversation about different paths to forgiveness while sharing
stories that deserve to be heard.

Andrea Awi
Graduate student, Department of Sociology
California State University, Los Angeles

A definite must-read for anyone who has lost a loved one to homicide. Discola
provides an eye-opening and stimulating view of how some people are able to
forgive even under the most unlikely of circumstances. Throughout the book, she
builds on each story, creating a refreshing opportunity for self-reflection. The more
I read, the more I felt that personal growth is possible. To me, the book held hope.

Claudia Guerrero, co-victim

Redefining Murder, Transforming Emotion

Offering insights based on years of original research, *Redefining Murder, Transforming Emotion: An Exploration of Forgiveness after Loss Due to Homicide* investigates the ideas and experiences of individuals who have lost loved ones to homicide (co-victims) in order to advance our understanding of the emotional transformation of forgiveness. It stands at the crux of two vibrant, growing fields: criminal victimology and the sociology of emotion. Analysis of 36 intensive interviews with co-victims and three years of participant observation of self-help groups and other victim-centered events offer a multidimensional understanding of forgiveness.

Specifically, this book answers the questions of "What?," "When?," "How?," and "Why?" forgiveness occurs by exploring co-victims' ideas about forgiveness, the differential experiences of various groups of people, the processes through which forgiveness occurs in a variety of extreme circumstances of homicide, and co-victims' motivations toward forgiveness. The book concludes with commentary on overarching conclusions based on this work; theoretical and practical implications; suggestions for directions for future inquiry; and an in-depth account of the methodological strategies employed to gather such rich and nuanced data.

This book will appeal to academics and students alike, within relevant fields, including sociology, criminology, restorative justice, victim services, psychology, and social welfare, as well as individuals seeking a better understanding of their own experiences, including co-victims or others whose lives have been altered by extreme forms of violence and upheaval. Its detailed postscript will also serve well those interested in qualitative methodology in social science research.

Kristen Lee Discola (formerly Hourigan) received her Ph.D. in Sociology from the State University of New York at Albany in 2017, and is now an Assistant Professor of Sociology at California State University, Los Angeles. Her areas of specialization are social psychology, with a focus on emotion and identity, and crime and deviance, with a focus on victimization and trauma. Demonstrating a profound commitment to scholarship and professional growth, Discola has won a number of awards for her in-depth, qualitative work investigating individuals' experiences following tragic loss, including the inaugural Siegel Graduate Fellowship for Victimology Studies through the American Society of Criminology, Division of Victimology; the Liska Dissertation Research Award; the Paul Meadows Award for Excellence in Research; and the Distinguished Doctoral Dissertation Award, from the State University of New York at Albany.

Routledge Studies in Crime and Society

Legalizing Cannabis
Experiences, Lessons and Scenarios
Edited by Tom Decorte, Simon Lenton and Chris Wilkins

Female Capital Punishment
From the Gallows to Unofficial Abolition in Connecticut

Risk and Harm in Youth Sexting
Young People's Perspectives
Emily Setty

Gendered Responses to Male Offending in Barbados
Patriarchal Perceptions and Their Effect on Offender Treatment
Corin Bailey

Crime and Fear in Public Places
Towards Safe, Inclusive and Sustainable Cities
Edited by Mahesh K Nalla and Vania Ceccato

Preventing Sexual Harm
Positive Criminology and Sexual Abuse
Stephanie Kewley, Sarah Pemberton and Mohammed Rahman

Female Capital Punishment
From the Gallows to Unofficial Abolition in Connecticut
Lawrence Goodheart

Redefining Murder, Transforming Emotion
An Exploration of Forgiveness after Loss Due to Homicide
Kristen Lee Discola

For more information about this series, please visit:
www.routledge.com/Routledge-Studies-in-Crime-and-Society/book-series/RSCS

Redefining Murder, Transforming Emotion

An Exploration of Forgiveness after Loss Due to Homicide

Kristen Lee Discola

Routledge
Taylor & Francis Group

NEW YORK AND LONDON

First published 2021
by Routledge
52 Vanderbilt Avenue, New York, NY 10017

and by Routledge
2 Park Square, Milton Park, Abingdon, Oxon OX14 4RN

Routledge is an imprint of the Taylor & Francis Group, an informa business

Library of Congress Cataloging-in-Publication Data
Names: Discola, Kristen Lee, author.
Title: Redefining murder, transforming emotion : an exploration of
forgiveness after loss due to homicide / Kristen Lee Discola.
Description: New York, NY : Routledge, 2021. |
Series: Routledge studies in crime and society |
Includes bibliographical references and index.
Identifiers: LCCN 2020028422 (print) | LCCN 2020028423 (ebook) |
ISBN 9781138061279 (hardback) | ISBN 9781315158372 (ebook)
Subjects: LCSH: Forgiveness. | Murder victims'
families–Psychology. | Restorative justice.
Classification: LCC BF637.F67 D57 2021 (print) |
LCC BF637.F67 (ebook) | DDC 362.88/2–dc23
LC record available at https://lccn.loc.gov/2020028422
LC ebook record available at https://lccn.loc.gov/2020028423

ISBN: 978-1-138-06127-9 (hbk)
ISBN: 978-1-315-15837-2 (ebk)

Typeset in Bembo
by Newgen Publishing UK

This book is dedicated to the 36 individuals who bared their souls for this project, sharing their stories, ideas, and emotions to make this work possible. I am forever grateful to each of you for your openness and candor. That which you have shared has humbled me, strengthened me, and driven me to create something meaningful out of tragedy.

Contents

List of Figures   xii
List of Tables   xiii
Acknowledgments   xiv

1   Introduction to the Research, Context, and Content
    of this Book   1
    Why Focus on Homicide? 4
    Taking a Sociological Approach 5
    Methodological Overview 7
    Research Context 8
    Participant Demographics 10
    Conceptualization of Forgiveness 13
    Avoiding Value Judgments 15
    Organization of this Book 16
    Questions for Further Discussion 17

2   Narrating Lived Experiences of Forgiveness and
    Unforgiveness   23
    Background 25
    Experiences of Unforgiveness 25
    Experiences of Forgiveness 28
    Experiences of Benevolent Forgiveness 31
    Concluding Remarks 34
    Questions for Further Discussion 34

3   Forgiveness Factors Salient within Narratives of
    Lived Experience   37
    Background 38
    Forgiveness Factors Raised during Direct Questioning 39
    Contradiction between Feeling Rules and Lived Experience 42

Forgiveness Factors within Narratives 44
Concluding Remarks 51
Questions for Further Discussion 53

4   *"I could've been the one in jail for murder"*: How Experiential
    Empathy Fosters Forgiveness in Cases of Close Cultural
    Proximity between Forgiver and Forgiven   56
    Background 58
    Conceptualization of Terms 58
    The Process of Forgiveness in Cases of Close Cultural Proximity:
       Experiential Empathy 60
    Concluding Remarks 72
    Questions for Further Discussion 72

5   *"We are all victims of victims"*: How Speculative Empathy
    Fosters Forgiveness in Cases of Distant Cultural Proximity
    between Forgiver and Forgiven   76
    Background 78
    The Process of Forgiveness in Cases of Distant Cultural
       Proximity: Speculative Empathy 80
    Lack of Empathy, Lack of Forgiveness 90
    Concluding Remarks 93
    Questions for Further Discussion 97

6   Constructing Victim, Survivor, and Transcender Identities   103
    Background 105
    Co-Victim Identities: Victim, Survivor, and Transcender 111
    Victim, Survivor, and Transcender as Person Identities 113
    Victim, Survivor, and Transcender as Role Identities 120
    Victim, Survivor, and Transcender as Social Identities 124
    Concluding Remarks 132
    Questions for Further Discussion 135

7   Unraveling Causal Order   140
    Omarr's Transition from Victim to Transcender 142
    Lauren's Transition from Victim to Survivor 145
    Exploring Causation 148
    Concluding Remarks 169
    Questions for Further Discussion 172

8   Conclusions and Future Directions   174
    Summary of Main Conclusions and Avenues for Future Work 174
    Final Thoughts 181

Postscript: Detailed Methodology   184
Positionality 184
Research Questions 194
Conceptualizing and Designating Terms 195
Methods 200
Ethics in Research with Human Subjects 216
Developing the Project 219
Limitations of Design 220
Strengths of Design 222
Questions for Further Discussion 228

Appendix: Changing the Causal Direction   232
Index   233

Figures

4.1 Forgiveness through experiential empathy (particularistic
     role-taking)   61
5.1 Forgiveness through speculative empathy
     (abstract role-taking)   81
5.2 Forgiveness through experiential and speculative empathy
     (particularistic and abstract role-taking)   89

Tables

1.1	Descriptive Statistics of Participants	11
2.1	Forgiveness Categorization	25
3.1	Forgiveness-Fostering and Forgiveness-Impeding Factors	40
6.1	Co-Victim Identity Typology	105
7.1	Co-Victim Identities by the Passage of Time since the Loss	149
7.2	Group Participation by Co-Victim Identities	152
7.3	Co-Victim Identities by Level of Education	162
7.4	Co-Victim Identities by Age	163
7.5	Co-Victim Identities by Gender	164
7.6	Co-Victim Identities by Religion	166
7.7	Co-Victim Identities by Social Class	167
7.8	Co-Victim Identities by Race	168
A	Co-Victim Identities by Group Participation	232

Acknowledgments

I would like to express my deepest gratitude to the incredible folks (who must remain nameless) in the various co-victim groups who embraced me as one of their own, offering me friendship, mutual trust, and authenticity.

A heartfelt thank you extends to several colleagues for the time and energy they dedicated to helping me develop the project that fueled this book: Dennis McCarty, for fostering the first relationships that blossomed into the networks that gave this research life and for reminding me to remain focused upon my goals and priorities; Joanne Kaufman, who sifted through innumerable versions of early phases of this project, offering critique as it unfolded and transformed over the years; Joanna Dreby, whose suggestions and praise motivated me to develop this work into a complex yet accessible product; Jamie Fader, whose insights and attention to detail have unquestionably made me into a more polished author; David Wagner, who established high expectations when we first met and encouraged me to not only meet those expectations but to exceed them; Ryan King, for asking the difficult questions and pushing me to aim higher; and Sujatha Baliga, for inspiration at the Capital Region Restorative Justice Conference and for proposing the word "transcender" to best signify the experience of those who have risen above extreme violence to foster understanding and create peace both internally and within the larger world.

When this book first came to fruition, several people stepped up to share their opinions and insights as I made revisions. Most notably, Linda Francis gave selflessly of her time and energy as she offered invaluable suggestions, emboldening me to dive deeper and expand upon theoretical insights. Lois Presser both inspired and encouraged me, paving my entrance into networks of narrative researchers whose work laid a foundation for my own. And several of my students also played a role in various stages of this book's development: Cynthia Giron, Lorraine Rodriguez, Ruth Castellanos, Claudia Guerrero, Romy Griepp, and Andrea Awi.

Special thanks go to Michael Hourigan, who believed in the value of this research and my ability to shoulder such an ambitious endeavor; Paola Ducoing, whose positive mindset, matter-of-fact approach, and calm spirit propelled me over the finish line; and my children, Cadence and Logan, who kept me present and grounded along this extended journey.

This project was supported by the Larry J. Siegel Graduate Fellowship, Division of Victimology, American Society of Criminology.

Portions and/or earlier versions of analyses presented here have been previously presented at the following conferences:

Society for the Study of Symbolic Interaction, 2019, New York, NY
American Sociological Association, 2018, Philadelphia, PA
Society for the Study of Social Problems, 2018, Philadelphia, PA
American Society of Criminology, 2017, Philadelphia, PA; 2016, New Orleans, LA; 2015, Washington, DC; 2014, San Francisco, CA; 2013, Atlanta, GA
Eastern Sociological Society, 2013, Boston, MA

and published in the following articles:
Hourigan, Kristen Lee. 2019. "'The gentleman who killed my daughter': Exploring the effects of cultural proximity on forgiveness after an extreme offense." *Journal of Ethnographic and Qualitative Research* 13:212–230.
Hourigan, Kristen Lee. 2018. "Forgiving the unforgivable: An exploration of contradictions between forgiveness-related feeling rules and lived experience of forgiveness of extreme harm." *Humanity & Society* 43(3):270–294.
Hourigan, Kristen Lee. 2016. "Homicide survivors' definitions of forgiveness: Intrapersonal, interpersonal, and extrapersonal orientations." *Violence and Victims* (31)5:869–887.

Chapter 1

Introduction to the Research, Context, and Content of this Book

Standing on the uneven sidewalk, sprinkled with broken glass, it is nearing 11 o'clock at night. Behind me is an abandoned lot, remnants of deteriorated concrete foundation visible through the overgrowth, littered with empty Keystone beer cans, wind-tattered plastic bags from the corner store, and crushed fast-food containers. Surrounded by strangers, I catch sideways glances as they take note of my pale skin and crisp-seamed slacks. These are people whose paths would likely never have crossed mine if it were not for Tanya[1] inviting me to this site, the corner where her son Malik was gunned down by a rival gang-member eight years prior. The adjacent building, with boarded front door and broken window panes, has become the backdrop for the evening, with the occasional smell of marijuana wafting out of open windows and the sounds of sirens as police rush along the bordering street and loud bass shaking the ground as cars slow in front of the ripped tent that serves as a cover for two long folding tables, passengers peering out of open windows to discern the meaning of this gathering.

This night, the anniversary of his death, also happens to be Malik's birthday, and Mother's Day. Each new arrival adheres to the unwritten expectations of the event. Tanya greets each with a long, purposeful hug, *"As-salāmu ʿalaykum."* *"Wa ʿalaykumu s-sal ān"* comes in response. It quickly becomes evident that this exchange is a part of the Islamic tradition, a customary greeting and also an expression of solidarity in this context. After appropriate displays of respect and condolence for Tanya, each arrival moves through the ever-growing crowd, hugging and talking with some, fist-bumping others, greeting a few from a more formal distance.

Soon, I note another familiar face moving through the ever-growing crowd: Sandra. Tanya greets Sandra, then leads her toward me with the intention of introducing us, in hopes that Sandra would be interested in taking part in an interview for my research. Tanya does not realize I recently met Sandra at another community event. After a few minutes of small talk,

Sandra introduces me to J. R., who would become an advocate for my research in the coming weeks, helping me to diversify my sample by setting up several interviews with local men.

Viewed by the local community as a powerful, compassionate, committed community advocate, Sandra's sponsorship further facilitates my acceptance into the community at this event. I am soon welcomed into the fold, most notably by the elder women in the space, as they insist upon my acceptance of large plates of food, homemade rice and beans, chicken wings, pasta salad, all the trappings of a backyard barbecue. In time, young girls join Tanya's youngest daughter, Aniyah, laughing and singing as they begin "stepping" along the sidewalk. With the sound of the girls' rhythmic dance, as they stomp their feet and slap their thighs in unison, and the smell of the meat sizzling on the grill, the backyard-barbecue feel of the event intensifies, and the size of the gathering swells, as people spill off the sidewalk, up the steps, and between the cars. Deion, who I had previously met and interviewed for this research, hangs a sign across the nearby stoop with the slogan of the anti-violence program of which he is a part, which sponsors this event every year by providing food and paper-goods. On two separate occasions throughout the night, Deion waves over a wandering soul, drawn near by the smell of burgers on the grill. He says to each, *"End violence, brother,"* and offers the passerby a plate of food. Later, Tanya approaches an elderly woman in threadbare garments and an overflowing pushcart, who was watching the event from a bit of a distance. Tanya asks her if she is hungry, to which the lady replies that she is. She says she had gone to the local church in search of food but the church was closed. Tanya reaches for a plate and piles it high with a large portion of every type of food lining the long folding tables. The stranger humbly takes the plate, nodding to show her gratitude, and edges toward the curbside, where she quickly consumes the offering, then shuffles off in the direction from which she emerged.

One would not have known this is a memorial for a teen, if not for the instant shift of emotional energy when the cake emerges and Tanya and her children gather in remembrance. Each child touches Tanya, putting their arms around her, gently squeezing her arm. The center of the cake is adorned with a picture of Malik, an image captured just weeks before his death, and Tanya says a short prayer in Arabic, attendees responding quietly in cadence. Tears well in Tanya's eyes, and she is encircled by all attendees, who stand facing Tanya and her children, silent, somber, reflecting on the life lost, the pain persisting. After a few moments of silence, an elder woman in the group begins cutting the cake, careful not to disturb Malik's image, at the insistence of Malik's eldest sister. Others pass out slices, and everyone eats in silence. Tanya has again become the focus of all those present, as they quietly make their exits, taking plates of food and pausing by Tanya's side to acknowledge her pain, offer their condolences, and hold her momentarily while she cries.

This "birthday" memorial was one of 96 group events and meetings I had the honor of attending and participating in as I gathered data for the project that will be explored in this book. These observations were coupled with 36 intensive interviews of individuals who have lost loved ones to homicide, including Tanya, Sandra, J. R., and Deion. The narratives these folks shared at the group events I attended and within their one-on-one interviews form the basis of the data that I will analyze here. Before each chapter unfolds, I will detail one of these observations or interviews, to give heart to the data you will be encountering and to promote a deep understanding of the context within which these stories were collected by constructing a vivid backdrop to the narratives.

This work stands at the crux of two vibrant, growing fields within sociology: emotion and criminal victimology. By investigating the ideas and experiences of individuals who have lost loved ones to homicide (co-victims), this research advances our understanding of the emotional transformation of forgiveness.[2] Analysis of intensive interviews with co-victims and over three years of participant observation of self-help groups and other victim-centered events offers rich accounts and a multidimensional understanding of forgiveness, answering the questions of "What?," "When?," "How?," and "Why?" by exploring co-victims' emotional experiences, the factors that influence forgiveness, the processes through which forgiveness occurs, and co-victims' motivations toward forgiveness.

We know a great deal about what factors people believe foster or impede forgiveness, many of which are related to the act itself or the transgressor's actions following commission of the act. However, we do not yet know how forgiveness is possible in cases in which all indicators point toward unforgiveness. For example, how can one come to release their intense, negative, other-directed emotion following a trauma that was severe, intentional, and perpetrated by an individual who lacks remorse, fails to accept responsibility, and continues to reoffend? People who have never experienced loss of a loved one to homicide often have trouble imagining themselves within such a circumstance. Could you forgive someone who took the life of your sister or son? What if the murder was unprovoked, intentional, heinous, and perpetrated by someone who expressed no remorse or regret, who continued to be violent, and who you could not identify with? Can one forgive such an act? If so, how? And, perhaps even more thought-provoking, what is the motivation behind such forgiveness? This book provides grounded empirical research to answer these questions by exploring the experiences of those who have lost loved ones in a variety of extreme circumstances of homicide.

Why Focus on Homicide?

Loss to homicide[3] is unique in several important ways, including the sudden and unexpected nature of the loss. For most, losing a loved one to homicide is unimaginable. Many who lose a loved one in this manner have never known anyone who has dealt with this type of loss, so there is a lack of normative guidance. In other words, when many people lose a loved one to violence they cannot rely on established networks of support to offer guidance as they grapple with the changes and challenges that follow their losses. Without normative standards, individuals do not know what is expected of them in terms of how to react or feel, nor do they know what they can expect from others in terms of supporting them or reacting to their experiences of this new reality.

Homicide is also unique in that it triggers events that result in a multiplicity of losses. The loss of the loved one is not the only loss that co-victims grapple with, and the effects of these losses upon one's overall state of well-being are severe, numerous, pervasive, and long-lasting.[4] Losses accompanying the violent death of a loved one may include loss of social support and financial stability as well as emotional and psychological trauma, including feelings of vulnerability, a loss of confidence in the safety and stability of one's world, post-traumatic stress, depression, and complicated grief. The psychological impact can also lead to other secondary effects, including changes to physical health, loss of employment, and deterioration of key relationships.

Though we all lose loved ones throughout our lives, these losses are typically private matters, dealt with among our closest relatives and friends. In contrast, loss to homicide is often a public spectacle. Media involvement can shift the narrative surrounding the death, as well as the life, of the individual killed. Although the current project does not investigate co-victims' experiences of media involvement, the public nature of the death and the judicial processes that follow undoubtedly affect the emotional realities of those closest to the homicide victim and therefore deserve mention here.

Based on previous research, we know a great deal about what factors influence the likelihood that an individual will forgive. These include factors related to the victim, the offender,[5] the relationship between the two, and the circumstances of the offense. Though our understanding of the factors that affect forgiveness has increased greatly in recent years, the majority of previous work places participants in hypothetical or imagined scenarios[6] or focuses upon transgressions that are relatively minor and/or non-criminal.[7] By focusing upon real-life, serious harm, this book aims to increase the breadth of our understanding of forgiveness. Homicide is, by definition, severe, deliberate, and within the offender's control. Homicide's status as one of the most severely punished criminal acts also indicates its dissension from the culture's moral code. Considering these factors, homicide should be one of the most difficult acts to forgive and therefore provides a meaningful vantage point from which to consider lived experiences of forgiveness.

In many cases, a co-victim will never know the identity of the individual who took the life of his or her loved one because the offender remains at large. In other instances, the co-victim may be aware of the offender's identity but will never be able to determine the truth about the offender's feelings or thoughts before, during, or since the crime. If an individual is charged with the murder, each stage of the criminal justice process imposes limitations upon his or her behavior. The accused may be advised by counsel not to admit guilt, or feelings of fear and shame may impede expression of blame-worthiness or remorse. Often there is no interaction between co-victim and offender or this interaction is limited to glances across a crowded courtroom during which the offender is under strict orders from his or her lawyer to remain stoic and unemotional, under no circumstances expressing remorse for the alleged crime, because such expressions would be a sign of guilt to the jurors witnessing courtroom interactions. Finally, once incarcerated, prison culture may dissuade inmates from being open and self-reflective in terms of their emotional states. For these reasons, forgiveness of a serious criminal act, such as murder, may be especially difficult, as factors such as offender acceptance of responsibility and expression of remorse may be highly unlikely. These factors make exploration of forgiveness after homicide particularly valuable, as such cases are inherently unlikely to result in forgiveness due to several factors shown in previous research to impede forgiveness (i.e., severe offense, intentionality, lack of expressed remorse, or acceptance of responsibility).

For the reasons outlined here, loss to homicide provides a powerful vantage point from which to study forgiveness. Forgiveness after offenses of this magnitude has not yet been investigated thoroughly[8] and offers the opportunity to increase our understanding of all types of forgiveness (as well as unforgiveness). The effects of homicide are most commonly studied from a psychological or criminal justice perspective,[9] which leaves key questions unanswered and important processes not fully understood. This book will explore the processes that lead to the most extreme forms of forgiveness from a sociological standpoint, so that we may come to better appreciate the nuances of forgiveness at all levels and the complexity of the array of factors affecting the likelihood of forgiveness as well as its consequences.

Taking a Sociological Approach

Since the likelihood of forgiveness relates to several inherently social factors, a sociological approach is well suited to investigate the process of such emotional transformation. Therefore, this project takes a symbolic interactionist perspective as its foundation. With a social psychological focus within sociology, symbolic interactionism focuses on the causes and consequences of the meaning-making processes that result from social interactions throughout the lifetime.[10] According to symbolic interactionists, people learn from others how to perceive, interpret, and evaluate reality, and the meaning they assign to each aspect of their social environment is determined by this prior learning. Action is seen as directed by the socially constructed meaning an individual assigns to objects in his or her environment (including events, symbols, emotions,[11] other people or groups, and the actions of self and others). Social action then involves making a series of adjustments and readjustments as one's interpretation and evaluation of a situation, their "definition of the situation," change. Social order is a product of ongoing social interaction and the shared meanings and behavioral expectations that emerge from that interaction.[12] Within society, individuals occupy various positions (or roles), and each position is associated with a set of expected behaviors and attitudes.[13] Taking this perspective while investigating co-victims' experiences allows us to consider various meaning-making processes alongside many relevant factors, including prior experience, social networks, roles, and expectations.

Within the symbolic interactionist framework, research investigating the sociology of emotion[14] is particularly useful for analyses presented here. Emotions are viewed as sociocultural constructs, developed through socialization, and emotional responses to events are seen as dependent upon culturally assigned labels and one's definition of the situation.[15] Emotion norms and feeling rules are foundational concepts that I will draw upon from within the sociology of emotion,[16] as they govern the way individuals experience and express emotion.[17]

Loss due to homicide is a non-normative[18] life event, meaning that it is a significant, unexpected event that lacks social structuring. Therefore, emotion norms have not been crystallized for the role of co-victim. Though we may expect individuals to initially feel emotions such as shock, anger, and sadness after loss to homicide, as time passes the emotions related to such loss are not governed by firmly established norms and feeling rules.[19] Most people have never experienced the loss of a loved one to homicide and do not have co-victims within their personal social circles from whom to learn such norms. The media portrays co-victims who are both vengeful and forgiving, both filled with hatred and with compassion, so both ends of the emotional spectrum are represented as appropriate responses to such loss. Since there are no widely accepted norms for the other-directed emotions associated with loss due to homicide, dominant ideologies surrounding forgiveness do not account for such non-normative types of harm. We do not yet understand what happens in the absence of normative guidance in regard to forgiveness in such cases. This book begins the process of developing this understanding.

Thirty years ago, Peggy Thoits[20] called for intensive interviews with samples of individuals going through non-normative life transitions, including the bereaved. The current study rises to this challenge, utilizing a symbolic interactionist perspective to explore the way individuals create (or re-create) meaning around their experiences and emotions. Specifically, it investigates how individuals who have lost loved ones to homicide understand and experience forgiveness, and how this varies by cultural distance from the offender. Particular attention is paid to the connection between emotion and identity as well as the way in which one's definition of the situation elicits an emotional response and how a shift in one's definition of the situation will in turn transform one's emotional reaction to the event.

Methodological Overview

The methods employed in this study include 36 semi-structured interviews of co-victims and participant observation of victim-centered events and meetings. Over the course of more than three years, I attended monthly meetings of three co-victim self-help groups; local charity events and fundraisers surrounding issues of victimization or loss; private and public memorials; advocacy and community outreach events; and holiday and celebratory family gatherings. I focus upon the stories, or narratives, individuals construct and communicate both within interviews and when interacting with others, including loved ones, neighbors, fellow co-victims, imprisoned offenders, at-risk youth, policy-makers, and advocates. It is through the construction and delivery of stories that people make sense of their experiences, including their own identities and the identities of those with whom they come into contact.[21] Therefore, by gathering and reflecting upon co-victims' stories, I hoped to glimpse the meaning-making processes that occur in the aftermath of homicide.

With the goal of exploring narrative, my interview script had less structure than is typically used in qualitative interviews, so that respondents were given greater control.[22] I opened interviews by saying, "*I'd like to start by asking you to tell me your story.*" This allowed respondents to construct their stories in ways they found meaningful. The interview usually then took on a conversational tone, peppered with probe questions I used to elicit further detail or clarification (for example, I often asked, "*Can you tell me more about that?*" or "*What was that experience like for you?*"). Many of the topics I was interested in studying arose organically, and those that did not arise were asked about specifically (the full interview script is included in the postscript of this book).

During co-victim meetings and events, participants also engaged in story-telling, or "narrativization." The process of storytelling can be viewed as a sort of performance[23] and, as such, during the telling of the story the speaker is essentially attempting to convince the listener, who was absent at the original event, of their interpretation of that event. Therefore we can use one's stories to learn not only about individuals' experiences but also about how each understands and gives meaning to those experiences, especially in cases of trauma or struggle.[24] Therefore, rather than looking to the narrative to understand the truth of what happened in an objective sense, by investigating the story itself we seek to uncover the meaning-making processes underneath and behind the story, its creation, and its delivery. Exploring narrative is particularly useful when investigating victimization, as stories of personal violation or harm have an inherent moral quality about them and the victimization event itself often becomes a defining historical event within the individual's life narrative.[25]

Combining intensive interviews and prolonged participant observa-tion in several contexts allowed for a focus upon intense emotion within naturally occurring social settings. In 2005, Jonathan Turner and Jan Stets noted the limitations generated by the methodological choices of the vast majority of research on the sociology of emotions. They called for more focused attention on intense emotions, often overlooked by experimental researchers and those who investigate the recollections of undergraduate students. They point out that these studies have focused on only one end of the emotional spectrum and suggest use of observational methods in order to gather data based on people in their natural settings. They note that studies of this sort would "help open up our theories to include emotions of a more intense kind" and that "[r]elatively few studies in social psychology actu-ally study the naturally occurring social contexts within which emotions arise."[26] Mine is a study of these more intense emotions and includes obser-vation of participants' natural social contexts, including those where strong emotions are often felt most intensely as individuals share their stories, help one another cope, and encounter emotional triggers related to the loss and the resultant trauma.

Research Context

This research was conducted in two counties in the northeastern region of the United States. These counties include cities with impoverished areas with relatively high rates of violence and gang activity as compared to the smaller towns in the area. The victim-centered events I observed and participated in took place in these cities, at times occurring at the loca-tion of recent shootings or the site where a life being honored was lost, as in the observation described at the start of this book. Observation at this type of event supplemented my interview data by helping me to understand the social context of the murder and the social support that followed, allowing me to witness such support as it occurred as well as the narration of participants' stories with an array of audiences.

The majority of data collected through participant observation comes from my attendance of monthly meetings of two local self-help groups. The first group I began attending in 2011. This group, Loved Ones Left Behind[27] (LOLB), was founded by Diane (an interviewee who you will get to know well throughout this book) as an alternative form of support for co-victims. After losing her sister to murder, Diane had become dissatisfied with her experiences in local self-help groups due to a narrow focus upon supporting parents of homicide victims. She said:

> I know that that's not [the group's] intent, but it always feels like when you're a sibling [you] kind of pick up the pieces, and it's not about you. What you're going through is not as important, and you don't have groups that are really addressing that sibling stuff. And even though [the group] is not only for parents but for any relationship, at the end of a meeting or even during the course of a meeting, you'll feel substandard. And I know it's not the intent, but it's just the way it is, you know? Like, you have parents saying "there's no greater loss than the loss of a child," but they don't understand that [as a sibling] you've lost [your sibling and also] a part of your parent. And everybody is concerned about [your parent], which I'm not saying they shouldn't be, but you kind of get lost, or you can kind of put all your stuff aside and go into this other role of caretaker [for your parent] … [You are not] able to express your feelings without having to worry and guard [your parent], because you don't want to cause further harm.

Diane therefore established a new group, founded upon an openness that allowed a wider variety of co-victims to join together in mutual support. These meetings were very informal and surprisingly upbeat. Most were attended only by regular members and myself, and involved lively discussions of recent news in each participant's life. Conversation focused upon loss to homicide only when a new attendee was present or when a regular member was struggling with a relevant issue, such as an upcoming victim–offender conference or a looming holiday. I continued attending these meetings until the group disbanded in 2014 but have remained in contact with several of the regular members.

The second self-help group, which I regularly attended between 2011 and late 2014, was Homicide Bereavement Circle (HBC). This is a local chapter of a national organization focused upon supporting individuals who have lost loved ones to violence. Monthly HBC meetings are very routinized, as compared to meetings of LOLB. Each meeting began with a recitation of the mission of the organization followed by a round of introductions, during which each person in attendance recounted the story of his or her loss to homicide, often in great detail. Each meeting remained focused upon issues relevant to such loss, including discussion of upcoming memorials and other local victim-centered events. The conclusion of the meeting entailed a moment of silence and fellowship, as we joined hands in a circle, bowed our heads, and allowed the weight of the moment to be acknowledged and the lives lost honored.

The third self-help group I attended for only a few months in 2016. Fellowship after Violent Loss (FVL) is an offshoot of the national organization of HBC, set within a major metropolitan city. Despite its connection to HBC, its meetings were reminiscent of LOLB meetings: unstructured, informal, often lighthearted, and focused less on the murder that initiated each participant's affiliation with the fellowship, and more on members' current circumstances. I participated in this third group to gain a better understanding of the two groups I had spent years involved within, by way of comparison. I was especially interested in connecting to FVL in order to explore how racial and cultural diversity affects the self-help group environment. The membership of LOLB and HBC was almost exclusively white and middle or upper-middle class, despite the minority racial status and socioeconomic disadvantage of the vast majority of co-victims in the area. When I sought a better understanding of co-victims' experiences across racial categories and social classes, I was led to FVL, whose membership was diverse in terms of both race and class. Through this additional participant observation,[28] I was able to begin to untangle issues of race and class, which I will return to later in this book.

In each of these self-help groups, there is a strong sense of community. Participants regularly spoke of one another as *"family"* and reported that the bonds among the group were like no other. This was a place where these co-victims could be seen and heard in their most vulnerable states, without being judged and without fear of pushing the listener away by expressing raw emotion. For these reasons, this research context was ripe with opportunities to witness unique and valuable forms of social support as well as the relatively unfiltered expression of emotion.

Participant Demographics

The length of time that had passed since each participant had lost his or her loved one varied substantially, ranging from 4 months to 48 years (with an average of 21 years), and the sample of interview participants for this study was demographically diverse (Table 1.1) (it is important to note that the

Table 1.1 Descriptive Statistics of Participants (n = 36)

Age (average: years)	52
Gender, percentage	
Male	33
Female	67
Racial identification, percentage	
White	58
Black	28
Latino/a	14
Religious affiliation, percentage	
Christian	44
Muslim	8
Other	8
Spiritual but not religious	17
Not religious	8
Unspecified	14
Education, percentage	
High school diploma or equivalent	20
Some college, associates, or technical/trade	50
BA/BS	17
MA/MS or more	14
Victim's relationship to participant, percentage[1]	
Daughter/son	31
Cousin	22
Sibling	14
Best friend	11
Parent	8
Other	17
Circumstances of crime, percentage	
Robbery	25
Street violence (not robbery- or gang-related)	22
Intimate-partner violence	11
Serial murderer (not gang-related)	11
Gang-related	8
Other	17
Unknown	6
Participant's previous relationship to offender, percentage	
Immediate family member	6
Extended family member	11
Acquaintance	11
No previous relationship	64
Unknown/unspecified	8
Forgiveness status, percentage	
Benevolent forgiveness	56
Non-benevolent forgiveness	22
Unforgiveness	22

1 Percentages do not add to 100% because one participant lost both her spouse and son in the same incident.

demographics of the sample do not represent the population of all residents in the recruitment areas who have lost loved ones to homicide). Participants ranged from 28 to 85 years old (with an average of 52 years), 33% were male, and 42% self-identified as people of color. Religious affiliations included Islam, Judaism, Santería, Buddhism, and various forms of Christianity, with a wide range in levels of religious participation. For example, one participant was a Deacon in a Roman Catholic parish while another was a pastor. On the other end of the spectrum, one interviewee reported that he did not *"indulge in religion"* and believes that religion is *"the institutionalization of principles and belief for control purposes."* Educational levels ranged from completing General Education Development (GED) classes while in prison to holding graduate-level degrees. Occupations included state and military administrative positions, social worker, parole officer, Deacon, nurse, secretary, waitress, and hair stylist. Seven participants had spent time in prison for drug-related, gang-related, or violent crimes. Most of these individuals had been incarcerated multiple times and served lengthy sentences. Eight other participants who had never been incarcerated spoke of their upbringing in areas of concentrated disadvantage, describing neighborhoods that were *"violent," "gang-infested,"* and/or *"poverty stricken."* These individuals spoke of witnessing various forms of violence throughout their lives including drug-trafficking and gang-related activity within their families. Other participants described their upbringings as taking place in *"very safe"* and *"sheltered"* areas.

Almost a third of participants had lost a son or daughter to homicide; others had lost parents, siblings, grandparents, grandchildren, cousins, uncles, nieces/nephews, and best friends. Ten participants had lost multiple loved ones in separate incidents.[29] The majority of those lost were murdered during incidents of street violence including robberies and drug- and gang-related crimes. Many of the individuals killed were bystanders, whereas others were willingly involved in the crimes leading to their deaths. Others were killed at the hands of serial murderers, during incidents of intimate-partner violence, as an act of terror, or for reasons of revenge or jealousy. The majority of cases (64%) involved offenders with no prior relationship to the victim or participant.[30] The majority of the homicides were intraracial (67%) and perpetrated by men (only four offenders were female, two of whom committed the homicide with male counterparts). Of those killed, 70% were male and 44% were identified by interviewees as black or Latino/a.

Approximately half of the sample consisted of active, or previously active, members of self-help groups. Recruitment methods created a sample consisting of a higher proportion of people likely to engage in victim-centered networks than is likely found in the population of all co-victims. It is reasonable to believe that these individuals feel differently, and have different experiences, than those who choose not to engage in such groups.

It should also be noted that, because the project explores forgiveness specifically, the sample is skewed in terms of the proportion of participants who had forgiven. Nearly 80% of participants had forgiven the person who took the lives of their loved ones and nearly three-quarters of these forgiving individuals also felt positive motivations or goodwill toward the offender. Since potential participants knew the focus of my work, those who were unforgiving may have been much less likely to approach me or agree to be interviewed than those who had forgiven the offender. It is also possible that individuals connected me to others who shared similar attitudes toward forgiveness and held similar identities.

Conceptualization of Forgiveness

Forgiveness can be an imprecise and ambiguous term as used in general conversation. For the sake of both clarity and sensitivity, it is crucial that I clarify what I do, and do not, mean when using the term forgiveness in this book. This is especially important given the emotionally charged nature of the word for many participants. By determining a clear definition of the term forgiveness, we can build a more solid foundation for investigating the reparation of social bonds as well as inform policies and services aimed at rebuilding relationships after conflict of all types.

Forgiveness versus Unforgiveness

Given the wide-ranging definitions that exist for the concept of forgiveness,[31] it is necessary to begin this exploration with a clear, precise definition of the term. This is especially important because I do not want to risk implying that the gravity of the loss has been underestimated or the act condoned in any way. I, therefore, did not take the conceptualization of this term lightly. The definition used here was developed through a lengthy process of consideration of the experiences of individuals taking part in this research as well as previous work on the topic (I describe this process in detail in the postscript of this book).

Forgiveness is conceptualized here as:

- *Forgiveness: the release of negative, other-directed emotions that resulted from harm caused by prior actions of the other which may or may not be replaced by positive, other-directed emotion.*

As such, forgiveness is not an emotion in and of itself. Rather, forgiveness is a process, an emotional transformation in which negative, other-directed emotions are released. These emotions may include anger, hatred, bitterness, contempt, avoidance, and vengefulness. This definition of forgiveness is best thought of as a process, often occurring in stages over time. Later sections of this book detail the process of forgiveness following homicide.

While forgiveness is an emotional transformation, unforgiveness is a lack of such transformation. Therefore, unforgiveness is conceptualized here as:

- *Unforgiveness: the persistence of negative, other-directed emotions that resulted from harm caused by prior actions of the other.*

When a harmed party is unforgiving, feelings such as rage and bitterness endure. Such individuals may also continue to act upon these emotions, seeking vengeance or avoiding contact with the offender.

Benevolent versus Non-Benevolent Forgiveness

Though all individuals who have suffered harm at the hands of another could be categorized into two groups, those who are forgiving and those who are unforgiving, there is another meaningful distinction that needs to be explained. This is the difference between forgiveness that is, and is not, benevolent. With the terms "benevolent forgiveness" and "non-benevolent forgiveness," I mean to differentiate between forgiveness that does, and does not, include the emergence or reestablishment of positive, other-directed emotions.

Benevolent comes from the Latin *bene*, meaning "well," and *volent* from the verb "to wish." Therefore benevolent means "to wish well," and benevolent forgiveness is a release of negative emotion accompanied by a sense of goodwill or kindly feelings toward the other. In other words, an individual who demonstrates benevolent forgiveness not only wishes the offender no harm, he or she also wishes the offender well. In the wake of harm, such an individual may experience feelings of caring, generosity, and sympathy toward the offender and his or her circumstances. If a prior relationship existed between the harmed party and the offender, there may be a reestablishment of positive sentiments once present within that relationship, such as friendship, trust, respect, pride, gratefulness, or love. Therefore, benevolent forgiveness is conceptualized here as:

- *Benevolent forgiveness: the release of negative, other-directed emotions that resulted from harm caused by prior actions of the other which are replaced by positive, other-directed emotion.*

This type of forgiveness may be accompanied by various helping behaviors, indicating feelings of compassion. Such compassion couples positive other-directed emotions with an awareness of, and sympathy toward, the suffering of the other and a motivation to alleviate that suffering.

When such positive emotions do not accompany the release of negative emotion, forgiveness is non-benevolent. Therefore, non-benevolent forgiveness is conceptualized as:

- *Non-benevolent forgiveness: the release of negative, other-directed emotions that resulted from harm caused by prior actions of the other which are not replaced by positive, other-directed emotion.*

The distinction between forgiveness that is and is not benevolent is an important one, because it has clear implications in the wake of extreme harm. Often, co-victims of homicide desire the positive, internal effects that they believe will come from forgiveness, or they are told by family, friends, counselors, or spiritual leaders that they would benefit from forgiving the offender or that forgiveness is necessary for their own healing. But for many, the generation of positive emotion toward the offender is unimaginable. Their anger and bitterness are too intense to imagine feeling sympathetic, caring, or loving toward the offender. If such positive emotions were required for forgiveness, these individuals may not perceive forgiveness as a realistic possibility, nor as desirable. Some, including participants in this project, may even feel that fostering positive emotions toward the offender is a betrayal of the loved one lost. In such cases, distinguishing between non-benevolent forgiveness, as a release of negative emotion, and benevolent forgiveness, as a release of negative emotion *and* establishment or reestablishment of positive emotion, may allow co-victims a restored sense of control and hope for emotional healing. Co-victims can therefore benefit from the advantages they may attach to forgiveness without feeling that they must reconcile with the offender or extend positive sentiments.

Avoiding Value Judgments

A final caveat is necessary as we unpack the various forgiveness definitions used in this book, and that relates to the need to avoid value judgments surrounding forgiveness, both benevolent and non-benevolent, and unforgiveness. There are co-victims, researchers, support networks, religious communities, counselors, and, undoubtedly, readers, who may feel that forgiveness is in some way better, more virtuous, or healthier than unforgiveness and that benevolent forgiveness, in turn, is better, more virtuous, or healthier than non-benevolent forgiveness. As a social scientist, symbolic interactionist, and friend of the participants who selflessly shared their experiences, narratives, and perspectives for this project, I cannot

support such a stance. This is not to say that forgiveness, and benevolent forgiveness in particular, cannot be positive, virtuous, and healing for all parties
involved or for those who stand at a distance but are nonetheless impacted
by the forgiveness taking place. Aspects of this work certainly stand as a testament to the benefits that can arise from such emotional transformation. But
it is necessary that I am clear in the lack of value judgments I attach to these
processes. Through this research I have met co-victims whose forgiveness is
non-benevolent as well as co-victims who remain unforgiving decades after
the murder of their loved ones. I do not want to imply that these individuals'
experiences are worse, less virtuous, or less healthy than those participants
who shared stories of benevolent forgiveness. Such investigations shall be left
to other researchers. Instead, within these pages, I hope to explicitly demonstrate and explain the processes involved in forgiveness and unforgiveness,
without judgment. I hope that such a candid, value-free approach will spark
conversations and inspire open communication across difference.

Organization of this Book

In Chapter 1, the reader is introduced to the content of the book. I discuss the research context and highlight the methods used in the research
that supports the findings put forth in these pages, justify the scope and
direction of the research, conceptualize the main terms, and outline the
objectives of each chapter. Chapter 2 then introduces the reader to several of the participants of this project, describing participants' experiences
of unforgiveness, benevolent forgiveness, and non-benevolent forgiveness.
Using co-victims' narratives, Chapter 3 demonstrates what factors make
forgiveness more or less likely to occur after homicide and examines the
ways in which co-victims navigate and make sense of contradictions in
order to forgive the unforgivable. This prepares the reader for a more theoretical analysis of the process of forgiveness, presented in Chapters 4 and
5. Chapter 4 focuses upon the ways in which experiential empathy fosters
forgiveness in cases of close cultural proximity between forgiver and forgiven. It demonstrates and explains the processes involved in generating
understanding through role-taking in groups and how such understanding
fosters forgiveness through redefinition of the situation. Chapter 5 engages
cases of distant cultural proximity, demonstrating and explaining speculative
empathy and the affect control processes involved in generating forgiveness in cases in which there is great cultural distance between forgiver and
forgiven. Chapters 6 and 7 pull identity into the discussion, answering the
question of why some co-victims forgive and others do not. In Chapter 6,
I introduce, describe, and differentiate between three co-victim identities
and explain how they connect to forgiveness. Chapter 7 explores the passage

of time, interaction within co-victim networks, and social position as potentially influential in the development of co-victim identities, ultimately unraveling issues of causality. The book culminates with overarching conclusions; theoretical and practical implications; and suggestions for future research (in Chapter 8) followed by a postscript detailing the methodological strategies undertaken in this work.

Questions for Further Discussion

1 How might varying definitions of forgiveness impede open, fruitful conversation across difference?
2 Do benevolent forgiveness, non-benevolent forgiveness, and unforgiveness fall along a spectrum or are they distinct processes?
3 Why might benevolent forgiveness be less likely than non-benevolent forgiveness when the harmed party and the individual who caused the harm had a close relationship prior to the offense?
4 Why might non-benevolent forgiveness be less likely than benevolent forgiveness when the harmed party and the individual who caused the harm had a close prior relationship prior to the offense?

Notes

1 Participants' names, and the names of their loved ones, have been changed to protect confidentiality.
2 Though this research is narrowly focused upon emotional transformations that take place after loss to homicide, there is a wide scholarship on homicide survivorship focused upon a range of important issues that are not addressed here. For example, see Armour, Marilyn. 2003. "Meaning making in the aftermath of homicide." *Death Studies* 27:519–540. https://doi.org/10.1080/07481180302884; Armour, Marilyn and Mark S. Umbreit. 2012. "Survivors of homicide victims: Factors that influence their well-being." *Journal of Forensic Social Work* 2(2–3):74–93. https://doi.org/10.1080/1936928X.2012.750253; Sharpe, Tanya L. 2008. "Sources of support for African-American family members of homicide victims." *Journal of Ethnic & Cultural Diversity in Social Work* 17(2):197–216. https://doi.org/10.1080/15313200801947231; Sharpe, Tanya L. 2013. "Understanding the sociocultural context of coping for African American family members of homicide victims: A conceptual model." *Trauma, Violence, & Abuse* 16(1):48–59. https://doi.org/10.1177/1524838013515760; Smith, Jocelyn R. 2015. "Unequal burdens of loss: Examining the frequency and timing of homicide deaths experienced by young Black men across the life course." *American Journal of Public Health* 105(Suppl 3):S483–S490. https://doi.org/10.2105/AJPH.2014.302535; Smith, Jocelyn R. and Desmond U. Patton. 2016. "Posttraumatic stress symptoms in context: Examining trauma responses to violent exposures and homicide death among Black males in urban

neighborhoods." *American Journal of Orthopsychiatry* 86(2):212–223. https://doi.org/10.1037/ort0000101; Zinzow, Heidi M., Alyssa A. Rheingold, Alesia O. Hawkins, Benjamin E. Saunders, and Dean G. Kilpatrick. 2009. "Losing a loved one to homicide: Prevalence and mental health correlates in a national sample of young adults." *Journal of Traumatic Stress* 22(1):20–27. https://doi.org/10.1002/jts.20377

3　In this book, the words "homicide" and "murder" are used interchangeably, despite the differences in their legal definitions. Cases were included in this sample when participants originally defined the death of their loved one as murder, even if they later came to define the act as a type of homicide that would not legally be considered murder (killing in self-defense, for example).

4　For a coherent review of the intra-personal and inter-personal effects of loss to violent death, see Currier, Joseph, Jason Holland, Rachel Coleman, and Robert Neimeyer. 2008. "Bereavement following violent death: An assault on life and meaning." pp. 177–202 in *Death, Value and Meaning series. Perspectives on Violence and Violent Death,* edited by R. G. Stevenson and G. R. Cox. Amityville, NY: Baywood Publishing.

5　Throughout this book, I use the term "offender" to indicate the individual who caused harm, regardless of whether or not the individual was arrested and convicted of an illegal act. Some parties avoid use of this term due to its negative connotation and connection to a retributive criminal justice system. With respect for this view, I use this term because it is currently widely accepted in academic research, policy, and general conversation about crime and its effects.

6　For examples, see Eaton, Judy, C. Ward Struthers, and Alexander G. Santelli. 2006. "The mediating role of perceptual validation in the repentance–forgiveness process." *Personality and Social Psychology Bulletin* 32:1389–1401. https://doi.org/10.1177/0146167206291005; Exline, Julie Juola, Roy F. Baumeister, Anne L. Zell, Amy J. Kraft, and Charlotte V. O. Witvliet. 2008. "Not so innocent: Does seeing one's own capability for wrongdoing predict forgiveness?" *Journal of Personality and Social Psychology* 94(3):495–515. https://doi.org/10.1037/0022-3514.94.3.495; Wallace, Harry M., Julia Juola Exline, and Roy F. Baumeister. 2008. "Interpersonal consequences of forgiveness: Does forgiveness deter or encourage repeat offenses?" *Journal of Experimental Social Psychology* 44(2):453–460. https://doi.org/10.1016/j.jesp.2007.02.012; Wenzel, Michael and Tyler G. Okimoto. 2010. "How acts of forgiveness restore a sense of justice: Addressing status/power and value concerns raised by transgressions." *European Journal of Social Psychology* 40:401–417. https://doi.org/10.1002/ejsp.629

7　For examples, see Bradfield, Murray and Karl Aquino. 1999. "The effects of blame attributions and offender likeableness on forgiveness and revenge in the workplace." *Journal of Management* 25:607–631. https://doi.org/10.1177/014920639902500501; Eaton, Judy, C. Ward Struthers, and Alexander G. Santelli. 2006. "The mediating role of perceptual validation in the repentance–forgiveness process." *Personality and Social Psychology Bulletin* 32:1389–1401. https://doi.org/10.1177/0146167206291005; Exline, Julie Juola, Roy F. Baumeister, Anne L. Zell, Amy J. Kraft, and Charlotte V. O. Witvliet. 2008. "Not so innocent: Does seeing one's own capability for wrongdoing predict forgiveness?" *Journal of Personality and Social Psychology* 94(3):495–515. https://doi.org/10.1037/0022-3514.94.3.495; McCullough, Michael E., Frank D. Fincham, and Jo-Ann Tsang. 2003. "Forgiveness, forbearance, and time: The temporal unfolding of transgression-related interpersonal motivations." *Journal of Personality and Social Psychology* 84:540–557. https://doi.org/10.1037/0022-3514.84.3.540; Struthers, C. Ward, Judy Eaton, Alexander G. Santelli, Melissa Uchiyama, and Nicole Shirvani. 2008. "The effects of attributions of intent and apology on forgiveness: When saying sorry may not help the story." *Journal of Experimental Social Psychology* 44(4):983–992. https://doi.org/10.1016/j.jesp.2008.02.006; Struthers, C. Ward, Judy Eaton, Rachelle Mendoza, Alexander G. Santelli, and Nicole Shirvani. 2010. "Interrelationship among injured parties' attributions of responsibility, appraisal of appropriateness to forgive the transgressor, forgiveness, and repentance." *Journal of Applied Social Psychology* 40(4):970–1002. https://doi.org/10.1111/j.1559-1816.2010.00607.x; Wallace, Harry M., Julia Juola Exline, and Roy F. Baumeister. 2008. "Interpersonal consequences of forgiveness: Does forgiveness deter or encourage repeat offenses?" *Journal of Experimental Social Psychology* 44(2):453–460. https://doi.org/10.1016/j.jesp.2007.02.012; Wenzel, Michael and Tyler G. Okimoto. 2010. "How acts of forgiveness restore a sense of justice: Addressing status/power and value concerns raised by transgressions." *European Journal of Social Psychology* 40:401–417. https://doi.org/10.1002/ejsp.629; Williamson, Iam, and Marti Hope Gonzales. 2007. "The subjective experience of forgiveness: Positive construals of the forgiveness experience." *Journal of Social and Clinical Psychology* 26(4):407–446. https://doi.org/10.1521/jscp.2007.26.4.407; Zechmeister, Jeanne S., and Catherine Romero. 2002. "Victim and offender accounts of interpersonal conflict: Autobiographical narratives of forgiveness and unforgiveness." *Journal of Personality and Social Psychology* 82(4):675–686. https://doi.org/10.1037//0022-3514.82.4.675

8 To the best of my knowledge, the only sociological exploration of forgiveness after homicide is focused upon the death penalty and restorative justice processes: Barrile, Leo G. 2015. "I forgive you, but you must die: Murder victim family members, the death penalty, and restorative justice." *Victims & Offenders* 10:239–269. https://doi.org/10.1080/15564886.2014.925022

9 There are several studies of the psychological effects of loss to homicide (for example, see Amick-McMullan, Angelynne, Dean G. Kilpatrick, and Heidi S. Resnick. 1991. "Homicide as a risk factor for PTSD among surviving family members." *Behavior Modification* 15:545–559. https://doi.org/10.1177/01454455910154005; Amick-McMullan, Angelynne, Dean G. Kilpatrick, Lois J. Veronen, and Susan Smith. 1989. "Family survivors of homicide victims: Theoretical perspectives and an exploratory study." *Journal of Traumatic Stress* 2:21–33. https://doi.org/10.1002/jts.2490020104; Beck, Elizabeth, Brenda Sims Blackwell, Pamela Blime Leonard, and Michael Mears. 2003. "Seeking sanctuary: Interviews with family members of capital defendants." *Cornell Law Review*, 88:382–418; Sharp, Susan F. 2005. *Hidden Victims: The Effects of the Death Penalty on Families of the Accused*. New Brunswick, NJ: Rutgers

University Press), the effects of sanctions upon co-victims (for example, see Armour, Marilyn Peterson and Mark S. Umbreit. 2012. "Assessing the impact of the ultimate penal sanction on homicide survivors: A two state comparison. " *Marquette Law Review* 96:1–131) and the effects of restorative justice processes upon co-victims (for example, see Umbreit, M. S., B. Vos, R. B. Coates, and Martin, K. A. 2006. "Facilitated dialogue on death row: Family members of murder victims and inmates share their experiences." pp. 349–375 in *Wounds That Do Not Bind: Victim-Based Perspectives on the Death Penalty,* edited by J. R. Acker and D. R. Karp. Durham, NC: Carolina Academic Press; Umbreit, Mark S., and Betty Vos. 2000. "Homicide survivors meet the offender prior to execution: Restorative justice through dialogue." *Homicide Studies* 4:63–87. https://doi.org/10.1177/1088767900004001004)

10 See Blumer, Herbert. 1969. *Symbolic Interactionism: Perspective and Methods.* Upper Saddle River, NJ: Prentice-Hal; Mead, George H. 1934. *Mind, Self and Society.* Chicago, IL: University of Chicago Press.

11 There are meaningful distinctions between the terms "emotion," "feeling," "sentiment," and "affect" within the literature on emotion. In order to construct arguments that are accessible to a wide audience, I do not distinguish between these terms in the current work, except when discussing Affect Control Theory. For a detailed discussion of the various terms, see Smith-Lovin, Lynn. 1995. "The Sociology of Affect and Emotion." pp. 118–148 in *Sociological Perspectives on Social Psychology,* edited by K. S. Cook, G. A. Fine, and J. S. House. Boston, MA: Allyn and Bacon.

12 Matsueda, Ross L. 1992. "Reflected appraisals, parental labeling, and delinquency: Specifying a symbolic interactionist theory." *American Journal of Sociology* 6:1577–1611. https://doi.org/10.1086/229940

13 Burke, Peter J. and Jan E. Stets. 2009. *Identity Theory.* New York, NY: Oxford University Press.

14 See Thoits, Peggy. 1989. "The sociology of emotions." *Annual Review of Sociology* 15:317–342. https://doi.org/10.1146/annurev.so.15.080189.001533

15 Hochschild, Arlie R. 1979. "Emotion work, feeling rules, and social structure." *American Journal of Sociology* 85(3):551–575. https://doi.org/10.1086/227049; Shott, Susan. 1979. "Emotion and social life: A symbolic interactionist analysis." *American Journal of Sociology* 84(6):1317–1334. https://doi.org/10.1086/226936

16 Hochschild, Arlie R. 1979. "Emotion work, feeling rules, and social structure." *American Journal of Sociology* 85(3):551–575. https://doi.org/10.1086/227049

17 It should be noted that I use the terms "emotion norms" and "feeling rules" interchangeably in this work. For a detailed explanation of each concept, see Hochschild, Arlie R. 1979. "Emotion work, feeling rules, and social structure." *American Journal of Sociology* 85(3):551–575. https://doi.org/10.1086/227049

18 Though some authors use the term "non-normative" to indicate something that is socially sanctioned or stigmatized, use of the term here is not meant to indicate any such negative connotation. I use the term "non-normative" throughout this book to indicate that something is unanticipated, socially unstructured, and unguided by firmly established norms. Others have utilized this term similarly.

For example, see Wrosch, Carsten, and Alexandra Freund. 2001. "Self-regulation of normative and non-normative developmental challenges." *Human Development* 44:264–283. https://doi.org/10.1159/000057066

19 Goodrum, Sarah. 2008. "When the management of grief becomes everyday life: The aftermath of murder." *Symbolic Interaction* 31(4):422–442. https://doi.org/10.1525/si.2008.31.4.422

20 Thoits, Peggy. 1990. "Emotional deviance: Research agendas." pp. 180–203 in *Research Agendas in the Sociology of Emotions*, edited by T. D. Kemper. New York, NY:State University of New York Press.

21 See McAdams, Dan P. 1993. *The Stories We Live By. Personal Myths and the Making of the Self.* New York, NY: Guilford Press; Neimeyer, Robert. A. and Adam Anderson. 2002. "Meaning reconstruction theory." pp. 45–64 in *Loss and Grief*, edited by N. Thompson. New York, NY: Palgrave.

22 This is a method successfully used by many researchers. For examples, see Riessman, Catherine Kohler. 2002. "Narrative analysis." pp. 217–270 in *The Qualitative Researcher's Companion*, edited by A. M. Huberman and M. B. Miles. Thousand Oaks, CA: Sage Publications; Mishler, Elliot. G. 1986. *Research Interviewing: Context and Narrative.* Cambridge, MA: Harvard University Press.

23 See Goffman, Erving. 1974. *Frame Analysis.* New York, NY: Harper & Row.

24 See Neimeyer, Robert A. and Adam Anderson. 2002. "Meaning reconstruction theory." pp. 45–64 in *Loss and Grief*, edited by N. Thompson. New York, NY: Palgrave; Riessman, Catherine Kohler. 2002. "Narrative analysis." pp. 217–270 in *The Qualitative Researcher's Companion*, edited by A. M. Huberman and M. B. Miles. Thousand Oaks, CA: Sage Publications (p. 232).

25 Pemberton, Anthony, Eva Mulder, and Pauline G. M. Aarten. 2018. "Stories of injustice: Towards a narrative victimology." *European Journal of Criminology* 16(4):391–412. https://doi.org/10.1177/1477370818770843

26 Turner, Jonathan H. and Jan E. Stets. 2005. *The Sociology of Emotions.* New York, NY: Cambridge University Press.

27 Self-help group names are pseudonyms, created in order to protect participant confidentiality.

28 I also engaged in interviews with three long-term members who took on leadership roles within FVL, as well as one new member. These interviews are not a part of the current dataset. Since the current analysis, I have conducted nine additional interviews with co-victims whose experiences will undoubtedly shed light upon the complex interplay between culture and structure, as they are from within minority racial groups and the upper-middle or upper social classes. Such a combination is relatively unique among co-victims and is therefore likely to provide valuable insights in future publications.

29 In cases in which participants had lost multiple loved ones, demographic categorization was based on the loved one that interviewees focused upon most during interviews.

30 This is disproportionate to the national average. While homicide involving a victim and offender with a previous relationship is more common than between strangers, individuals who knew the person who took the lives of their loved ones may have been less likely to agree to be interviewed for this research.

31 For examples of the wide-ranging definitions of forgiveness used in relevant literature, see Enright, Robert D. and Joanna North (Eds). 1998. *Exploring Forgiveness*. Madison, WI: University of Wisconsin Press; Enright, Robert D., Elizabeth A. Gassin, and Ching-Ru Wu. 1992. "Forgiveness: A developmental view." *Journal of Moral Education* 21:99–114. https://doi.org/10.1080/0305724920210202; Forster, Daniel E., Joseph Billingsley, V. Michelle Russell, Thomas G. McCauley, Adam Smith, Jeni L. Burnette, Yohsuke Ohtsubo, Joanna Schug, Debra Lieberman, and Michael E. McCullough. 2019. "Forgiveness takes place on an attitudinal continuum from hostility to friendliness: Toward a closer union of forgiveness theory and measurement." *Journal of Personality and Social Psychology.* https://doi.org/10.1037/pspi0000227; Hourigan, Kristen L. 2016. "Homicide survivors' definitions of forgiveness: Intrapersonal, interpersonal, and extrapersonal orientations." *Violence and Victims* (31)5:869–887. https://doi.org/10.1891/0886-6708.VV-D-15-00015; McCullough, Michael E. 2001. "Forgiveness: Who does it and how do they do it?" *Current Directions in Psychological Science* 10:194–197. https://doi.org/10.1111/1467-8721.00147; McCullough, Michael E., Kenneth I. Pargament, and Carl E. Thoresen. 2000. "The psychology of forgiveness: History, conceptual issues, and overview." pp. 1–14 in *Forgiveness: Theory, research, and practice*, edited by M. E. McCullough, K. I. Pargament, and C. E. Thoresen. New York, NY: Guilford Press.; McCullough, Michael E., Everett L. Worthington, and Kenneth C. Rachal. 1997. "Interpersonal forgiving in close relationships." *Journal of Personality and Social Psychology* 73:321–336. https://doi.org/10.1037/0022-3514.73.2.321; Worthington, Everett L. (Ed.). 1998. *Dimensions of Forgiveness: Psychological Research and Theological Perspectives.* Philadelphia, PA: Templeton.

Chapter 2

Narrating Lived Experiences of Forgiveness and Unforgiveness

I wanted him to suffer all this time and now I got to see what that actually looked like. For the first time in 13 years, to see my dad as a person, as my father again ... I told him that I loved him and I forgave him ... it was as if those 13 years of anger and hopelessness and victimization went away, and it changed my life.—Alex

I slowly walk the wide gravel path alongside Glenda, a middle-aged white woman with a peaceful yet solemn presence about her. She might be described as eclectic, with her colorful flowing garbs and strappy sandals, so her presence at this event seems fitting. This is a trauma and resilience retreat. The venue is a Tibetan Buddhist monastery tucked among the towering oak trees on the edge of a Catskill mountainside. After a full day of guided meditation; resilience workshops focused upon movement, drumming, creative practice, and companionship; one-on-one sessions with Lama Jogen; and a vegan lunch, we stroll along this path, mindfully, as was the instruction of the monk leading this walk by babbling streams. High in the trees lining the path hang long strands of prayer flags, beautiful in their patterns and color, yet tattered and frayed from the wind. Several young children lead the pack, running ahead and doubling back, squealing with their excitement to take part in the traditional prayer that will take place at the lake shore at the foot of the hill followed by the symbolic release of a cup of earthworms, bought by the monks from the local bait and tackle shop for this purpose.

As Glenda and I walk, she tells me of her struggles to forgive. She has come to this retreat to *"learn about forgiveness."* She is not having difficulty forgiving the men who shot and killed her brother as he shopped inside a busy electronics store, oblivious of the gang retaliation unfolding in the street outside. As a matter of fact, she never mentions those men in our conversations during this event. Rather, she is struggling to forgive her sister-in-law, whose decisions surrounding Glenda's late brothers' belongings and funeral services seem, to Glenda, beyond reason. I am intrigued. Glenda has already asked if she can take part in an interview for this research, so I look forward to asking her more about her forgiveness process of the men who shot her brother, and her struggle to release the anger she harbors toward her sister-in-law.

On the walk back from the lake-side ceremonial release, Glenda asks me about Loved Ones Left Behind (LOLB). Diane, the founder of LOLB, is a panelist at the trauma and resilience retreat, and she suggested Glenda attend an LOLB meeting when she had met Glenda at the retreat earlier that day and learned of her brother's murder 16 months prior. When I had arrived at the retreat, Diane told Glenda that I was a regular attendee of LOLB meetings, so Glenda takes the opportunity during our wooded jaunt to inquire about the self-help group. I assure her that the group is made up of compassionate, open-minded, and resilient folks who will be eager to offer emotional support as she processes her difficult feelings and experiences.

Weeks after meeting Glenda at the trauma and resilience retreat, and days after my interview of her which also took place at the monastery, I have a third opportunity to hear Glenda narrate her experience, this time to a different audience and in a different context, as she recounts her story of loss to the folks at LOLB. As I listen, I continue to reflect upon the differences between the way Glenda describes the acceptance and sympathy she feels toward two strangers after their act of killing her brother, and the anger and bitterness she continues to feel toward her sister-in-law after she had discarded her brother's possessions before Glenda had time to sort through them.

The differences between these two emotional states, forgiveness and unforgiveness, will form the crux of this chapter, as I offer candid accounts of each. Within the sample of participants in this study, there were clearly distinguishable cases of forgiveness and unforgiveness as well as marked differences between the experiences of those whose forgiveness I identify as "benevolent" versus "non-benevolent." This distinction is crucial in a study of this sort, given the emotionally charged nature of one's experiences of traumatic loss, and the miscommunications and conflicts that can arise if individuals are not careful to convey what they do, and do not, mean when they use the word forgiveness. For example, some co-victims within this study found the word forgiveness offensive because they felt it implied a sense of condoning of the behavior or of acceptance of the act.

As shown in Table 2.1, eight participants (22% of the full sample) described experiences indicative of unforgiveness at the time of the interview and observations. Eight (22%) indicated non-benevolent forgiveness, and 20 (56%) indicated benevolent forgiveness. What follows is a discussion of each of these emotional states as they relate to loss to homicide. This will establish a clearer picture of forgiveness and unforgiveness in the context of homicide

Table 2.1 Forgiveness Categorization (*n* = 36)

Forgiveness categorization	
Unforgiveness	8 (22%)
Non-benevolent forgiveness	8 (22%)
Benevolent forgiveness	20 (56%)
Total	36 (100%)

and set the foundation upon which I can then build an explanation of how co-victims come to forgive as well as a discussion of why some forgive and others do not.

Background

There has been a great deal of research investigating forgiveness, but it could be argued that previous work has been more effective in solidifying understanding of feeling rules associated with forgiveness than of actual lived experience of forgiveness. Feeling rules[1] specify the intensity, direction, and duration of the emotion that is *expected* to be felt in each situation (from strong to weak, positive to negative, and fleeting to lasting). Much of the previous work on forgiveness has involved placing participants in hypothetical or imagined scenarios.[2] In effect, these authors have investigated forgiveness-related feeling rules, analyzing participants' cognitive constructions and prescriptive ideas rather than descriptions of actual lived experiences of forgiveness. Studies focusing upon participant recall of transgressions that are relatively minor[3] also inform our understanding of forgiveness-related feeling rules, as the factors individuals recall and articulate as having impacted their likelihood of forgiveness of minor transgressions demonstrate the way they think about forgiveness and which transgressions/transgressors they deem forgiveness-worthy. This book offers an opportunity for a deeper level of understanding of the *lived experience* of forgiveness, particularly in cases of extreme harm.

Experiences of Unforgiveness

During interviews and while engaging in victim-centered events, co-victims described both past and current experiences of other-directed emotions that were extremely intense and negative, including rage, hatred, and vengefulness. During self-help group meetings, participants described their anger as *"boiling"* and *"seeing red."* Rose, a 78-year-old who had lost her daughter to murder 40 years earlier, described her experience of living in a constant state of rage as *"an awful hell."* And Carol, a 60-year-old who once co-chaired a co-victim self-help group, said about the young man who killed both her son and husband 21 years earlier, *"I was pissed! ... I absolutely hated him."* Carol shared how her therapist and doctor continually asked her if she felt like she was going to commit suicide after the tragedy that befell her family. She said she told them that she was simply *"too angry"* to take her own life. She said, *"Believe me, it would not be me [who I killed]."* During one self-help group meeting, a couple remembered their feelings toward the man who killed their daughter. They wished for both his death and his continued suffering, despite the contradiction: *"We wished he'd killed himself. Although we wanted him to suffer all sorts of horrible things in prison."*

For many participants, feelings of anger extended beyond the offender. Some felt intense rage toward police, attorneys, witnesses, family, friends, or God. Others described an anger that encompassed everyone they encountered. Mark, a 49-year-old whose brother was killed during a robbery, offered a vivid description of his emotional experience: *"The first nine or ten years I basically just ground my teeth and hated the world 24 hours a day, I actively made an effort to hate everything and everyone."*

These participants' rage was often so intense that they found it overwhelming, sharing stories of how it affected their behavior and mood within other relationships and with strangers.

Elena, a 39-year-old who lost a close childhood friend to murder 18 years earlier, described how her anger was so intense following the homicide that it made her act in ways she would never have imagined. Soon after the homicide, tragedy befell her community again, when an infant's life was lost. She said:

> *I remember even yelling at a nun, a sister, and I will never forget how she came up to me at the wake and it was just heart-wrenching. I literally felt like a knife was going into my heart, like somebody was stabbing, like it was bleeding. I just looked at her and she was like, "Oh, he is an angel now," and I go, "Shut up!" I was so mean to her. I was like, "I don't want to hear this! How can you say, after what we have went through this year, this beautiful baby was born and he is to die, for what?" I was just livid, and it was really hard.*

Other participants spoke of not being able to watch the evening news because their feelings of rage would surface when they heard stories of others being harmed. For example, Sue, a 54-year-old woman who lost her infant grandson to homicide, shared how her anger would emerge when she watched the news. She said:

> *Sometimes I'll get angry at things not even related to [my grandson's death]. Just all of a sudden, when I hear about like a kid or a child or whatever being murdered, or animals too, it's like I get so involved, and so ticked!*

Such all-encompassing anger was often accompanied by revenge fantasies or motivations. Several participants described their experiences seeing the offender in the courtroom and feeling motivated to kill. Elena recalled her feelings toward the offender in the courtroom: *"I was like, 'I want to chop you up and see how you feel.'"* And Jeanne, a 59-year-old whose adult son was shot by a 15-year-old during a street robbery, recalled how she felt at the trial of the man who killed her son:

> *If I had a gun in my hand, I could have walked in the courtroom and shot him, and you could have at that time, walk in with a gun. They didn't put you through a metal detector or anything else for that matter, you know? And [they] got some quarter-pound sheriff sleeping in the corner that would've tripped over themselves trying to get you anyway; you know what I'm saying? ... I would've walked right at him and fired that gun, no hesitation whatsoever.*

After the murder of his sister and her unborn child, J. R. said, *"I wanted revenge. You know, like aggression meets aggression. And I was very aggressive then. I just felt like someone had to pay for this. I was not thinking then that the law needs to apprehend or make an arrest."*

Others longed to be the person carrying out the death penalty on the offender. One participant had even written to the author of an editorial in a major newspaper who purported the inhumane nature of the death penalty. She said,

> *I wrote him a letter and said I would be very willing to push the button. And who is [the author] to say it's inhumane? They're put to sleep first. Their heart is stopped. I said, "What they do to their victim is what is inhumane." That never comes up, the inhumane treatment of a victim, the torture they go through. So how can they say anything that happens to [the offender] is inhumane?*

Other participants explained that, if they had had the means, they would have sought revenge. During one self-help group meeting, a new member described with great passion how she was seeking *"the resources"* to take revenge against the man who had killed her son. She said she had considered purchasing a gun or commissioning someone to take the offender's life.[4] Another participant described how he had once put his thoughts of revenge into action: *"I made a phone call and I got my people on the scene. And I gave them instructions and what we called an S.O.S., shoot on sight. When you see him, kill him."*

Others were more passive in their actions with regard to revenge. Ronald, a 73-year-old whose son was an innocent victim to a fatal gang initiation, said:

I keep hoping to look online, I look [the offender] *up online on the corrections site, and I hope to see "deceased." I am sorry to say it, but my son is not coming back ... Whatever happens to* [the offender], *I hope it's painful.*

A few participants shared how their vengefulness extended beyond the offender, often to the offender's parents or to individuals within the criminal justice system. Tanya said, *"I was so angry, I wanted something done to him, I wanted something done to his parents, to the people that he knows. I wanted them to know how I felt."* At her second self-help group meeting, another woman expressed her profound, all-encompassing rage directed at the *"corrupt"* officials charged with investigating the murder of her son in the Dominican Republic. She told the group how she had researched ways to construct bombs, similar to those she had heard about in the news, and looked into purchasing the necessary components in order to *"blow up the whole fucking police department."*

It should be noted that, although not all co-victims had felt a desire for revenge, all participants noted during interviews that they had experienced anger or a similar emotion immediately following, or soon after, the murder of their loved one. For some, such emotions were temporary and they later came to release their negative, other-directed emotions, demonstrating forgiveness, as conceptualized here. The next section will describe those participants' experiences of forgiveness.

Experiences of Forgiveness

Overall, 78% of interviewees in this sample had forgiven the individuals who took the lives of their loved ones. These participants described previous, other-directed emotions that were extremely intense and negative, including hatred, rage, and vengefulness. However, these co-victims shared how they had *"put down"* or *"let go of"* the emotional investment in the person who caused the harm and the negative, other-directed emotions, indicating forgiveness, as conceptualized here. As Sandra, a 49-year-old graduate school student who had lost several loved ones to homicide, noted, *"Forgiveness means that I do not harbor anything."* And, Glenda, whose story was introduced at the start of this chapter, offered, *"[Forgiveness] is letting go. Like, okay, it happened, my brother was shot, I cannot do anything about it."* Carol shared how she had visited the prison seven years after the murder to see the young man who killed her son and husband. She said, *"I did tell him I didn't hate him any more. I did hug him and say goodbye."* And Omarr, whose case will become a demonstration of the process of forgiveness later in this book, said,

I forgave him actually once the eye witness told me the accounts ... Once I realized from the eye witness what took place, there was no blame on [the offender]. *It was just hurt for the absence … I feel as if there is no animosity, no grudge … from that point forward. That helped me to feel that much more of a closure or a satisfaction, a sense of forgiveness, if you will, to that whole piece … It was a forgiveness in that I didn't pursue his life, you know, so he was forgiven. At the time of his apology, I can say forgiveness came in at that point. Even though there were five of 'em, and I only spoke to one, for me it was like that one spoke as a representative of that group, which moved me past that point.*

These individuals described forgiveness as a dynamic process, not occurring in one moment in time. Letishia, a 40-year-old nurse who had lost several loved ones to street violence, stated, *"Forgiveness for* [murder] *don't happen in a day, sometimes it takes years."* And, Sandra, who had spent a great deal of time contemplating the effects of loss to homicide, explained:

Forgiveness can occur in stages, it's a process. The more you pull the shade up, the more you see in terms of what you lost, what you miss, the more there is to forgive. Sometimes because our bodies and our minds can only handle so much, the shade can only be cracked a little bit. And that little bit I see, I can work with. That I can forgive. And then as time goes on and I get more perspective on the loss, I become aware that there are other things related to this homicide that I need to forgive … Having more to forgive later on does not negate the forgiving that I have done for today.

After forgiveness, many co-victims found solace in the fact that they had come to realize that it was acceptable to enjoy life and to relish in festive moments, celebratory events, or the simple things that once brought them happiness. Often this realization came when they met other co-victims who were at points in their healing processes in which they could experience joy and peace of mind. On several occasions, members of self-help groups reflected during interviews upon their early experiences of attending meetings and the revelation that there was hope for a future free of intense, negative emotions. Witnessing the laughter of other co-victims was often a key moment in the lives of those attending self-help groups. Many said they were comforted by witnessing other co-victims laughing and enjoying time spent chatting with fellow co-victims. In those moments, they realized that they too would some day laugh again. During one meeting, Gloria said Homicide Bereavement Circle (HBC) was *"a savior."* She said, *"I thought I'd never smile again 'til I saw light at HBC. I thought, 'If these people can laugh and smile, then maybe some day I'll be able to laugh and smile and not feel guilty.'"* Others talked about how the laughter of fellow co-victims symbolized hope that healing was in store. It functioned as a gesture that signified their right to reenter the social world apart from their co-victim statuses. It was acceptable to set aside the grief for one moment and feel joy.

Benefits of Forgiveness

Though I wish to remain value-free in my analysis of the data generated through this project, in order to fully detail the depth and variety of experiences of my participants, it is necessary that I include discussion of the benefits forgiving co-victims offered in their interviews and when in conversation with other co-victims.[5] Participants commonly described the forgiveness process as associated with a healing within themselves. Lorraine, an 81-year-old retiree who lost her son when he was killed during an armed robbery, explained: *"If someone forgives, they have a burden lifted off of them."* Deion, a 33-year-old man who had lost four loved ones to homicide in separate incidents relating to street violence, stated, *"You have to forgive people in order to be able to live peacefully with yourself."* And Tanya offered,

> I'm past that anger, bitter stage because that just would keep me from growing as a person. It would keep me stuck, and I'm not going to do anything that's going to do that, because I lost a lot already ... You can't let these things hold you down because emotionally resentment and anger and those are all the things that tear at us, away from the good things that we have.

She later shared,

> Forgiveness is good because it allows you to grow as a person and get past all of those inadequacies that we feel when we are vengeful. Those are inadequacies. I don't want those things holding me down. Because I want to move forward and, you know, create a better life for myself and my children.

Finally, Glenda, who struggled with forgiving her sister-in-law for her actions after the murder of Glenda's brother explained,

> The more you can forgive, the better it is on you, because it is hard to harbor resentment, you know, it weighs you down. It is not bothering [my sister-in-law] that I hold these resentments against her, it is bothering me. So it is my work to do, to let them go and give them up. It is not her work, it is my work. I think as long as I go around thinking she did something wrong ... I am holding a grudge. It is going to cause me agitation and I am still going to have that wound that I am carrying around.

Forgiving participants often discussed the importance they saw in releasing negative emotion. Florence, a 71-year-old whose son was murdered by a female who was carrying out the murder for purposes of a gang initiation, noted, *"If you stay bitter, you are ruining your own life too, you are hurting yourself and everybody around you."* Letishia explained that the *"negative energy vibrates all through you."* She said:

> You gotta incorporate forgiveness into your activities of daily living. Because if you don't, it will consume you and you will become that which you despise. You won't see it initially 'cause it's in the abstract, but it's subtle. It's there and it grows.

Participants explained that forgiveness allows individuals to heal or move forward with their lives. Lisha, a 28-year-old nursing student who lost her best friend to murder, explained, *"Forgiveness means healing your soul. That's how I define* [forgiveness], *because once you forgive somebody, you let it go. You never forget but* [you] *let it go."* And Roshaun, a 28-year-old outreach worker who had lost his best friend to homicide when they were both gang-affiliated, noted, *"I don't think I'd be able to move forward in life if I just held grudges. Because* [I'd] *be carrying all that."* Omarr, a 42-year-old who had lost several loved ones to gang violence during a time when he was heavily involved in drug-trafficking, stated, *"Forgiveness has to be part of the healing. You can't heal without forgiving."* And, finally, Alex, a 33-year-old woman who spoke about her healing process as a long and challenging journey during which she was able to forgive her father for the murder of her mother, said, *"Forgiveness is kind of like a byproduct of healing, but at the same time, to me, it's like a byproduct of love and understanding. And then healing is like the whole thing.* [Forgiveness is] *also the journey."*

Participants were most likely to note benefits of forgiveness when their forgiveness involved not only a release of negative emotion but also the generation of positive emotion. This type of forgiveness is what I have termed "benevolent forgiveness." For such participants, the release of negative, other-directed emotion allowed them to establish what many referred to as *"a new normal"* and to feel a range of emotions they had not felt since their loved ones' deaths. Many described current, positive emotions, including happiness, acceptance, calm, relief, satisfaction, and hope. Some participants spoke of having *"peace of mind,"* being *"excited about life,"* and feeling *"motivated to succeed,"* *"lucky to be alive,"* and grateful for the time they had with their loved ones before their untimely deaths.

Experiences of Benevolent Forgiveness

The release of negative, other-directed emotion was often accompanied by the development, or reestablishment, of positive, other-directed emotions, such as compassion, concern, respect, sympathy, and even renewed love, as seen in two cases in which the participants' fathers had killed their mothers. In these cases, the co-victims' forgiveness was what I refer to here as "benevolent."

Development of Positive Other-Directed Emotion

For some participants who entered a state of benevolent forgiveness, the offenders were strangers prior to taking the lives of their loved ones, so their forgiveness included the *development* of positive other-directed emotion. For example, Glenda shared how she wished the offenders well and hoped that they found ways in prison to *"somehow better themselves."* Letishia worried about *"the psychological effects"* that result from taking a life, and Diane explained how she held back during her victim–offender dialogue out of concern for the offender and his well-being. She said,

> Some questions I didn't ask because I felt more in the role of caretaker for him, like I didn't want to make him uncomfortable. Like there was one time something came up and I could have really called him out on it. But I was more in that other role of trying not to push [his] buttons or anything like that and trying to be cautious.

She explained how she was *"really concerned"* about his emotional state when she agreed to take part in a victim–offender dialogue:

> Everything dated back [to] seeing him in shackles [at the arraignment] and without having any family there through anything. So it was like this whole forced caretaker kind of role. I started getting worried [that] I would open all this up for him, and what is he going to do? You know? He's got to be like sweating bullets now, just knowing that this family is coming … It's got to be eating him up inside and, like, how is he processing all that?

She explained that, as the date of the dialogue drew closer, she became increasingly concerned about the quality of emotional support within the prison available to the man who killed her sister.

These cases illustrate the development of positive, offender-directed emotions. These emotions accompanied the release of previously felt anger and vengefulness, demonstrating benevolent forgiveness. In other cases, there was a preexisting, positive relationship between the co-victim and the offender. Benevolent forgiveness in these cases involved the *reestablishment* of positive, other-directed emotions, discussed in the next section.

Reestablishment of Positive Other-Directed Emotion

Some co-victims had prior positive relationships with the person who killed their loved ones, so their forgiveness included a reestablishment of positive emotions once shared between co-victim and offender. For example, Alex described what it was like to see her father suffering in the end of this life, handcuffed to his hospital bed, and the way that experience engendered compassion, which then allowed her to move forward with a sense of general peace. She said through tears:

> *It just really changed everything because I had to see what I consider what judgment looks like. I wanted him to suffer all this time and now I got to see what that actually looked like. For the first time in 13 years, to see my dad as a person, as my father again. And it kind of bottom-lined it for me ... So I told him that I loved him and I forgave him ... And from the moment I walked in and saw him to when I left [the hospital] it was as if those 13 years of anger and hopelessness and victimization went away and it changed my life. I got my life back. I still grieve the loss of my mom just as much, and that will never go away, but it's almost like now I get to grieve my dad too.*

Alex had previously felt intense anger toward her father and had not had any contact with him for 13 years. She said, *"I had never talked to him. I didn't want to talk to him. The way I saw it, you know, what he did was unforgivable, and I didn't want him to ever get pleasure from seeing or hearing from me again."* Upon witnessing his suffering during her ten-minute supervised visit in his hospital room, Alex was motivated to ease her father's suffering. She traveled back to the hospital the next day to spend another ten minutes by his side. During that time, she told him *"over and over again"* that she forgave him for his actions and that she and her sister loved him. She was told that, as his next of kin, she had the right to sign a "do not resuscitate" order on his behalf. Given his condition, Alex saw this as a means of easing his suffering. She said:

> [He was] *being kept alive on all these machines ... Later, from the death report, the autopsy said he had AIDS in addition to just severe malnutrition and, like, if you were to see his condition you know that he's in the physical state [that we'd be] prolonging his life unnecessarily. So [my sister, my aunt, and I] talked at length about it and [we decided to] keep him on pain medication and all that, but just take him off all these extra machines ... He's staring at a plain wall, you know, he's handcuffed to a bed. He's in terrible condition ... I signed the thing and he died two days later, because he was ready to go.*

Alex's case clearly demonstrates compassionate forgiveness. Compassion involves a recognition of one's suffering and a motivation to relieve that suffering. During these visits with her dying father, Alex was able to generate compassion and act upon that emotion. This is a prime example of benevolent forgiveness in its pairing of the release of intense, negative other-directed emotion and reemergence of positive, other-directed emotion.

Concluding Remarks

This chapter has been foundational in that it lays the groundwork for coming chapters. As we travel along a path of increasing complexity, it kickstarts our investigation by answering the question of "What?" What is forgiveness, in the context of murder? By demonstrating cases of unforgiveness and forgiveness, including benevolent forgiveness, it creates a common understanding from which we can turn to an investigation of "When?" When do co-victims forgive the person who took the lives of their loved ones? In the next chapter, I will highlight the various factors that play a part in determining whether or not a person forgives someone who causes extreme harm. I will then narrow in on two factors, understanding and empathy, to develop an explanation of how individuals forgive after homicide and where their motivations to forgive arise from.

Questions for Further Discussion

1 How may forgiveness after minor transgressions be experienced differently than forgiveness after more serious offenses?
2 Can intense negative and positive other-directed emotions exist simultaneously and, if so, how might this change our understanding of forgiveness?
3 How is forgiveness of self different from forgiveness of others?
4 What factors make an offense more or less forgiveness-worthy? Do ideas about forgiveness-worthiness vary by culture?

Notes

1 Hochschild, Arlie R. 1979. "Emotion work, feeling rules, and social structure." *American Journal of Sociology* 85(3):551–575. https://doi.org/ https://doi.org/ 10.1086/227049.
2 For example, see Eaton, Judy, C. Ward Struthers, and Alexander G. Santelli. 2006. "The mediating role of perceptual validation in the repentance–forgiveness process." *Personality and Social Psychology Bulletin* 32(10):1389–1401. https://doi.org/ 10.1177%2F0146167206291005; Exline, Julie Juola, Roy F. Baumeister, Anne L. Zell, Amy J. Kraft, and Charlotte V. O. Witvliet. 2008. "Not so innocent: Does

seeing one's own capability for wrongdoing predict forgiveness?" *Journal of Personality and Social Psychology* 94(3):495–515. https://doi.org/10.1037/0022-3514.94.3.495; Wallace, Harry M., Julia Juola Exline, and Roy F. Baumeister. 2008. "Interpersonal consequences of forgiveness: Does forgiveness deter or encourage repeat offenses?" *Journal of Experimental Social Psychology* 44(2):453–460. https://doi.org/10.1016/j.jesp.2007.02.012; Wenzel, M. and T. Okimoto. 2010. "How acts of forgiveness restore a sense of justice: Addressing status/power and value concerns raised by transgressions." *European Journal of Social Psychology* 40(3):401–417. https://doi.org/10.1002/ejsp.629

3   For example, see Bradfield, M. and K. Aquino. 1999. "The effects of blame attributions and offender likeableness on forgiveness and revenge in the workplace." *Journal of Management* 25(5):607–631. https://doi.org/10.1177/014920639902500501; Eaton, Judy, C. Ward Struthers, and Alexander G. Santelli. 2006. "The mediating role of perceptual validation in the repentance–forgiveness process." *Personality and Social Psychology Bulletin* 32(10):1389–1401. https://doi.org/10.1177%2F0146167206291005; Exline, Julie Juola, Roy F. Baumeister, Anne L. Zell, Amy J. Kraft, and Charlotte V. O. Witvliet. 2008. "Not so innocent: Does seeing one's own capability for wrongdoing predict forgiveness?" *Journal of Personality and Social Psychology* 94(3):495–515. https://doi.org/10.1037/0022-3514.94.3.495; McCullough, Michael E., F. D. Fincham, and J. Tsang. 2003. "Forgiveness, forbearance, and time: The temporal unfolding of transgression-related interpersonal motivations." *Journal of Personality and Social Psychology* 84(3):540–557. https://doi.org/10.1037/0022-3514.84.3.540; Struthers, C. Ward, Judy Eaton, Alexander G. Santelli, Melissa Uchiyama, and Nicole Shirvani. 2008. "The effects of attributions of intent and apology on forgiveness: When saying sorry may not help the story." *Journal of Experimental Social Psychology* 44(4):983–992. https://doi.org/10.1016/j.jesp.2008.02.006; Struthers, C. Ward, Judy Eaton, Rachelle Mendoza, Alexander G. Santelli, and Nicole Shirvani. 2010. "Interrelationship among injured parties' attributions of responsibility, appraisal of appropriateness to forgive the transgressor, forgiveness, and repentance." *Journal of Applied Social Psychology* 40(4):970–1002. https://doi.org/10.1111/j.1559-1816.2010.00607.x; Wallace, Harry M., Julia Juola Exline, and Roy F. Baumeister. 2008. "Interpersonal consequences of forgiveness: Does forgiveness deter or encourage repeat offenses?" *Journal of Experimental Social Psychology* 44(2):453–460. https://doi.org/10.1016/j.jesp.2007.02.012; Wenzel, M. and T. Okimoto. 2010. "How acts of forgiveness restore a sense of justice: Addressing status/power and value concerns raised by transgressions." *European Journal of Social Psychology* 40(3):401–417 https://doi.org/10.1002/ejsp.629; Williamson, Ian and M. H. Gonzales. 2007. "The subjective experience of forgiveness: Positive construals of the forgiveness experience." *Journal of Social and Clinical Psychology* 26(4):407–446. https://doi.org/10.1521/jscp.2007.26.4.407; Zechmeister, Jeanne S. and Catherine Romero. 2002. "Victim and offender accounts of interpersonal conflict: Autobiographical narratives of forgiveness and unforgiveness." *Journal of Personality and Social Psychology* 82(4):675–686. https://doi.org/10.1037/0022-3514.82.4.675

4   It is important to note here that I never had the sense that the co-victims who
    spoke of current thoughts of revenge were capable of following through on their
    ideas. Rather, they used self-help group meetings as safe spaces to vent their
    vengeful *fantasies*, which individuals outside the co-victim networks may not
    have understood or sympathized with. These admissions of emotion were met
    with acknowledgment and understanding from other co-victims, followed by
    reminders about why the speaker should not, or could not, follow through. Often
    these reminders surrounded the speaker's obligations to their surviving children
    or suggestions that taking such action makes the revenge-seeker too much like
    the murderer.

5   Several empirical studies have also noted a variety of physical and mental health
    benefits to forgiveness. See Kaplan, Berton H. 1992. "Social health and the forgiving
    heart: The Type B story." *Journal of Behavioral Medicine* 15(1):3–14. https://doi.org/
    10.1007/BF00848374; Kiecolt-Glaser, Janice K., Lynanne McGuire, Theodore
    F. Robles, and Ronald Glaser. 2002. "Emotions, morbidity, and mortality: New
    perspectives from psychoneuroimmunology." *Annual Review of Psychology* 53(1):83–
    107. https://doi.org/10.1146/annurev.psych.53.100901.135217; Martinčeková,
    Lucia, and John Klatt. 2017. "Mothers' grief, forgiveness, and posttraumatic
    growth after loss of a child." *Omega – Journal of Death and Dying* 75(3):248–
    265. https://doi.org/10.1177%2F0030222816652803; McCullough, Michael E.,
    Kenneth I. Pargament, and Carl E. Thoresen. 2000. "The psychology of forgive-
    ness: History, conceptual issues, and overview." pp. 1–14 in *Forgiveness: Theory,
    Research, and Practice,* edited by M. E. McCullough, K. I. Pargament, and C. E.
    Thoresen. New York, NY: Guilford.; Subkoviak, Michael J., Robert D. Enright,
    Ching-Ru Wu, Elizabeth A. Gassin, Suzanne Freedman, Leanne M. Olson, and
    Issidoros Sarinopoulas. 1995. "Measuring interpersonal forgiveness in late ado-
    lescence and middle adulthood." *Journal of Adolescence* 18(6):641–655. https://
    doi.org/10.1006/jado.1995.1045; Wemmers, Jo-Anne, and Katie Cyr. 2006.
    "What fairness means to crime victims: A social psychological perspective on
    victim–offender mediation." *Applied Psychology in Criminal Justice* 2(2):102–128;
    Williamson, Ian, and M. H. Gonzales. 2007. "The subjective experience of for-
    giveness: Positive construals of the forgiveness experience." *Journal of Social and
    Clinical Psychology* 26(4):407–446. https://doi.org10.1521/jscp.2007.26.4.407;
    Witvliet, Charlotte V. O. and Michael E. McCullough. 2007. "Forgiveness and
    health: A review and theoretical exploration of emotion pathways." pp. 259–
    276 in *Altruism and Health: Perspectives from Empirical Research,* edited by S. G.
    Post. Oxford, England: Oxford University Press; Williams, R. and V. Williams.
    1993. *Anger Kills: Seventeen Strategies for Controlling the Hostility that can Harm
    your Health.* New York, NY: Harper Perennial; Záhorcová, Lucia, Peter Halma,
    and Robert D. Enright. 2019. "Forgiveness as a factor of adjustment in bereaved
    parents." *Journal of Loss and Trauma* 25(2):188–203. https://doi.org/10.1080/
    15325024.2019.1664786

Chapter 3

Forgiveness Factors Salient within Narratives of Lived Experience

I saw his family. I saw how he was raised ... So in some ways I felt bad for him ... he was just a kid with no real family who was just a part of that [street culture], that was his family's life. You were ready to kill somebody at all times.—Renee

I had spent countless hours in Omarr's company over the last year and a half, chatting prior to the start of the Restorative Justice Alliance meetings that we both attended monthly, debating and collaborating during these meetings, and witnessing him doing the same with Diane, Roger, and Renee, each of whom was a regular attendee of Loved Ones Left Behind (LOLB) meetings. So when Omarr mentions the lack of such support networks in the area during his second interview for this research, I am puzzled. Omarr speaks at length about the need for this type of support in the community and his efforts to launch what he refers to as a *"violence support group."* Because this is my second time interviewing Omarr (his first interview had lasted over two hours and we both felt there was still a great deal we wanted to discuss), I know he lost his cousin to murder and that this has been a defining event for Omarr. So, I decide to ask why he did not take part in LOLB. I say:

> *I was at an LOLB meeting recently, and they were talking about the Restorative Justice Alliance and all of these things that I know you're very involved in, and it dawned on me, I thought, "Why isn't Omarr here?" Because you mentioned, when we talked before, how important that type of support is and how you see a need for that in the community. You know people in the room of LOLB, from the Restorative Justice Alliance, and yet you don't go to LOLB meetings. And you lost a loved one to homicide. So I was curious as to what your thoughts are on that.*

Omarr replies, *"I was not aware of their meetings."* After a pause, he adds, *"So, I'm not absent based on no interest, I'm absent because I'm unaware of the meetings."* I press, *"So, if you had known, do you think that that's something you would be interested in?"* To which Omarr replies forcefully, *"Definitely!"* I am intrigued by the idea that Omarr has spent so much time in the company of people who regularly attend and promote LOLB, discussing many relevant topics, but they have never mentioned the group to Omarr. It was only when Omarr inquired about my research, and consequently told me that he was a co-victim, that he came to learn of LOLB, which is held in the same building as the Restorative Justice Alliance meetings he attends each month, whose leaders sit with Omarr month after month, collaborating on projects and community programs focused upon interrupting patterns of violence. All those meetings, all those conversations, yet no one had mentioned LOLB to Omarr. How odd. He explains:

> *Well, I think part of it, too, is that not many people know my story, that part of my story. Most people, like Diane and the likes of them, are more familiar with my history in the streets and my incarceration and, you know, that whole violence intervention piece. Not many people are familiar with my background situation with the homicide of my cousin.*

I had (incorrectly) assumed that Omarr shared his story of loss with others, given his direct involvement within so many relevant programs in the community and his candor during his interview. As it turns out, I am one of only two people to whom Omarr has disclosed the full depth of his story, who know about the forgiveness process he underwent while behind bars with the man who took his cousin's life. The only people who Omarr has told are myself and Omarr's wife.

Omarr's story will become an invaluable piece of this exploration, in this chapter and the next, as his words highlight the connection between understanding, empathy, and forgiveness. Before approaching the process of forgiveness, answering the question of "How?," we must first explore "When?" When does forgiveness occur? When is unforgiveness more likely to persist? This will be the focus of the current chapter.[1]

Background

Previous research has uncovered several variables that affect the likelihood of forgiveness. These include the forgiver's ability to empathize with and understand the offender[2] and the forgiver's ability to view him- or herself as similar to the offender or as capable of committing similar transgressions, in both severity and type.[3] Individuals who feel guilt for their own transgressions are also more likely to forgive the transgressions of others.[4] Acts perceived as especially severe are unlikely to be forgiven[5] as are those seen as immoral or deliberately cruel.[6] Finally, we know that variables related to the offender's actions after the offense also influence the likelihood of forgiveness. Forgiveness becomes more likely if the offender acknowledges responsibility for the act and accepts blame.[7] And, whether symbolic or verbal, studies show that expressions of offender remorse correspond to an increased likelihood of forgiveness.[8]

Given the wealth of knowledge that exists about what factors influence forgiveness, I began to question how forgiveness is possible in cases in which all indicators point toward unforgiveness. For example, how can one come to release their intense, negative, other-directed emotion following a trauma that was severe, intentional, and perpetrated by an individual who lacks remorse, fails to accept responsibility, and continues to reoffend? The first step in determining how this is possible was to uncover the forgiveness ideologies (the integrated systems of concepts and ideals) of co-victims to determine if their ideas are aligned with the ideas of others who have never experienced such tragic loss at the hands of another person. With this aim, I analyzed a subsample of 30 interviews from this dataset. This subsample consisted of those participants who included reference to, or discussion of, factors fostering or impeding forgiveness either in response to direct questions during interviews or during the narration of their stories. What follows is a discussion of these factors as they were made relevant in participants' interviews and as they appeared within their narrations of lived experiences of forgiveness or unforgiveness. In this chapter, the distinction between participants' narratives and their answers to direct questioning during interviews becomes important, because the presence, or absence, of various factors is suggestive of the contrast between participants' ideas, their "feeling rules,"[9] and their actual lived experiences. I will first discuss those factors participants noted as capable of influencing the likelihood of forgiveness, when answering direct questions during interviews, such as, *"Are there certain things that would make you more or less likely to forgive a person?," "Is there anything that you feel is absolutely necessary in order for you to forgive?,"* and *"Do you feel as if there is anything that is unforgivable?"* I will then turn to an exploration of the factors that arose within participants' narratives, both at the start of interviews, when each participant was asked to *"share* [his/her] *story,"* and during relevant events, when sharing his or her story among others, including fellow co-victims, policy-makers, offenders, and at-risk youth.

Forgiveness Factors Raised during Direct Questioning

During interviews, several factors fostering or impeding forgiveness were mentioned when participants were asked directly about forgiveness. Table 3.1

Table 3.1 Forgiveness-Fostering and Forgiveness-Impeding Factors (*n* = 30)

Factor raised	Count (percentage)
Forgiveness-fostering factors	
Remorse	21 (70%)
Understanding	13 (43%)
Evidence of pro-social change	7 (23%)
Empathy	6 (20%)
Acceptance of responsibility	4 (13%)
Forgiveness-impeding factors	
Severity	11 (37%)
Intentionality	9 (30%)
Victim innocence	5 (17%)
Total	30

shows the total number and percentage of participants who raised each of the forgiveness-fostering and -impeding factors.

During interviews, the forgiveness-fostering factor most commonly named was remorse. In fact, when asked *"Are there certain things that would make you more/less likely to forgive?,"* nearly three-quarters (21) of interviewees said remorse, and some indicated that expression of remorse was *"necessary"* or even *"essential"* in order to forgive. Diane, whose sister was brutally slain, explained how remorse is crucial in order to bring about forgiveness and how, without genuine remorse, forgiveness loses its meaning. She described remorse as a *"thirst"* for forgiveness and questioned why anyone would forgive someone who *"doesn't even want or need your forgiveness."* Roger, a 57-year-old whose grandfather was killed when Roger was a child, said, *"Part of forgiveness, to me at least, implies that whoever has harmed you has remorse for their actions, thus allowing you to forgive. I have always seen them as connected somehow."* When asked if she needed the offender's remorse or apology, Renee, a 60-year-old restorative justice advocate, answered:

> *That's the core sequence. To get complete forgiveness you have to see that genuine remorse and, to me, it has to be eye-to-eye. There's something about the eye-to-eye and that's why I told my therapist years ago, "I just need for him to see me." There's something that I think I need to see.*

Others felt remorse was helpful but not absolutely necessary. Glenda, whose brother was killed by a bullet intended for the killers' rival gang member, said when describing forgiveness, *"In its purest form, you would hold no resentments towards that person, even if they showed no remorse."* She later said in regard to her brother's killers, *"I don't think I can really expect or require remorse from them.*

I don't think that you have to have remorse, you know, in order to forgive." This type of forgiveness is what Trudy Govier refers to as "unilateral" forgiveness, meaning that it is unconditional and therefore does not require the expression of remorse from the offender.[10]

Some participants explained that remorse could be expressed without words. Letishia, who had lost several loved ones to homicide, said *"a tear, the body language, it is very important—not necessarily what you say but how you say it, the tone, the pitch."* Omarr offered another example, describing the communication of forgiveness that took place between himself and the person who took his cousin's life when they were both *"housed in the same block"* while imprisoned within the same facility:

OMARR: *Walking away from that conversation, yes, there was forgiveness. There was forgiveness.*
INTERVIEWER: *Did you tell him that you forgave him?*
O: *In our own street language, yeah.*
I: *Just in different words?*
O: *Right. Just in different words. But he definitely understood that he was being forgiven and relieved of the burden of having to carry that weight of, ya know, "I harmed you and how can I repair that loss?" It was very clear, getting the different lingo from that code of the street, that street talk, he understood that there was forgiveness being extended. There was an embrace and we conversed thereafter, 'til I was relocated after I was sentenced.*

Never did participants indicate that interaction was necessary between self and other to foster forgiveness. Participants suggested that the offender *having* remorse or *being* remorseful would foster forgiveness. However, even those co-victims who saw remorse as crucial in the forgiveness process did not indicate that *expression* of remorse was needed. In other words, an important distinction was uncovered here between perceptions of a sense of genuine *felt* remorse and the witnessing of a *demonstration* of remorse. This clarification may have been overlooked in previous research showing that expression of remorse through apology or repentance was a key factor in promoting forgiveness. This clarification may help to explain research indicating that apologies perceived as disingenuous are less likely to lead to forgiveness.[11]

Other forgiveness-fostering factors mentioned during interviews included the co-victim's ability to understand the circumstances of the homicide and empathize with the offender, the offender taking responsibility for his or her actions, and the offender demonstrating evidence of pro-social change (e.g., completing educational programs while imprisoned, engaging in religious practices, becoming sober, volunteering in the community). The latter factor is noteworthy in that it had yet to be uncovered by previous research as an influential factor in fostering forgiveness. This factor was mentioned by a quarter (7) of participants during direct questioning, and some indicated that this factor was not only important in their decision to forgive but was the most important factor. For example, Roger explained how this factor was even more impactful than remorse: *"I mean, OK, say you're sorry, that's great, but* show *me by your actions that you are sorry ... Modify your behavior,* [show me] *you are not that type of person any more."*

When asked directly about forgiveness, severity of the offense was the most commonly raised forgiveness-impeding factor, followed by intentionality of the act and the victim being *"innocent."* Many participants said that killings that were particularly heinous and brutal, that included torture or rape, or that involved children were among those acts that they considered unforgivable. The presence of an innocent victim (e.g., uninvolved bystanders or vulnerable groups like children or elderly people) had not yet been effectively considered in previous research, but interpretation of offense severity may encompass perceptions of victim innocence. Those crimes that involve an innocent victim are likely to be judged as more severe than crimes of a similar nature that are committed against an individual who the forgiver/unforgiver labels as deserving of harm or punishment. For example, the murder of a rival gang member may be judged as much less severe than a similar act committed against a child, elder, or someone perceived as living a pro-social lifestyle. Future research is needed to determine if these variables can be disentangled or are inherently confounded.

Overall, participants' forgiveness-related feeling rules were very similar to, or the same as, those whose feeling rules were investigated in previous work focused on lesser harms. This is evidence that the experience of extreme harm and resulting intense emotion does not substantially alter one's general ideologies surrounding the emotion norms associated with forgiveness.

Contradiction between Feeling Rules and Lived Experience

It is striking that the majority of participants in this subsample had forgiven the offender, despite the intentionality and severity of the offenses (many were described as especially brutal, involved children or other *"innocent"* victims, and/or included torture or rape) and the lack of expressions of remorse (only three offenders had displayed remorse), acceptance of responsibility, or evidence of pro-social change, all factors that make forgiveness less likely. In fact, the factors related to the offender (remorse, acceptance of responsibility, evidence of pro-social change) or the act (offense severity, intentionality, and victim innocence) that were raised in response to direct interview questions were rarely included in the narrated experiences of forgiveness in this subsample.

This indicates that the feeling rules held by the vast majority of co-victims in the subsample were not aligned with their lived experiences, as measured through personal narrative. In some cases, even factors participants felt were *"essential"* to forgiveness (such as remorse) were lacking in their experiences, yet they had forgiven.

On a few occasions, interviewees began to offer responses to the question, *"Do you feel as if there is anything that is unforgivable?,"* and quickly realized that they were contradicting themselves, as they had forgiven the act that they had just begun to describe as unforgivable. Sue, whose grandson was killed in infancy, answered, *"Probably the taking of someone's life. I mean, I know that sounds weird after all I said about* [how] *I could forgive our offender."* After our conversation, Sue continued to mull over the contradiction in her thinking. I received an email from her a few days after her interview. In it she told me that she had looked up the definition of forgiveness. She wrote,

> *The dictionary definition is basically to give up the resentment to an offender. How very interesting! So, basically, maybe I have done that and not realized?! I had mentioned to you that I don't hate the one who killed our grandson, that all I wanted was justice and for him to think about what he did … The opposite of forgive is to hate, and* [wanting] *to seek some kind of revenge. When I saw that dictionary definition, I wonder how many others have looked that up. How interesting!*

Sue continued to bring up the contradiction in her thinking for years after our initial conversation. As of our last discussion, she still had not settled the contradiction, as her definition of forgiveness mirrored her experience, but she continued to feel averse to the idea of labeling her experience as forgiveness.

A similar contradiction presented itself in my conversation with Whitney, a 50-year-old middle-school social worker who had lost several loved ones to homicide. When asked if she felt there is anything that is unforgivable, Whitney initially said it would be unforgivable to cause harm to her child or parent. She then stopped herself, realizing that she *"might still forgive"* in those instances (in fact, she had already forgiven the man who murdered her father). She then said, after several false starts, *"That's a difficult question … I wouldn't dare say that there's anything that's unforgivable, while in my heart I believe everything is forgivable."* Giving the question more thought, Whitney offered another instance of an unforgivable act: kidnapping and torturing a child. She said, *"I think it's almost worse to lose your child not knowing where they are, 'cause then you don't know the atrocities that are being done to them*

… There are things worse than death." Realizing her continued contradiction, she then resigned to say lightheartedly, *"So, tsk, I can't answer that!"*

Such contradiction highlights the discrepancy between participants' feeling rules surrounding forgiveness and lived experiences of forgiveness (or unforgiveness). Future research is needed to investigate the effects of potential cognitive dissonance[12] and deflection resulting from such contradiction following extreme harm, as well as the potential social impact of displaying emotion that is contradictory to emotion norms, such as rejection or inter-personal conflict, including within essential support networks such as families and religious communities.

The current findings may indicate that the dominant emotion norms surrounding forgiveness are prescriptive, leading individuals to note expectations associated with the forgiveness process when asked directly about their ideas, but these factors are not relevant when describing actual lived experiences of forgiveness. Perhaps this is evidence that, when asked about forgiveness, individuals offer their ideas on what factors *should* foster or impede forgiveness (describing forgiveness-related feeling rules) with limited awareness or consideration of what factors actually affected their ability to forgive (in lived experience). This may also serve as evidence that forgiveness-related feeling rules are multiple, diverse, ambiguous, and/or contextual. Therefore, continued exploratory work is warranted.

Contradiction between feeling rules and lived experience may also indicate that factors related to the act or offender are of less importance in instances of extreme harm relative to factors related to the forgiver/ unforgiver's personal experience (understanding and empathy), demonstrating that factors are weighed differently depending on level of harm or presence/absence of other relevant factors. That is to say, perhaps factors associated with the forgiver/unforgiver become more influential if factors related to the act or offender are impeding forgiveness, despite the level of harm. If this is the case, this knowledge may serve well those in helping professions and those who want to forgive but who were harmed in severe and/or intentional ways by offenders who are not remorseful or accepting of responsibility and/or do not intend to make pro-social changes to their life paths. The existence of prescribed feeling rules does not guarantee that people's lived experiences will align with those rules, and alternative resolutions may be preferred in some cases or under certain circumstances.

Forgiveness Factors within Narratives

Given my focus upon individuals' lived experiences following extreme harm, the most intriguing aspect of my data were the narratives co-victims constructed and shared both during interviews and when engaging in events relevant to participants' identities as co-victims.[13] Forgiveness or unforgiveness was a salient aspect of many participants' stories, which I witnessed at different times and in multiple social contexts. It is interesting to note that the majority of the factors that previous research indicates foster or impede forgiveness were not included in participants' narratives. Below, I briefly note those infrequently raised factors, then focus upon the two factors most commonly included in participants' stories: understanding and empathy. This will solidify the foundation upon which the remainder of this book will stand, as I illuminate the processes through which forgiveness occurs following extreme harm in later chapters.

Forgiveness Factors Not Present in Narratives

The severity of the offense or innocence of the victim was no more likely to be included within narratives of unforgiveness than those of forgiveness. In other words, both forgiving and unforgiving participants described heinous, brutal murders, often involving children, the elderly, or innocent bystanders. Forgiveness narratives did not include mention of offender acceptance of responsibility and on only one occasion was remorse and evidence of pro-social change salient in the participant's narrative. This co-victim's story was viewed by others foremost as a story of forgiveness, and she shared it in multiple venues, including self-help group meetings, memorials, and at-risk youth outreach programs. In order to explore the relevance of remorse, all participants whose offenders were known were asked directly if they had ever perceived remorse from the offender. In total, only three co-victims had perceived offender remorse (but this remorse was only salient in one co-victim's personal narrative).

Forgiveness Factors Present in Narratives

The only forgiveness-fostering factors that were salient within the vast majority of participants' narratives were those related to the co-victim's experience: his or her abilities to understand the offender's actions and empathize with the offender. The co-victim's ability to understand the circumstances of the offense was the most common forgiveness-fostering factor salient in participants' narratives. Participants who spoke of understanding often considered the deaths of their loved ones in light of contextual factors such as their loved ones' actions and chosen lifestyle; the relevant street culture, including reputation-building and retribution; the offenders' limitations, including mental illness, drug addiction, youthfulness, and ignorance; and the offenders' intense emotions, including panic, jealousy, and desire for control.

A few cases are illustrative of these factors being made salient within narratives of forgiveness based on understanding. Omarr explained that he blames his cousin for his own death, given this cousin's chosen lifestyle and violent history. In regard to the man who killed his cousin, Omarr said, *"it was not his fault"* because he was acting within the *"rules and principles of the street,"* to which he and his cousin both subscribed. Omarr explained that in order to understand one's actions, it is necessary to consider the factors leading up to the act. He said:

> *I believe the only way you will be able to forgive is going through that process of stepping back and not just seeing the immediate offense and action versus the root. What would put a person in a state of mind that they can do something offensive? That's whether it's a verbal statement, a physical attack, or something fatal. You know? There's something that took them, that altered their natural state of being humane and civil, to get them to act uncivilized.*

Though she did not have intimate knowledge of street culture like Omarr, Renee shared a similar sentiment during her narrative in regard to the man who killed her nephew:

> *I understand why this happened ... I understand who* [he was] *at that time ... I saw his family. I saw how he was raised ... So in some ways I felt bad for him ... he was just a kid with no real family who was just a part of that* [street culture], *that was his family's life. You were ready to kill somebody at all times.*

Glenda explained that she understood that the shooter who killed her brother was trying to *"make his name"* within his gang. She said, *"It was not like they robbed* [my brother] *and he gave them his wallet, and they just decided to shoot him anyway. I think that would be, there would be an extra level of choice on their part,* [which] *would make it harder to be understanding of."* She explained that she believed that *"the killers were acting according to the rules of their culture."*

Although empathy was not often mentioned as influential when participants were asked directly what factors they believed influence forgiveness, several stories of forgiveness included mention of empathy, and this empathy was often born from the co-victim's ability to understand. (Empathy is defined here as *the ability to recognize, or cognitively construct, the emotional experience of another, understand that emotional experience, and subsequently experience parallel or reactive emotions.* Empathy, and its connection to forgiveness, is discussed in greater detail in Chapters 4 and 5.) Lauren, a 29-year-old whose step-father killed her mother and then himself, explained that she empathized with her step-father, *"I put myself in his position before, and I tried to see through his eyes what made him do this. And, you know, that was a powerful thing. I just feel wiser because of this."* She later said she was sure her step-father *"felt he had to do what he did."*

Many participants viewed the offenders as victims themselves. Roger said that he believes that offenders often *"have a more compelling story than the victims."* And during Glenda's narrative, she described her belief that the men who murdered her brother were victims of their circumstances and societal injustices. She said they *"did not have a lot of options,"* given their social environment. Finally, Alex, whose father killed her mother, shared how she became able to take on others' *"point of view"* when she accepted the similarities between people and the fact that all people are capable of harming others:

> *I saw* [my father] *as a person capable of making a mistake, and, granted, it's a major mistake, but it is still a mistake. We are all dealing with stuff. We are all figuring out this life as we go along and, you know, the people who make major mistakes are also figuring it out as they go along … [I] understand that, you know, you were clearly in a bad place … I guess it just changed my outlook because I saw him as a victim too. Like a victim of his circumstances. And what kind of mind-frame does someone have to be in where murder makes sense to you? So I kind of just saw him as an equal. Like, "Oh, we are both dealing with stuff just like everyone in the world does." And that kind of just changed the context of right and wrong.*

Empathizing with the struggles and suffering of the offenders allowed these co-victims to release their negative feelings toward those who killed their loved ones (indicating forgiveness as conceptualized in this book). Some also came to feel positive emotions toward the offender, including sympathy, concern, and compassion. For example, Diane explained how she felt she had entered a *"caregiver role"* in regard to the offender when she saw him in the courtroom *"in shackles and without having any family there."* These individuals had come to see commonality between themselves and the individuals who took their loved ones' lives, allowing them to recognize the offenders' suffering, empathize with that suffering, and ultimately forgive.

Forgiving the Unforgivable

The current findings serve as evidence that the internal emotional transformation of forgiveness remains possible despite all of the factors that may make forgiveness of extreme harm more challenging and/or less likely than forgiveness of more minor harm. In such cases, it is still possible to forgive through understanding and empathy. This may indicate that the locus of control for the release of intense, negative, other-directed emotion lies within the harmed party and does not require direct interaction between parties. At least in cases of extreme harm, forgiveness, as conceptualized here, is fundamentally an intra-personal process, meaning that forgiveness takes place entirely within oneself. It therefore does not necessitate social inter-action between individuals. This is indicated in the fact that most participants did not mention interaction between self and other as relevant or necessary in the forgiveness process, either when answering interview questions or during narration of their stories. This was true even in cases in which the participant defined forgiveness inter-personally. In other words, those who believe forgiveness is an interactional process still go through a process of releasing negative, other-directed emotion that is entirely internal and does not necessitate such interaction. Therefore, regardless of the circumstances of the harm or the perpetrator's subsequent actions, the harmed party can alter his or her emotional response through processes related to understanding and empathy, potentially reclaiming some of their power lost through victimization (the processes involved in such emotional transformation are discussed in detail in Chapters 4 and 5).

In my sample of co-victims, contradictions between feeling rules and lived experience were overcome through a process in which participants shifted their "definition of the situation."[14] For example, when participants felt remorse was necessary for forgiveness, but they did not have the opportunity to witness remorse from the offender, whether because the offender was unknown, dead, or never given the opportunity to express remorse, some would *imagine* the offender as remorseful. Those participants who felt the offender displayed an explicit lack of remorse when shown on the media, during the trial, or in direct interaction explained how they felt this may be indicative of an inability or unwillingness to express felt remorse, rather than an actual lack of remorse. These participants justified a lack of expression of remorse by imagining factors that would make a remorseful individual unable to express those emotions. Some participants assumed that the offenders in their cases were advised by attorneys not to show remorse; that the offenders were afraid remorse would indicate guilt and thereby lead to incarceration; or that the offenders needed to maintain a reputation of stoic indifference in order to preserve their roles within gang hierarchies. For example, during a self-help group meeting, Jeanne shared how the young man who killed her son remained *"emotionless"* during the trial, failing to indicate any remorse for his actions. When asked by another group member how she was able to forgive the offender even though he *"wasn't even sorry for what he did,"* Jeanne explained that she did not see his actions in the courtroom as indicative of his actual emotional state. She assumed he was *"probably terrified"* and *"in shock."* She also explained that she believed that attorneys counsel defendants to avoid any expression of guilt as well as direct them not to make eye contact or speak to the loved ones of the deceased. Carol shared similar sentiments within her interview. She said with regard to the young man who took the lives of her husband and son, *"He said he wanted to tell the truth, but the lawyer said he needed to leave it the way it was."*

Other participants justified a lack of remorse by qualifying the offender's identity. For example, by noting mental illness or drug use, co-victims defined the perpetrators as blameless with respect to their emotional responses to the killing. As Cathy, a 66-year-old social worker who had lost her cousin to homicide several years earlier, explained, *"Some people are incapable of remorse."* In such cases, participants were redefining the situation in order to attach new meaning to the offenders' actions, or lack thereof (these ideas are revisited in detail in coming chapters).

Another factor impeding forgiveness that often required participants to redefine the situation was severity. Given the extreme nature of the harm caused, the actions of the offenders were often initially judged by participants as unforgivable, yet many came to release their negative emotions. After spending time with others who had lost to homicide, several interviewees utilized the narratives of others to shape their own narratives by comparison. For example, interviewees indicated that they believed they would be unable to forgive if their loved ones had been, for example, dismembered, raped, or held captive, as had happened to the loved ones of others within their social networks of co-victims. Forgiveness in their own cases seemed more attainable in light of such atrocities (and the forgiveness displayed in those cases), as the deaths of their own loved ones were less severe in comparison. Utilizing a new comparison group broadened the range of severity, allowing participants to judge what they once considered unforgivable as relatively less severe and therefore within the spectrum of forgivable acts.

Glenda's feelings surrounding the issue of intent clearly exemplified this process of redefining the situation to align feeling rules and experience. During her interview, Glenda spontaneously raised intentionality of the act as a factor that would decrease forgiveness-worthiness. Later in the interview and during a self-help group meeting, Glenda raised the issue of intention, making it clear that she felt that her brother's death was *"unintentional."* She explained that this lack of intention made her forgiveness substantially easier. Though the men who killed her brother intended to kill the other victim during an act of gang-related revenge, Glenda felt that they did not intend to take her brother's life, since he was killed by a stray bullet. She said, *"It is almost like it was an accident, an accidental murder* [by] *someone who was doing the intentional murder."* During her first LOLB meeting, Glenda explained that she was not sure if she would have forgiven if she was the sister of the other man killed in the event, because his murder was intentional. Other members of the self-help group had trouble understanding how Glenda defined her brother's killing as unintentional, given the offenders' lack of regard for the lives of those around their intended victim when they began firing shots outside a busy store. But the unintentional nature of the act was a definitive aspect of Glenda's narrative, indicating its salience and importance in the way she gave meaning to the event and her emotional reactions to it.

Other co-victims focused on mitigating factors within their own cases to reduce perceived intentionality. They pointed out that, if not for those factors, they could not forgive. Mitigating factors included drug use, age, and mental illness. For example, before learning of his drug addiction, Camila, a 44-year-old whose cousin killed his sister and his sister's children, was incapable of understanding her cousin's actions because they were so out of character. Factoring in his altered mental state allowed her to create meaning around the event and understand how such a heinous act, aimed at his family, could be committed by someone she had always known as religious and family-oriented. Camila said in reference to his drug use:

> That makes more sense. I mean, when somebody is on drugs, they don't know what they are doing ... So it makes sense to me that he was on drugs and he just didn't know what he was doing ... Somebody in a regular mind would never do something like that ... You don't know who you are any more [when you are under the influence of drugs] ... That's the only way it makes sense. He would have never done that if he was in his right mind.

Jeanne, who had forgiven the 15-year-old who shot her adult son, said during a self-help group meeting, "He didn't mean to kill my son. He was scared, so he just turned and shot as he ran away. He didn't even know he'd hit [my son]. He was just a kid making bad choices." The age of the young man who killed her son was a salient aspect of Jeanne's story and she regularly raised this point while sharing her story in various venues. She said during her interview:

> If this was a grown man or grown woman that committed a crime, I don't know if I could forgive. I have to say that, well, because he was a kid, I thought about how kids do stupid stuff. They're little, they don't think.

Here it is clear that Jeanne considered the age of the offender as a meaningful aspect of her story, as well as her forgiveness process, because the offender's youthfulness made him more worthy of forgiveness than he would have otherwise been.

Like in cases in which co-victims reconsidered severity, in examples such as these, it is clear that co-victims were redefining their own experiences by considering their cases relative to cases they believed were less forgiveness-worthy by comparison. Such re-interpretation based on social comparison is well aligned with the symbolic interactionist perspective, as individuals come to evaluate their experiences based on the meanings they learn through social interaction.[15]

As Peggy Thoits has shown,[16] changes to one's definition of the situation can result in transformation of emotion. In the cases analyzed here, participants redefined the situation in such a way as to better align their forgiveness-related feeling rules with their lived experiences. In cases in which forgiveness did occur, shifting the way one gave meaning to the events surrounding the homicide, or its aftermath, justified the release of intense, negative, other-directed emotion that participants experienced. By engaging in more qualitative research of this sort, we can bolster theories of emotion by more fully considering the shifting nature of definitions of situations, as individuals move through their social worlds and interact with influential others.

Concluding Remarks

This chapter highlights the importance of studying cases at the emotional fringes. Despite all indicators pointing toward a high likelihood of unforgiveness in these cases (i.e., severe, intentional acts often perpetrated against innocent victims and by offenders who do not express remorse and continue to reoffend), many participants in this sample had forgiven. There is, therefore, a contradiction between the factors that individuals believe influence their likelihood of forgiveness (their forgiveness-related feeling rules) and their lived (and narrated) experiences of forgiveness of extreme harm. It shows that the internal emotional transformation of forgiveness remains possible despite factors that may make forgiveness of extreme harm less likely than forgiveness of minor harm. In such cases, forgiveness remains possible through understanding and empathy, factors that will be further explored in coming chapters.

Contradictions may exist between the emotion norms associated with other life events as compared to individuals' experiences of non-normative instances of those events. For example, emotion norms undoubtedly exist for experiences of luck, but there may be contradiction between the way individuals expect they will feel and their actual emotional experiences of non-normative life events involving luck, such as winning a tremendous amount of money. Such an event affects multiple aspects of one's social world, perhaps including loss of work-related identities and unanticipated negative effects to social relationships. Therefore, emotional transformations following such non-normative luck may contradict one's luck-related feeling rules. Instead of feeling happy, excited, emancipated, or secure, as may be anticipated based on one's luck-related feeling rules, one may feel a sense of loss, anxiety, loneliness, and insecurity after such a windfall. Therefore, future research should expand upon the current focus by comparing instances of other non-normative, lived experiences to one's feeling rules. Continued exploration of non-normative emotional experiences will increase the validity of future research and expand the scope of current theories surrounding emotion.

The analyses presented here highlight how contradiction between forgiveness-related feeling rules and lived experience is overcome through a redefinition of the situation, potentially informing future research on feeling rules, emotion norms, and emotion management. These findings raise our awareness to the need to operationalize feeling rules and experienced emotion separately, considering where one's ideas and ideals about emotion may confirm or contrast with their lived and narrated experiences. As the subfield of emotion grows within sociology, we must bolster our understanding by moving beyond the laboratory, where we generally hear from undergraduate students recollecting relatively minor emotional experiences or anticipating their reactions to hypothetical situations, and investigating the real-world experiences of a range of emotions in context.

In order to continue investigating these issues, further research is needed to compare forgiveness-related feeling rules to lived experiences of forgiveness of various levels of harm. Comparative work is needed to determine if forgiveness of extreme harm is fundamentally distinct from forgiveness of lesser harms and if it involves different processes. Longitudinal work could also elucidate processes related to the establishment and transformation of feeling rules. As Arlie Hochschild eloquently noted with regard to feeling rules, "What is early and what is late is as profoundly a social affair as what is too much and what is too little."[17] Researchers should continue to investigate relevant change, as one moves in and out of social groups and positions, interacting with various influential others. Co-victims and others who have experienced extreme harm could provide a valuable perspective on such change, as we could explore how their feeling rules may change as they experience the raw emotion following such events, which may be less governed than other, less intense emotions. Perhaps feeling rules have not been crystallized for those who are experiencing such traumatic loss, offering a vantage point from which to explore establishment and communication of feeling rules as well. This could be investigated with further observational research in self-help groups such as those explored here.

Similarly, we must take into consideration such factors as previous social interaction and current social position. Research indicates that emotion norms may vary based on social identities[18] and status characteristics,[19] therefore future investigations of emotion generally, and forgiveness narratives in particular, should include demographic considerations to determine if people in various positions or with various social histories hold different ideologies and indicate more or less congruence between feeling rules and lived experience.[20]

In the next two chapters, I concentrate on the two forgiveness-fostering factors most salient in participants' narratives: understanding and empathy. Analyses surrounding these factors will provide answers to the question of *how* individuals come to forgive extreme harm, after which point I will take up the question of *why*.

Questions for Further Discussion

1   How might the severity of the offense affect what factors foster or impede forgiveness?
2   How might the relationship between the harmed party and the person who caused the harm affect the forgiveness process?
3   Which is more influential toward fostering forgiveness, the offender feeling remorse or expressing remorse? Why?
4   Is it possible to fully understand the mindset of a violent offender if one has never engaged in a violent act? Is such understanding necessary for forgiveness?

Notes

1   Analyses presented in this chapter were previously published: Hourigan, Kristen Lee. 2018. "Forgiving the unforgivable: An exploration of contradictions between forgiveness-related feeling rules and lived experience of forgiveness of extreme harm." *Humanity & Society* 43(3):270–294. https://doi.org/10.1177/ 0160597618801049
2   Zechmeister, Jeanne S. and Catherine Romero. 2002. "Victim and offender accounts of interpersonal conflict: Autobiographical narratives of forgiveness and unforgiveness." *Journal of Personality and Social Psychology* 82(4):675–686. https:// doi.org/10.1037//0022-3514.82.4.675
3   Exline, Julie Juola, Roy F. Baumeister, Anne L. Zell, Amy J. Kraft, and Charlotte V. O. Witvliet. 2008. "Not so innocent: Does seeing one's own capability for wrongdoing predict forgiveness?" *Journal of Personality and Social Psychology* 94(3):495–515. https://doi.org/10.1037/0022-3514.94.3.495
4   Jordan, Jennifer, Francis J. Flynn, and Taya R. Cohen. 2015. "Forgiven them for I have sinned: The relationship between guilt and forgiveness of others' transgressions." *European Journal of Social Psychology* 45:441–459. https://doi.org/ 10.1002/ejsp.2101
5   Exline, Julie Juola, Roy F. Baumeister, Anne L. Zell, Amy J. Kraft, and Charlotte V. O. Witvliet. 2008. "Not so innocent: Does seeing one's own capability for wrongdoing predict forgiveness?" *Journal of Personality and Social Psychology* 94(3):495–515. https://doi.org/10.1037/0022-3514.94.3.495

6 Zechmeister, Jeanne S. and Catherine Romero. 2002. "Victim and offender accounts of interpersonal conflict: Autobiographical narratives of forgiveness and unforgiveness." *Journal of Personality and Social Psychology* 82(4):675–686. https://doi.org/10.1037//0022-3514.82.4.675

7 Eaton, Judy, C. Ward Struthers, and Alexander G. Santelli. 2006. "The mediating role of perceptual validation in the repentance–forgiveness process." *Personality and Social Psychology Bulletin* 32:1389–1401. https://doi.org/10.1177/0146167206291005

8 Struthers, C. Ward, Judy Eaton, Rachelle Mendoza, Alexander G. Santelli, and Nicole Shirvani. 2010. "Interrelationship among injured parties' attributions of responsibility, appraisal of appropriateness to forgive the transgressor, forgiveness, and repentance." *Journal of Applied Social Psychology* 40(4):970–1002. https://doi.org/10.1111/j.1559-1816.2010.00607.x

9 Hochschild, Arlie R. 1979. "Emotion work, feeling rules, and social structure." *American Journal of Sociology* 85(3):551–575. https://doi.org/10.1086/227049

10 Govier, Trudy. 2012. "Public forgiveness: A modest defense." pp. 25–36 in *Public Forgiveness in Post-Conflict Contexts,* edited by B. Van Stokkom, N. Doorn, and P. Van Tongeren. Antwerp: Intersentia.

11 Struthers, C. Ward, Judy Eaton, Alexander G. Santelli, Melissa Uchiyama, and Nicole Shirvani. 2008. "The effects of attributions of intent and apology on forgiveness: When saying sorry may not help the story." *Journal of Experimental Social Psychology* 44(4):983–992. https://doi.org/10.1016/j.jesp.2008.02.006

12 Festinger, Leon. 1957. *A Theory of Cognitive Dissonance.* New York, NY: Harper & Row.

13 The value of such narratives in studies of victimization, and methodological strategies for exploring them, are discussed at length in Hourigan, Kristen Lee. 2019. "Narrative victimology: Speaker, audience, timing." pp. 259–277 in *The Emerald Handbook of Narrative Criminology,* edited by Jennifer Fleetwood, Lois Presser, Sveinung Sandberg, and Thomas Ugelvik. Bingley, UK: Emerald Publishing. https://doi/org/10.1108/978-1-78769-005-920191024

14 Smith-Lovin, Lynn. 1990. "Emotions as the confirmation and disconfirmation of identity. An affect control model." pp. 238–270 in *Research Agendas in the Sociology of Emotions,* edited by Theodore Kemper. New York, NY: SUNY Press.

15 Blumer, Herbert. 1969. *Symbolic Interactionism: Perspective and Methods.* Upper Saddle River, NJ: Prentice-Hall; Mead, George H. 1934. *Mind, Self and Society.* Chicago, IL: University of Chicago Press.

16 Thoits, Peggy. 1995. "Managing the emotions of others." *Symbolic Interaction* 19(2):85–109. https://doi.org/10.1525/si.1996.19.2.85

17 Hochschild, Arlie R. [1983]2012. *The Managed Heart: Commercialization of Human Feeling.* Oakland, CA: University of California Press (p. 67).

18 Pierce, Jennifer L. 1995. *Gender Trials: Emotional Lives in Contemporary Law Firms.* Berkeley, CA: University of California Press; Seery, B. L. and M. S. Crowley. 2000. "Women's emotion work in the family: Relationship management and the process of building father–child relationships." *Journal of Family Issues* 21(1):100–127. https://doi.org/10.1177/019251300021001005

19 Harlow, R. 2003. "Race doesn't matter, but ...: The effect of race on professors' experiences and emotion management in the undergraduate college classroom." *Social Psychology Quarterly* 66(4):348–363. https://doi.org/10.2307/1519834; Presser, Lois. 2013. *Why We Harm*. London: Rutgers University Press; Wingfield, A. H. 2010. "Are some emotions marked 'whites only'? Racialized feeling rules in professional workplaces." *Social Problems* 57(2):251–268. https://doi.org/10.1525/sp.2010.57.2.251

20 In order to first develop an articulate discussion of feeling rules versus lived experience of forgiveness, demographic variation across participants' experiences was not included here. Future analyses of the larger project from which the current sample emerged will be forthcoming. That analysis will allow for expansion upon the current findings by considering variation across race, religion, gender, social class, age, time since the loss, and the circumstances of the homicide.

Chapter 4

"I could've been the one in jail for murder"

How Experiential Empathy Fosters Forgiveness in Cases of Close Cultural Proximity between Forgiver and Forgiven

A lot of my people from where I grew up are doing 50, 60 years in prison [for murder], so I was kinda spared from that situation. I could've been the one in jail for murder.—Deion

"I forgave the gentleman who killed my daughter …" Her next words fall on deaf ears. I am staggered and intrigued by her use of the word "gentleman," coupled with her polite, respectful attitude toward the man who had brutally slain her daughter and seven other young women in the area. To me, "gentleman" implies a degree of esteem. I wonder, does she afford this man such respect?

I sit beside her at a small dining table, the single-bedroom apartment bright with the afternoon sun. The comfortable simplicity of the space and her warm nature remind me of my maternal grandmother, who would have also been in her 80s if she were alive on this day. With a similar calm, open poise that made all those in her presence feel accepted and welcome, my grandmother often said *"a place for everything, and everything in its place."* Perhaps this saying was a testament to the times in which both women came of age, not only as it relates to the practice of ensuring there is an allotted space for winter quilts and soup ladles, but also as it relates to governing one's emotional space. There is no doubt that Barbara continues to mourn the loss of her daughter and still feels deeply the anguish, sorrow, and helplessness that accompany the memory of her daughter's life, cut short before she had the opportunity to fully realize her own potential. In conversation about her daughter's murder, Barbara's pain is clear. But as she speaks, whether in conversation with me, sitting among co-victims at self-help group meetings, or when poised in front of a semicircle of inmates, it is difficult to question the authenticity of her words, which communicate an unwavering and, at times, astounding level of acceptance of the man who others refer to as *"a monster."* Barbara does not harbor anger, hatred, or contempt; she does not seek or fantasize of revenge. It is as if she has created an emotional "place" for the man to exist, separate from his heinous acts. I think, *"A place for everything, and everything in its place."* It is as if, in Barbara's heart, there are separate "places" for her love for her daughter, for her pain of loss, for her motivation to create good from tragedy, and for her compassion for the man who she has come to regard as incapable of remorse or moral action. The separation of these emotional spaces allows for their simultaneous existence. Just as her tidy apartment holds multiple spaces, separate yet all within reach, her heart provides countless recesses within which her emotions can reside, each distinct in their focus, nature, and strength, yet connected by an underlying sensitivity and acceptance of both self and others.

Barbara's forgiveness was remarkable and, in many ways, inspired the writing of this book, sparking within me a level of intrigue that fueled my work and motivated me to open myself up to the heart-wrenching stories of so many people, who would become my friends. I was determined to understand her forgiveness and share that understanding with the world. During the writing of this chapter, Barbara passed away. When I received the call, I was heartbroken; but I was also honored. I was honored to have known this incredible woman, honored to have become her friend, and honored to have been given the gift of her story. During her life, Barbara touched countless others, using her story of loss and forgiveness to inspire change and promote inner serenity and outward compassion despite the traumas and tragedies that befall us. It is my hope that this book, and her words within it, will continue that legacy, bringing a sense of inner calm and outward acceptance to readers from all walks of life.

A year after I first heard Barbara refer to the man who took so many lives as *"the gentleman who killed my daughter,"* a man explained to me how he had forgiven the man who killed his cousin but could never forgive the man who killed his grandmother. He said resolutely that the difference was in the perpetrators' varying levels of adherence to *"the rules and the principles of the streets."* Stories such as these are at the heart of this chapter and the next. I have long been fascinated by the use of language, but these were more than cases of interesting word choices. These individuals had clearly redefined the situations surrounding the homicides of their loved ones to align their emotions with their interpretations of reality. But, how? And, why? In the pages that follow, I will show how these individuals, and others like them, enter a state of forgiveness for what many consider an unforgivable crime. I argue that, at least in cases of extreme harm, individuals may redefine the actor (the offender), object person (the lost loved one), or behavior (the killing) through processes related to role-taking, thereby generating empathy for the offender and ultimately forgiving. These targets of redefinition developed from the theoretical categories of Affect Control

Theory (actor, object person, and behavior), a perspective to which I will return in more detail in Chapter 5.

In this chapter and the next, I investigate the forgiveness process in cases of varying cultural distance and consider the roles played by identity and emotion, applying a symbolic interactionist framework, including applying the above categories of redefinition. In doing so, I offer insight into two distinct types of empathy, which I call "experiential empathy" and "speculative empathy," and I demonstrate the paths co-victims take to enter these two states of empathy. As I will show, these two forms of empathy are distinct in their processes, although similar in their effects.[1]

Background

Based on previous research, one would not expect an individual to forgive an act that was vicious, intentional, and perpetrated by an individual who lacks remorse and fails to accept responsibility.[2] Yet, forgiveness in such cases can, and does, occur. In this chapter, I will show how such forgiveness may be based on the forgiver's ability to understand the circumstances of the event and therefore empathize with the offender.

Several empirical studies have established a strong connection between forgiveness, understanding, and empathy. We know that higher levels of empathy are related to a stronger likelihood of forgiveness[3] and that empathy is most likely to result when an individual recognizes similarities between self and other or perceives a common cultural background or group membership.[4] This explains why individuals are more likely to forgive when they are able to understand the perspective of the offender,[5] when they believe the offender has a shared history,[6] or when they view themselves as similar to the offender or as capable of committing similar transgressions (in both severity and type) as those committed against them.[7]

Conceptualization of Terms

Empathy

As is the case with forgiveness, various definitions exist for the concept of empathy and social scientists do not agree as to what it does, and does not, include. Therefore, it is important here that I clearly delineate what I mean when using the term empathy.

One aspect of empathy that is widely accepted is the ability to take on the perspective of the other and thereby perceive the situation as it is perceived *by* the other.[8] Hoffman explains that this is based on the empathizer's ability to relate the situation of the other to one he or she has personally experienced.[9] This ability may or may not be accompanied by cognitive, motivational, or behavioral outcomes[10] as well as both parallel and reactive emotion.[11] Using a sociological lens, Turner and Stets[12] note that empathy should be viewed not as an emotion but as a "meta-emotion," a mechanism that allows for a deeply intersubjective form of role-taking.

In light of the most current sociological research, empathy is conceptualized here as:

- *Empathy: the ability to recognize, or cognitively construct, the emotional experience of another, understand that emotional experience, and subsequently experience parallel or reactive emotions.*

As such, empathy is not an emotion, rather it is a cognitive facility that engenders emotion in response to one's perceptions and interpretations of the experience of another. Empathy therefore has both cognitive and affective features. The emotions generated may be reflective, as in "*I shared in her joy as she accepted her diploma,*" which indicates the empathizer is also feeling the emotion of joy (parallel emotional response). Alternately, the empathizer's emotions may be reactive in nature, as in "*I felt sorry for her as she expressed her struggles with jealousy.*" Here, the empathizer is not feeling a parallel emotion (she is not sharing the feeling of jealousy) but a reactive emotion (sympathy for the other, which may be based on the empathizer's previous experiences of jealousy).

Though the majority of previous research exploring empathy utilizes a psychological framework, sociologists have recently begun elaborating upon early work by explicitly employing a symbolic interactionist framework.[13] Building upon this foundation, I argue that empathy occurring at varying cultural distances can be explained by use of this perspective.

Since empathy is inter-personal by definition, it is well suited for an individual-level, sociological investigation. Also, its direct connection to inter-personal understanding and perceived similarity make it an inherently sociological phenomenon and well supported by a symbolic interactionist viewpoint. Symbolic interactionists explain that people's perceptions, interpretations, and evaluations of reality, including the actions of others, are determined by learning that took place during previous interactions within social groups.[14] People's reactions to events are determined by these perceptions, interpretations, and evaluations,[15] and therein lies the key to understanding and predicting behavior and emotion. Identities are assigned to self and other, and each identity is associated with sets of meanings and role expectations, which serve as a standard for evaluating behavior.[16] Behavior is evaluated through the process of role-taking.[17] Such role-taking is conceptualized here as:

- *Role-taking: projecting oneself into the roles of others and appraising the situation, oneself in the situation, and possible lines of action from the standpoint of others.*

Through role-taking, shared social histories lead to understanding, which fosters the empathy that results in forgiveness.

But we do not yet understand what separates those who do and do not forgive offenders who are culturally close, nor do we know how forgiveness occurs in cases of great cultural distance and if empathy is involved in such cases. Here, I investigate role-taking processes at varying levels of cultural distance in order to clarify differences in the empathic processes in cases of varying cultural distance between actors. The current chapter focuses upon the way in which understanding and empathy foster forgiveness in cases of close cultural proximity between forgiver and forgiven. The subsequent chapter will then take up the questions of how such processes unfold in cases of distant cultural proximity.

The Process of Forgiveness in Cases of Close Cultural Proximity: Experiential Empathy

Early in my data collection process, it became clear that the stories of those who spoke of forgiveness often included themes of understanding and empathy, whereas those who were unforgiving spoke of a lack of empathy and inability to understand the offender's perspective. In order to more clearly explore both situations, I separated data into cases by cultural proximity.

"Close cultural proximity" refers to cases in which participants spoke of offenders sharing a common or similar culture. For example, participants spoke of following a shared *"code,"* holding the same *"principles,"* having a common *"lifestyle,"* living within a similar *"environment,"* or identifying with a common group. Shared groups included gangs, families, neighborhoods, and *"blocks."* Participants classified as "close cultural proximity" often also shared several demographic and/or structurally based characteristics with the offenders in their cases, such as gender, race/ethnicity, social class, religion, and educational attainment level, but it is important to note that classification was based on participants' references to cultural commonality rather than demographic information.

"Distant cultural proximity" refers to cases in which no similarities were shared in the participant's narrative or during victim-centered events in terms of values, role expectations, behavioral norms, group membership, upbringing, or lifestyle. In most of these cases, participants also highlighted stark distinctions between the groups they considered themselves a part of and those to which they believed the offenders belonged.

In total, 20 cases in my sample were categorized as "close" and 16 as "distant." In each of these categories, there were cases of both forgiveness and unforgiveness, and in each case of forgiveness there was evidence of empathy. However, as I will show in this chapter and the next, the process by which participants entered a state of empathy varied depending on their cultural distance from the offender.

Understanding through Role-Taking in Groups

The first aspect of the forgiveness process that deserves attention is the development of understanding through role-taking that occurs within groups of similar others. As seen in studies of forgiveness of minor offenses, co-victims in this sample who perceived themselves or their lived experiences as similar to the offenders' or as belonging (or having belonged) to a similar social environment often entered a state of forgiveness through what I call "experiential empathy." This was the case for 12 participants in the sample. Though their early emotional reactions to the homicides included intense anger, desire for revenge, and avoidance motivations, all indicative of initial unforgiveness, these emotions were quelled when co-victims redefined the event (Figure 4.1). Based on a specific understanding of the social context within which the homicide occurred, these participants were able to take on the role of the offender, consider his or her perspective, and create meaning. For some, this involved redefining the act of killing as an appropriate response to the specific circumstances leading up to the event; for others the loved one lost was redefined as an antagonist in the event. Such redefinition facilitated empathy and thereby forgiveness.

This empathic process was dependent upon the co-victim's ability to view the self as capable of making the same behavioral choices if facing

Figure 4.1 Forgiveness through experiential empathy (particularistic role-taking)

Source: Figures are replicated, with permission, from previously published analyses from this project: Hourigan, K. L. 2019. "'The gentleman who killed my daughter': Exploring the effects of cultural proximity on forgiveness after an extreme offense." *Journal of Ethnographic and Qualitative Research* 13:212–230..

similar circumstances and a personal understanding of the social environment that fostered the violence leading to the murder. I refer to this type of empathy as "experiential" because of its dependence upon direct, personal experience. Those co-victims who entered a state of forgiveness through empathy in this manner discussed a period in which they sought understanding of the offender's circumstances. There was clear evidence of role-taking, as participants discussed putting themselves *"in* [the offender's] *shoes,"* viewing the circumstances from *"the other side,"* and trying to *"see through* [the offender's] *eyes."*

Several participants described a direct, personal understanding of the circumstances within which the murder occurred based on their social histories and/or prior involvement in violent lifestyles. This is directly aligned with the work of Michael McCullough and colleagues,[18] who found that forgiveness is more likely in inter-personal situations in which the forgiver perceives a shared history with the forgiven, as well as with Martin Hoffman's[19] findings that empathy is based on the empathizer's ability to relate the situation of the other to one he or she has personally experienced. These individuals understood the roles the offender was acting within at the time of the murder, the "code of the street," as described by Elijah Anderson.[20] When the actions leading up to and including the homicide adhered to shared behavioral standards associated with these roles, empathy resulted and led to forgiveness.

Roshaun talked about how he may have been the one in prison for murder if the circumstances were different. He described his neighborhood where violence was commonplace, saying, *"You could get jumped, shot, or stabbed."* Roshaun had lost many loved ones to homicide and had several close friends and family members imprisoned for murder. Roshaun explained that he understood the circumstances of such violence because he had *"seen the dark side of life."* Roshaun discussed how his time *"on the streets,"* living a life of violence, fostered a deep understanding for the offender's actions. He said, *"I get it, because I was there."* He shared how he eventually came to see himself as a *"villain,"* saying, *"You look at that mirror, in your face, and you start thinking about everything that you've done did in the past that are haunting you."* In his view, his forgiveness was a result of that understanding: *"I've forgiven* [the offender]. *I mean, you got to understand to forgive."*

Deion, who had also lost several loved ones to homicide, shared a similar story, describing what he referred to as *"a tough life"* involving *"lots of gun play"* and discussing how his time dealing drugs, *"hustling,"* and *"running"* in gangs could have resulted in a very different life course. Not only did Deion regularly interact with people who engaged in acts of serious violence, he had also acted within the role of a violent offender. He shared how he and his brother *"grew up doing things that we wasn't supposed to do,"* saying it *"felt right at the time."* Although Deion had been imprisoned multiple times for gang- and drug-related crimes, he had never taken a life, despite his involvement in activities which, for others, led to such events. At a local community event, Deion told me that he was effective in his current role as an anti-violence outreach worker because he had *"lived that life"* and therefore understood the roles associated with violent groups. He said, *"A lot of my people from where I grew up are doing 50, 60 years in prison* [for murder], *so I was kinda spared from that situation. I could've been the one in jail for murder."* Like Roshaun, Deion's first-hand experiences within the environment in which the offenders lived resulted in forgiveness of those responsible for taking the lives of those he loved.

Daniel, a 30-year-old anti-violence outreach worker raised within the same environment in which his cousin was killed, also had an intimate knowledge of the *"street life"* that fostered his forgiveness. He said, *"I seen things, I've done things that I'll never want to think about, I will never want to even go through again. I even get chills because of the things that I done did."* Daniel said, *"That ain't the life for me,"* and he had begun using his experience to bring about change for future generations. These participants had an intimate knowledge of the standards of behavior associated with gang involvement, drug dealing, or violence in general. Their forgiveness was born from an ability to role-take and understand the specific circumstances of the homicide and the role expectations within the social environment, having acted within such roles in the past. Doing so led these participants to deem the offenders who had taken the lives of their loved ones as empathy-worthy.

Though the majority of participants had ceased all criminal behavior in lieu of pro-social opportunities by the time of their interviews, proudly serving as a *"role model"* or *"asset to the community,"* their past experiences surviving within an area of concentrated poverty, with high levels of drug- and gang-related activity, left them with an acute understanding of the standards of behavior within such an environment. When they engaged in role-taking, many redefined the actions of the offender as within the limits of such standards. Omarr, who lost several loved ones to violence during a time when he was heavily involved in drug-trafficking, redefined his cousin's homicide as an act of self-defense, ultimately blaming his cousin for his own death. However, this redefinition of the situation occurred only after Omarr heard from a direct witness to the event. During his first interview, Omarr explained how he viewed his cousin's role in his own death based on the principles he and his cousin lived by, what he called the *"code of the street."* He explained that if someone draws a weapon they are expected to use it and, therefore, a lethal response is acceptable:

> One of the rules was that a gun was not a show-and-tell toy. If someone had to know that you had a gun it was with the deliberate intention of using it and full

> *follow through. It wasn't a threatening tool ... So the violation for* [my cousin]
> *was that ... he pulled the weapon out and he didn't follow through with what*
> *weapons are used for ... According to the game and the rules, he was overpowered*
> *and the person who was initially the victim of his attack ended up with the*
> *weapon ... According to the rules and the principles of the streets of that time, he*
> *died as a consequence of his own error and misjudgment.*

When Omarr learned of his cousin's involvement in his own death, his feelings of rage toward the offender were mollified, as were his plans for revenge. When he saw the offender years later, while he and the offender were both imprisoned, he expressed his understanding of the event and offered his forgiveness.

Omarr later told me, in a second interview, that he had lost five other family members since his cousin's death. When I asked about the circumstances, he said:

> [They] *were pretty much the same in principle. Different dynamics, one was a*
> *robbery versus this or that, but pretty much the same in principle in that it was*
> *the attitude and activities of the street. For example, one of my other cousins*
> *who lost his life, this was at a time when* [there] *was a lot of territorial con-*
> *frontation ... And with this particular cousin, he was one that had fed into that*
> [territorial] *mindset. And days preceding* [his death], *the same group that was*
> *responsible for his homicide were uptown* [in his cousin's territory]. *And, he*
> *was made aware that they were up there. He came out, there was words, and*
> *he chased them off the street, shooting at them. Maybe a week later,* [my
> cousin] *was at a nightclub downtown* [in rival territory], *and a female who*
> *is associated with this group sees him there and sees him leaving by hisself. So,*
> *she makes a phone call to the guys and says, "so and so just left, he's heading*
> *down this direction." So they went down, caught him on one of the side streets,*
> *stepped out of their vehicles, no words exchanged, just gunned him down ... By*
> *the accounts of everyone in the neighborhood, they said all they could hear is*
> *maybe a minute and a half of gunfire and then silence and then laughing. And*
> *then car doors shut and you could hear the car speed off. And* [my cousin] *was*
> *riddled with bullets from his head all the way down to his feet. I can't remember*
> *if it was 15, 25, whatever, but there was no part of his body that was not, you*
> *know, suffering from gunshot wounds.*

As in the case of his other cousin, at first Omarr was enraged when he learned of the death. In this case, his anger stemmed from *"the degree"* of violence used. He said, *"In the moment, of course, I'm ready to respond and react."* As Omarr received more information about the murder, his feelings shifted as his definition of the situation changed:

As I got more information, and more details, by the rules, what can you do? You know? This is something [my cousin] brought upon hisself. He stepped out, he attacked them with guns, they survived it, and they returned the favor, so to say. So what can you do? … 'Cause it's like, the rule is, you pull a gun … you don't leave them to come back to you. You know? You pull it out, you use it, you get the job complete and that's it. So therefore you don't have to worry about these kinda things, at least from that source. So, by that rule alone, that's to say, "You know what, you guys, you put yourselves in a predicament that you didn't finish what you started and you paid the price for it." You know? That's just the rules.

These accounts offer prime examples of how one's emotional response to an event depends upon the definition one assigns to the situation and how altering one's interpretation of the situation will change the resultant emotional response. In each of these instances, Omarr's definition of the event shifted from "*man killed my cousin*" to "*man defended himself against my cousin.*" This redefinition resulted in forgiveness, which Omarr described in a moving account:

The [case] I just described with my cousin that was gunned down, um, I ended up in the same prison with that individual, with one of the individuals actually. And we didn't know who each other was, for probably almost a year of day-to-day interactions, sitting with each other, talking with each other, everything … So this particular prison is structured where there is no floor in between the tiers, so you can yell from the third tier down to the bottom, and so on and so forth. So a conversation was happening from floor to floor … And then one day, one of my, as we use to call them, one of my "soldiers" [heard that] the person who was responsible for my cousin's murder was in that cell unit range, where they were talking. And he mentioned it: "We had these dudes from the city, and they came up and killed my man's cousin and, you know, these dudes ain't gon' be able to live in the system. Wherever they go, they gon' get it and they'll never make it out of the system." Bla bla bla bla, and so on and so forth. And after that period of lockdown for count, when it came out, his partner came and got him and told him, "Yo, that dude that you talkin' 'bout is in cell so and so."… So he immediately came to my office, where I had one of the inmate organization offices. He came to my office and told me what transpired, and that the guy was on the range with 'em, told me where he was, and he had been with me every day. And his response was, "I'm letting you know that he's here. And who he is. And I'm ready to get rid of him for you." And, I'm in a different place in many ways at that time, even with my own case and the frustration and anger, I had moved beyond that, even with that dark period within my own self. And now he's pulling me back into a dark space. And it's even more dangerous in there because this guy [the man who killed his cousin] can perceive me to be a threat and try to get rid of me, to make sure he's not hit. So I was mad at my soldier and the situation, and my response to him was, you know, I blasted him first and foremost: "This is why you had no business on the gate, [you] shouldn't have had the conversation." And I read him on that. And my response to the situation was, "I want you to just take your ass home," 'cause he was getting released on parole in like maybe 40 days. And, it's like, "You could really jeopardize staying in here just because you running your mouth on the gate, like you wasn't supposed to. And you put everybody else in jeopardy." Because [the man who killed my cousin] *was a Latino and it's very racially tense in the system. So it was just a big thing, a big mess. I told* [my soldier] *to leave it alone and shut his mouth and let it go. And I didn't want to hear nothing else about it. But now I'm in a position that I'm carrying this knowledge* [about] *somebody that's with me every day. And, it was a lot of mixed emotions, I spoke to absolutely no one about it for a few months, then I had one person that I knew I could trust and confide in, and I shared it with him. He helped me process it out and make a rational or a right decision. And, you know, it wasn't long after that that we separated, um, to different prisons, we were both shipped out.*

Omarr explained that several years after being sent to different prisons, the man who killed Omarr's cousin was transferred to the institution Omarr was housed in. He explained that this prison was *"extremely tense"* and *"extremely divided by gangs and by race."* His account continued:

Everybody stayed in their lane and their zone, so to say. I mean literally, it's undescribable. And, with him being a Latino, and associated with the [international Latin gang] *… you didn't see Latinos walking and talking with the blacks. You didn't. It just didn't happen. As cool as they may have been, unless your name really was heavy enough, that didn't happen, because there was suspicion. You know, if there was an incident where a black was attacked by the Latino, there was a suspicion that you, as a black person, gave them the "up" on how to get to this person. And vice versa. So everybody just stayed amongst themselves. But me and this guy was cool, and I always challenged ignorant attitudes and atmospheres, so I did engage with the whole population of groups, whether they were gang-related, Latino, white, or whatever the case may be. But, one of my cousin's guys that he ran with was also at the prison and on the range with me, with us. And he was very bitter about it. I mean, extremely bitter, like, you know, "If I find out who these dudes are, I'm killin' 'em." And they moved the guy right on the range with him. So now I'm stuck on "where's my loyalty, allegiance gonna go?" You know, and where* [do] *the principles stand? So I went and I told the Latino brother, they called him "Red," I went and told Red, when we went out to the yard, I wanted to walk and talk with him. So, he said, "No big deal." You know, he respected me, so we get outside to the rec yard. They see me* *and him walking, so now the yard tenses up. Because it's like, "OK, somebody's getting ready to get stabbed." And we walking, we just talking, just general conversation as we always did at other facilities. And once I got him where I felt his guard was comfortable with me, I just told him, I said, "I want to share something with you. But, as far as I'm concerned, it doesn't change how I feel and what I think. The only thing that will change the dynamics is how you respond to what I'm gonna share with you." I said, "Now, we've been together for almost 16, 18 months. And I've looked out for you, I've provided for you, I've helped you whenever you turned a corner, even when there were potential conflicts." I said, "So, never can you believe that there's any type of animosity or ill will in my heart towards you." And I was a minister for the Nation of Islam in there, in the system, so his response, "Nah, brother, nah minister, you know I got much respect and love for you. Nobody could ever say that," and I said, "Alright, but listen." I said, "Listen to me close and careful. You caught your case in [city]." And he kinda like tensed a little bit but kept walking, but he slowed, he slowed his step down. I said, "Nah, let's just keep walking." He says, "How you know about that?" I said, "Well, we find out what we wanna know." ... I said, "Your case was with so and so." He's like, "Yeah." I said, "Well, that was my cousin." And he stopped, immediately, and like put some space between us. I said, "Don't do that. Just keep walking. Act like everything is cool. Don't bring attention to it. Just keep walking." He didn't know where anything was gonna come from, so all he could do at that moment is do as I said. And as we walked, I told him, I said, "You know, principles—," you know the same thing I just explained to you, "I found out everything that happened, you know, and that's what has allowed me to move past it." I said, "And as far as I'm concerned, I don't see you any different now that I've told you this, as I did before I told you. Now, the disrespect will come (a) in you trying to maneuver to feel like I'm a threat and get rid of me, or (b) that you wear it as a badge of honor in my face. Almost tossing it in my face, that you're proud of it. Either one of them is gonna bring a bad outcome." And his response was, "When did you find out?" And I told him how long I'd known and I said, "And that tells you I could have gotten you myself, or I could have sent somebody at you a long time ago if that was my intention." He says, "So, why you bringing it up now?" I said, "Because there's someone else on the range who was very close to [my cousin], extremely close to him. He's out lookin' for the perpetrators. And I don't want you to feel that I betrayed my relationship and trust and respect that is built between us by not telling you to watch yourself and watch your mouth." I said, "So, it'll be in your best interest, it'll behoove you, to not speak about this case in this environment." And he stopped for a second, and he just started crying.*

Omarr told me about how this man then apologized *"in his own way"* for taking Omarr's cousin's life, and how Omarr accepted his apology. Omarr's candid account offers a valuable example of expression of benevolent for-giveness. Not only had Omarr released his initial feelings of anger and vengefulness, he also took action to warn this man of an impending threat, demonstrating that Omarr also felt goodwill toward this man, despite the fact that this was the man who had so violently taken his cousin's life many years earlier.

Several other participants who had lost loved ones during street crimes or gang altercations described choices their loved ones had made that placed them within a violent situation, redefining the victim of the homicide as a blameworthy party, as Omarr had done in both cases of his cousins' deaths. Tanya, who lost her first-born son to street violence, said, *"My son lived a life of crime in the streets and he was a victim of his own circumstance and … then he became a victim of the streets."* Others emphasized how their loved ones had *"chosen a life of crime in the streets."* Sandra, who had lost several family members to homicide, said, *"You live by the sword and you die by the sword, and not everybody makes it out, and so I understand that … I mean, they understand that there are certain consequences that go with certain lifestyles."* Here, co-victims are reassessing the level of innocence of their loved ones and, in doing so, shifting some of the blame off the offenders by redefining the act, thereby cognitively constructing an empathy-worthy offender.

Several participants who had never personally engaged in serious, violent acts also had an intimate understanding of the violence found within the social environment they shared with the offender, and such understanding also facilitated role-taking. Participants talked about being *"all in the same community"* and their sense that individuals within the area were *"united."* One participant said, *"We're a family in the neighborhood."* These participants had experienced hardships and disadvantages similar to those who committed murder. The resultant empathy was, therefore, also experi-ential in nature. Letishia described her experience growing up in what she described as a *"rough environment"* where prostitution, drugs, and violence were commonplace:

> *I saw people being stabbed because of the drugs and all that … I've seen violence, people gettin' hurt up, stabbed out, I've seen it as a child … Sometimes my mom and her friends had to rally us kids and hide us into a safe place … we used to run into the abandoned buildings to shelter us from the chaos that was going on out in the street.*

Such participants viewed the offenders' cultures and social histories as con-sequential in leading to the homicides. Having experienced those envir-onments, they understood the relevant group norms and role expectations, including those ultimately leading to murder. Tanya, whose son grew up in the same environment in which he was killed, said:

> *This boy that murdered my son was a 17-year-old kid that grew up on the streets, who comes from a violent background where his father is in jail. And he has guns, and his father has guns, and this is how he was raised up. People say, "I remember that boy when he was two years old, he had a gold chain on his neck." They glorified certain things in this child's mind. That made him come out to be the child that he is today, a murderer ... When you are living the certain type of lifestyle, this is what it is ... My son could have been on the other side where he would have took somebody's life.*

These participants considered themselves members of the shared communities within which the murders took place and had an intimate knowledge of the role expectations within these situations, even if they had never been perpetrators of violence. When they redefined the actors and/or actions of the offender so that the interaction fell within the shared expectations of behavior within the group, empathy ensued, leading to forgiveness. For example, *"man killed my brother"* became *"rival gang member killed my brother,"* or *"John killed my best friend"* became *"John retaliated against my best friend."* Such perspective-taking was based on a direct, personal knowledge of the social environment in which the homicide occurred. The shared cultural understandings and common values in these cases structured participants' definitions of the situation. The moral claim[21] for empathy was therefore available to these co-victims.

Forgiveness through Redefinition of the Event

Forgiveness in cases of close cultural proximity resulted when co-victims redefined the circumstances of the event as adhering to role expectations within relevant social contexts. For example, when asked if he had forgiven the man who killed his best friend, Roshaun said he had. His forgiveness was a result of understanding role expectations in the neighborhood. He said, *"You can't understand when you're outside looking in. It's when you're inside, now you got a different outlook ... You got to understand to forgive."* He explained how he came to understand the offender's actions because he *"realized* [the offender] *had an image to uphold,"* which made violence necessary. Here, Roshaun's first-hand experiences resulted in forgiveness born from an ability to role-take. By assuming the role of the offender, Roshaun was able to redefine the act, viewing it as an act of impression management rather than heinous murder. This reevaluation resulted in a release of anger and vengefulness.

This is a prime example of how one's emotional response depends upon one's definition of the situation[22] and how altering one's interpretation will change the resultant emotional response.[23]

Several other participants who had lost loved ones during street crimes or gang altercations also described choices their loved ones made that placed them within a violent situation, saying things like, *"He was a victim of his own circumstances"* or *"He chose a life of crime."* Here, co-victims were reassessing the level of innocence of their loved ones and, in doing so, shifting the blame by redefining the victim within the event.

Though shared group membership facilitated role-taking, the current findings show that the key to forgiveness lies in redefining the event to foster understanding and empathy. If participants perceived the offenders' actions as conforming to role expectations, forgiveness resulted. But if participants defined the act as senseless, they remained unforgiving. Never was this more apparent than in cases in which participants had lost multiple loved ones and were forgiving in one case and unforgiving in another. Two such cases, described next, arose in the current sample.

Lack of Understanding, Lack of Empathy, Lack of Forgiveness

During his second interview, Omarr explained the difference between his forgiveness of the man who took his cousin's life (described earlier) and the unforgiveness he felt for the man he blames for his grandmother's death. He described what he called *"the balance between gentleman and gangster."* Because his cousin was killed after he pulled a gun during a robbery, Omarr defined his homicide as justified and he was able to empathize and forgive. He viewed the offender as within his rights when he overpowered his cousin. His actions fell within the *"rules and principles"* that Omarr continually referenced throughout our conversations. Within the same narrative, Omarr spoke of the man he held responsible for his grandmother's death. He called the man *"my grandmother's son"* and, when asked for clarification, he hesitantly admitted that the man was Omarr's father, saying *"I can't even use the term 'father' in the same sentence."* Also taking part in the violent subculture within their neighborhood, Omarr's father belonged to the same social group as Omarr, but from Omarr's perspective he had not acted within the standards of that group. Omarr defined his father's actions as immoral and unforgivable: *"I can say totally and absolutely that anything outside of the rules, outside the principles, is unforgivable."* This indicates that, at least in Omarr's case, the definition of the act as adhering to group norms was more important in leading to empathy, and ultimately forgiveness, than was common group membership itself. Therefore, similarity is important in that it allows for more effective role-taking, but it is not the similarity itself that fosters forgiveness. Instead, it is the forgiver's definition of the action as understandable.[24]

Another prime example of this distinction was shared by Vin, a 45-year-old military veteran who differentiated between two losses: his uncle's murder and the loss of his comrades during war, who he described as "[my] *brothers and sisters in arms … like a second family."* Vin said that he would never forgive his uncle's murderer *"because it was something senseless, there was no meaning, no reason for it."* But when lives were lost during war, Vin felt there was opportunity for understanding and sense-making. He said, *"There was a purpose to* [a soldier's] *death, compared to my uncle, there was no purpose there."* Vin believed the enemy soldiers who killed his comrades were acting within the role expectations associated with combat, therefore Vin did not feel vengeful or angry as a result of those deaths. In those cases, he was understanding despite the dissimilarities between the American troops and enemy forces. Soldiers shared common standards of behavior during war, and those who killed his comrades were acting within those standards, understood within the culture of war. Rather than defining the event as *"an Iraqi killed Scott,"* Vin redefined the death of his comrade as *"a soldier killed his enemy."* But since the man who killed his uncle was not acting in accordance with accepted group standards, Vin viewed his actions as unforgivable. Again, this case makes clear that it is understanding based on the perception of adherence to role expectations that is impactful in the empathy–forgiveness sequence, even more so than common group membership. These findings indicate that the crux of the connection between understanding, empathy, and forgiveness may not be in similarity or shared group membership itself, but rather may reside in the particularistic understanding based on role-taking fostered by shared standards of behavior within a common culture, a clarification that may have been previously overlooked.

These findings can best be understood by considering role-taking[25] and its connection to identity.[26] Through a process of role-taking, individuals assess the actions of the other within the framework provided by the identities they perceive the offender (and victim) as holding. If they judge the actions as adhering to role expectations, empathy may ensue, leading to forgiveness. Therefore, though it is true that an individual who views him- or herself as similar to the offender, as belonging to a common or similar group, and/ or as capable of committing similar acts, may forgive through empathy, this analysis shows that this may only occur if the individual (re)defines the event so that the offender's actions are seen as falling within expected standards of behavior. Though previous research shows that shared group member- ship and perceived commonality lead to a higher likelihood of empathy and forgiveness,[27] the current findings explain why empathy and forgiveness occur in some instances of shared group membership or similarity but not in others.

Concluding Remarks

These cases of close cultural proximity between forgiver and forgiven show that the connection between forgiveness and both similarity and understanding that has been shown to exist in cases of lesser transgressions also exists in cases of more severe, life-altering harm. It further supports previous work showing that empathy is a key process involved in forgiveness, that such empathy is rooted in the ability to role-take, and that empathy is largely dependent upon perceived similarities, commonality, or shared group membership. We now know that such connections are relevant beyond cases of minor or non-criminal harm. Most importantly, this analysis offers a clearer understanding of when forgiveness between culturally close others is likely, and unlikely, to occur. It shows that the distinction lies in whether or not the individual in the position to forgive (re)defines the actor(s) or action within the event, thereby interpreting the event as understandable (and therefore empathy-worthy) based on role-taking fostered by a personal, direct understanding of the situation in which the act occurred.

The current chapter has begun the process of explaining the connection between empathy and forgiveness, but there are more questions to be answered. What happens when the cultural distance between people is so great that it seems impossible for understanding to exist? What if direct understanding is not possible due to a lack of common experience, values, or social history? Can empathy still be generated? Is forgiveness still possible? For example, if an individual comes from a social environment in which there is no knowledge of the "*code of the street*," as described by Elijah Anderson,[28] how can he or she empathize when his or her loved one is killed in a violent robbery or by a stray bullet from a gang altercation?

The simple answer is yes, forgiveness remains possible, through empathy, despite dissimilarity between people and great cultural distance. Chapter 5 offers explanation of the processes involved in such cases, introducing the idea of "speculative empathy" and showing how it can foster forgiveness in cases of distant cultural proximity between forgiver and forgiven.

Questions for Further Discussion

1   How might close cultural proximity (such as cases of familial relationship or strong friendship) make understanding more difficult?
2   What role does understanding play in the process of forgiving oneself?

3 How can forgiveness occur if the offender and circumstances are unknown?
4 Is compassion necessary for forgiveness to occur? Is justice?

Notes

1 Sections of this chapter and the next are based on a previous publication from this project: Hourigan, Kristen Lee. 2019. "'The gentleman who killed my daughter': Exploring the effects of cultural proximity on forgiveness after an extreme offense." *Journal of Ethnographic and Qualitative Research* 13:212–230.
2 See Eaton, Judy, C. Ward Struthers, and Alexander G. Santelli. 2006. "The mediating role of perceptual validation in the repentance–forgiveness process." *Personality and Social Psychology Bulletin* 32:1389–1401 https://doi.org/10.1177/0146167206291005; Exline, Julie Juola, Roy F. Baumeister, Anne L. Zell, Amy J. Kraft, and Charlotte V. O. Witvliet. 2008. "Not so innocent: Does seeing one's own capability for wrongdoing predict forgiveness?" *Journal of Personality and Social Psychology* 94(3):495–515. https://doi.org/10.1037/0022-3514.94.3.495; Struthers, C. Ward, Judy Eaton, Alexander G. Santelli, Melissa Uchiyama, and Nicole Shirvani. 2008. "The effects of attributions of intent and apology on forgiveness: When saying sorry may not help the story." *Journal of Experimental Social Psychology* 44(4):983–992. https://doi.org/10.1016/j.jesp.2008.02.006; Zechmeister, Jeanne S. and Catherine Romero. 2002. "Victim and offender accounts of interpersonal conflict: Autobiographical narratives of forgiveness and unforgiveness." *Journal of Personality and Social Psychology* 82(4):675–686. https://doi.org/10.1037//0022-3514.82.4.675
3 Zechmeister, Jeanne S. and Catherine Romero. 2002. "Victim and offender accounts of interpersonal conflict: Autobiographical narratives of forgiveness and unforgiveness." *Journal of Personality and Social Psychology* 82(4):675–686. https://doi.org/10.1037//0022-3514.82.4.675
4 See Sturmer, Stefan, Mark Snyder, Alexandra Kropp, and Birte Siem. 2006. "Empathy-motivated helping: The moderating role of group membership." *Personality and Social Psychology Bulletin* 32(7):943–956. https://doi.org/10.1177/0146167206287363
5 Zechmeister, Jeanne S. and Catherine Romero. 2002. "Victim and offender accounts of interpersonal conflict: Autobiographical narratives of forgiveness and unforgiveness." *Journal of Personality and Social Psychology* 82(4):675–686. https://doi.org/10.1037//0022-3514.82.4.675
6 McCullough, Michael E., E. L. Worthington, and K. C. Rachal. 1997. "Interpersonal forgiving in close relationships." *Journal of Personality and Social Psychology* 73:321–336. https://doi.org/10.1037//0022-3514.73.2.321
7 Exline, Julie Juola, Roy F. Baumeister, Anne L. Zell, Amy J. Kraft, and Charlotte V. O. Witvliet. 2008. "Not so innocent: Does seeing one's own capability for wrongdoing predict forgiveness?" *Journal of Personality and Social Psychology* 94(3):495–515. https://doi.org/10.1037/0022- 3514.94.3.495

8 See Hakamsson, Jakob and Henry Montgomery. 2003. "Empathy as an interpersonal phenomenon." *Journal of Social and Personal Relationships* 20(3):267–284. https://doi.org/10.1177/0265407503020003001

9 Hoffman, Martin. L. 2000. *Empathy and Moral Development: Implications for Caring and Justice.* Cambridge, MA: Cambridge University Press.

10 Davis, Mark. 2006. "Empathy." pp. 443–465 in *Handbook of the Sociology of Emotions*, edited by J. Stets and J. H. Turner. New York, NY: Springer.

11 Davis, Mark. 1996. *Empathy: A Social Psychological Approach.* Boulder, CO: Westview Press.

12 Turner, Jonathan H. and Jan E. Stets. 2005. *The Sociology of Emotions.* New York, NY: Cambridge University Press.

13 For a comprehensive discussion of the development of an interactionist understanding of empathy, see Ruiz-Junco, Natalia. 2017. "Advancing the sociology of empathy: A proposal." *Symbolic Interaction* 40(3):414–435. https://doi.org/10.1002/symb.306

14 Stryker, Sheldon. 1980[2002]. *Symbolic Interactionism: A Social Structured Version.* Caldwell, NJ: Blackburn Press.

15 Blumer, Herbert. 1969. *Symbolic Interactionism: Perspective and Methods.* Upper Saddle River, NJ: Prentice-Hall; Stryker, Sheldon. 1980[2002]. *Symbolic Interactionism: A Social Structured Version.* Caldwell, NJ: Blackburn Press.

16 Stryker, Sheldon. 1980[2002]. *Symbolic Interactionism: A Social Structured Version.* Caldwell, NJ: Blackburn Press.

17 Blumer, Herbert. 1969. *Symbolic Interactionism: Perspective and Methods.* Upper Saddle River, NJ: Prentice-Hall; Mead, George H. 1934. *Mind, Self and Society.* Chicago, IL: University of Chicago Press.

18 McCullough, Michael E., E. L. Worthington, and K. C. Rachal. 1997. "Interpersonal forgiving in close relationships." *Journal of Personality and Social Psychology* 73:321–336. https://doi.org/10.1037//0022-3514.73.2.321

19 Hoffman, Martin. L. 2000. *Empathy and Moral Development: Implications for Caring and Justice.* Cambridge, MA: Cambridge University Press.

20 Anderson, Elijah. 2000. *Code of the Street: Decency, Violence, and the Moral Life of the Inner City.* New York, NY: W. W. Norton.

21 For an explanation of the moral claim's place within the empathic process, see Ruiz-Junco, Natalia. 2017. "Advancing the sociology of empathy." *Symbolic Interaction* 40(3):414–435. https://doi.org/10.1002/symb.306

22 Smith-Lovin, Lynn. 1990. "Emotions as the confirmation and disconfirmation of identity. An affect control model." in *Research Agendas in the Sociology of Emotions,* edited by Theodore Kemper. Albany, NY: SUNY Press.

23 Thoits, Peggy. 1995. "Managing the emotions of others." *Symbolic Interaction* 19(2):85–109. https://doi.org/ 10.1525/si.1996.19.2.85

24 This supports previous work indicating that individuals are more likely to forgive when they understand the offender's perspective: Zechmeister, Jeanne S. and Catherine Romero. 2002. "Victim and offender accounts of interpersonal conflict: Autobiographical narratives of forgiveness and unforgiveness." *Journal of Personality and Social Psychology* 82(4):675–686. https://doi.org/10.1037//0022-3514.82.4.675

25 Blumer, Herbert. 1969. *Symbolic Interactionism: Perspective and Methods.* Upper Saddle River, NJ: Prentice-Hall; Mead, George H. 1934. *Mind, Self and Society.* Chicago, IL: University of Chicago Press.

26 Burke, Peter J. and Jan E. Stets. 2009. *Identity Theory.* New York, NY: Oxford University Press; Stryker, Sheldon. 1980[2002]. *Symbolic Interactionism: A Social Structured Version.* Caldwell, NJ: Blackburn Press.

27 Sturmer, Stefan, Mark Snyder, Alexandra Kropp, and Birte Siem. 2006. "Empathy-motivated helping: The moderating role of group membership." *Personality and Social Psychology Bulletin* 32(7):943–956. https://doi.org/10.1177/0146167206287363

28 Anderson, Elijah. 2000. *Code of the Street: Decency, Violence, and the Moral Life of the Inner City.* New York: W. W. Norton.

Chapter 5

"We are all victims of victims"
How Speculative Empathy Fosters Forgiveness in Cases of Distant Cultural Proximity between Forgiver and Forgiven

Offenders, a lot of times, have a more compelling story than the victims ... They have been victimized themselves ... Basically, people are trying to do the best they can and sometimes they make some horrible, horrible decisions.—Roger

Though all of the accounts of loss that I have heard thus far have been heart-wrenching, Carol's story is especially disquieting. As I sit across from her in a busy diner, I am captivated by her ability to describe her experiences, which must have been nothing less than world-shattering, then turn with a genuine smile and upbeat tone to thank the waitress approaching with soda refills in hand. How could this woman, who had lost both her son and husband 20 years prior, recount her story of tragedy while simultaneously maintaining a positive, sunny emotional state?

Carol explains her motivation to take in a wayward 16-year-old, in order to provide a stable and supportive environment. She says, *"This was not a stranger ... this kid we'd known since the age of four ... He used to run away from home, shoplifted, [and he was] truant from school."* She explains how he had ended up *"on the streets"* and was then sent to a maximum-security juvenile detention center for *"mostly hardened cases, rapists, arsonists ... the bigger stuff."* When he was due to be released a few months later, Carol and her family offered to take him in. She describes how she had come to care for him: *"As far as I was concerned* [he was] *as much my family as* [my nieces and nephews] *were."* She says, *"All we did was try to help somebody, and his payback was to kill my husband and son."* As if such tragedy was not enough for one family to endure, Carol's younger son had been the one to come upon his father and brother's bodies, a trauma that would undoubtedly come with unimaginable effects.

Surviving tragedies such as these is inconceivable. And some believe forgiving those who cause these tragic events is equally unimaginable. In Carol's case, forgiveness did not grow from a personal understanding of the circumstances leading up to the event. Though she welcomed this young man into her home, she had not experienced the sort of social environment from which he had come, in which he was abused and subsequently left unprotected by the criminal justice system. Carol was therefore unable to generate forgiveness based on experiential empathy, as described in the previous chapter. Yet Carol had released all anger and resentment toward this young man. She did not harbor hatred nor did she fantasize about revenge. She had forgiven, but how?

Thus far, I have shown when cultural similarity and common group membership lead to experiential empathy and forgiveness through role-taking. But what happens when this type of particularistic understanding is not possible due to great cultural distance between individuals? Empathy, and therefore forgiveness, may be especially unlikely in cases in which the harmed party and transgressor have very different social environments and histories, and there is, therefore, a lack of understanding of the circumstances leading up to the offense on the part of the forgiver. The current chapter addresses such circumstances.[1]

Here, I argue that affect control allows for a release of these emotions (forgiveness) through what I call "speculative empathy." Through speculative empathy, the transformation of forgiveness remains possible even in cases in which understanding based on similar experience is not possible due to a lack of shared cultural scripts caused by great cultural distance between forgiver and forgiven. I argue that when there is a lack of direct understanding of a specific role being played (e.g., one's role as leader of a local gang) one can move to a higher level of abstraction to facilitate role-taking of a more general nature (e.g., recognizing one's role as a member of a shared humanity). I will show how role-taking at varying levels of abstraction connects to cultural distance between actors, to more clearly explain the forgiveness process. As I will show, role-taking, and therefore forgiveness, does not necessarily require understanding of the act or context. If one can imagine possible circumstances of another, one may role-take in a more abstract manner and therefore empathize through the understanding of emotion. I argue that the motivation for such abstract role-taking comes from processes related to affect control.

It is important to note that Affect Control Theory does not currently encompass the phenomenon of empathy nor do affect control theorists currently model cultural proximity between individuals.[2] However, I argue that such expansion of these facets of symbolic interactionist theorizing could lead to valuable insights into the processes involved in generating empathy and thereby fostering emotional transformation, such as forgiveness, by incorporating more complex nuances of social interaction than previously considered.

Background

Affect Control Theory

First developed in 1979 by David Heise, Affect Control Theory is particularly well suited for explanation of the processes I will describe here, because it is a substantiated theory allowing for consideration of the complex interplay between emotion and identity. I use it here to explain the empathic process relevant to cases of distant cultural proximity between forgiver and forgiven.

Affect Control Theory takes as its focal point the ABO (actor, behavior, object) event. Examples of ABO events for the current analysis may be "my father kills my mother" or "gangster kills Justin." In these examples, the actors are "my father" and "gangster." The behavior is killing. And the objects of that behavior are "my mother" and "Justin." The actor, inter-personal behavior, and object person associated with an event are only artificially separable, as one's definition of the situation, and response to it, depends on the combination of these three elements. According to Affect Control Theory, emotions emerge automatically in response to socially defined situations, and one's emotional reaction to an event is determined by the identity he or she sees each actor in the situation occupying.[3]

Every identity has both cognitive and affective meanings which are internalized from the larger culture within society[4] and aligned with corresponding characteristic emotions.[5] Each emotion can be categorized along continua of three fundamental dimensions of affective meaning: evaluation, potency, and activity.[6] Evaluation refers to the emotion's meaning in terms of good versus bad. Potency is related to the emotion's impact or relative power. And activity concerns the level of animation associated with the emotion. Therefore, all emotions can be described relative to one another, as if falling along three spectra simultaneously: from negative to positive, from vulnerable to powerful, and from passive to lively. Individuals reflect upon who they perceive themselves to be and come to associate core emotions with their culturally defined identities, such as when one is acting in a student-identity and feels proud, as a Buddhist and feels humble, or as a loving individual and feels compassion.

Affect control theorists postulate that emotions emerge in response to internal comparisons made between the transient affective meanings associated with one's identity within the relevant social context (situational self-sentiments) and the individual's fundamental self-sentiments. Such self-sentiments are relatively stable over the life course and across social contexts[7] and individuals seek to maintain these self-sentiments. This is accomplished by embodying identities that confirm self-sentiments. For example, if I generally view myself as confident (my fundamental self-sentiment) I will seek out situations in which I can act within identities that will cause me to feel confident (transient affective meanings) in various situations (the relevant social contexts), such as acting in the identity of "qualitative researcher" by attending conferences to present my latest research or assuming the role of "teacher" by volunteering to guest lecture on a topic I am particularly passionate about. Here, the conference and class session are the relevant social contexts, and the situation-specific emotion of confidence that I feel while acting within the roles of "qualitative researcher" and "teacher" (the transient affective meanings) sustain my fundamental self-sentiment (my general sense of confidence).

Affect control involves behavioral or cognitive changes aimed at maintaining congruence between one's fundamental impressions of self and the transient sentiments generated by one's interpretation of an event's actor, behavior, and object person. When an individual perceives his or her situation-specific emotions as deviating from those sentiments that are characteristic to his or her sense of self (a process known as "deflection"), he or she will be motivated to correct the deviance in order to protect the sense of self. In such cases, one may instigate restorative behavior by embodiment of a compensatory identity that reaffirms his or her self-sentiments.[8] In other words, if the current situation is causing me to feel emotions that are misaligned with the emotions I feel are typical of me, then I will seek out another opportunity to feel the emotions that coincide with my sense of self. For example, I may begin volunteering on weekends to give myself opportunities to feel generous or join a kickboxing gym to create opportunities to feel powerful.

When deflections occur that are unresolvable through changes to behavior, an individual may redefine the situation in such a way as to infer identities to the actors that would result in alignment of transient and fundamental affective meanings (thereby reducing deflections).[9] For example, if I see myself as a generally peaceful person and I become angry when a driver cuts me off on the highway, I will either engage in a particularly peaceful act, intentionally reconfirming my peaceful sense of self in response to my initial anger, or I will qualify the elements of the event by reinterpreting the acts and/or identities of the actors involved in the event, thus invoking new emotions and/or emotion norms. In this example, I may change my interpretation of the event from "driver cuts me off" to "reckless driver endangers my family." In this example, by thinking of the driver as reckless, and viewing the victim of his recklessness as my family, I am invoking my identity as a mother. Because the emotion of anger fits with my ideas as to what it means to protect one's children, the anger I felt toward the driver no longer causes deflection. I can see myself as a peaceful person while also being a mother whose anger is justified in response to a potential threat to her children. In this example, I would be redefining the event that is causing the mismatched emotion, so that my emotional reaction in the situation would align with my fundamental self-sentiments.

I argue that it is through the latter process that empathy is possible in cases of extreme harm and great cultural distance between forgiver and forgiven. In particular, I draw upon previous research which shows that our emotional response to any event depends upon our definition of the situation and how we identify actors and define actions.[10] Therefore, changing one's interpretation of the situation will change one's emotional response.[11] This may include qualifying an identity or assigning an entirely new identity to self or others in order to make meaning of events in terms of revised role expectations.[12] Cognitively framing, or reframing, the relevant situation allows one to construct meaning that naturally engenders emotions in line with one's fundamental conceptions of self.[13]

Though Affect Control Theory was constructed as a means of quantifying emotional experience to predict behavior and vice versa, in 1997 Linda Francis[14] highlighted its usefulness in explaining qualitative data, especially in cases of intense, negative emotion following loss of a loved one. For many, homicide generates prolonged, intensely negative emotions that may conflict with positive self-sentiments. This research focus is therefore well suited for utilizing Affect Control Theory to make sense of qualitative data.[15] As Linda Francis and Richard Adams point out,[16] such inductive research practices provide the opportunity to examine dynamic processes and further enrich established quantitative theories.

The Process of Forgiveness in Cases of Distant Cultural Proximity: Speculative Empathy

Many participants in my work did not perceive a shared social identity with the offenders in their cases. In fact, in several cases the cultural distance between the offenders and participants was multidimensional: the offenders were within minority racial groups, were raised in areas of concentrated disadvantage, and had experienced such social realities as parental incarceration, low educational attainment, gang involvement, drug addiction, and incarceration, whereas the co-victims associated with these offenders were white, were raised in what they described as *"sheltered"* and *"privileged"* areas, and had experienced such social realities as college educations and financial security. Such variation in experience yields important differences in culture found within the communities participants lived within.

This cultural distance eliminated the ability for the particularistic imaginings that fostered forgiveness when co-victims had a direct understanding of the social environment in which the homicide occurred.

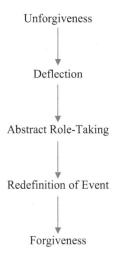

Figure 5.1 Forgiveness through speculative empathy (abstract role-taking).

Previous work has shown that empathy is based on the individual's ability to relate the situation of the other to one he or she has experienced personally[17] and that inhibiting one's ability to take on the perspective of the other reduces empathic concern.[18] However, 12 participants in this study who stood at a great cultural distance from the offenders in their cases had forgiven, and the theme of empathy was still present within their narratives, despite an inability for these individuals to understand the actions of the offender based on shared or similar identities and, therefore, a lack of opportunity for experiential empathy. This lack of direct experience indicates that a separate and distinct process leads to empathy within such cases of great social distance (Figure 5.1). I will show in this chapter that the key process resulting in these participants entering a state of empathy, and ultimately forgiveness, involved engaging in a higher level of abstraction in order to find commonality that could lead to empathy. In particular, I will demonstrate how such co-victims assigned a victim identity to the offender, creating the opportunity for what I call "speculative empathy."

When participants were faced with their original, reactive feelings of prolonged anger, hatred, and vengefulness, they often felt these emotions did not fit with their authentic selves. Such participants often referred to identities they regularly occupied, such as being a mother or a Catholic. Their identity standards included corresponding characteristic emotions that were positive and ranked relatively low on scales of activity,[19] such as compassion and caring. For example, during a meeting of Loved Ones Left Behind

(LOLB), Barbara, who lost her daughter to murder said, *"As a mother, I can't hold hatred in my heart."* Walking together after a trauma and resilience retreat at the local monastery, Glenda explained to me how she felt she *"must be compassionate"* toward the men who killed her brother because compassion is the *"cornerstone"* of her Buddhist beliefs. Others referred to being a *"good Catholic"* or striving to be *"Christ-like."*

When murder caused prolonged feelings that were extremely negative and highly active, this caused deflection from the individuals' fundamental positive self-sentiments. In other words, these intense negative emotions did not align with these co-victims' images of themselves. These emotions were not consistent with those that participants associated with their identities, for example, as a "mourning mother." Such an identity was viewed as less active and more positive than, for example, a "vengeful victim" identity, with its corresponding emotion of rage and motivation to punish. Rage and retribution were misaligned with these participants' self-sentiments and therefore caused deflection. Exemplifying this, participants said things like, *"This was not me,"* and they remembered asking themselves, *"What was I thinking?"*

In these situations, a redefinition of the situation was necessary to combat deflection. In order to feel positive, less active emotions (such as those commonly associated with the process of forgiveness), these participants redefined the offenders as members of a common humanity, diminishing the boundary between self and other. They viewed the offenders as people who had endured great suffering, attaching a qualifying victim identity with revised role expectations. This shift was often made evident through the language used to describe the offender. Rather than using terms such as *"murderer,"* *"heinous,"* or *"evil,"* co-victims began referring to the offender as *"the kid,"* *"the guy"* or, as noted in the opening section of Chapter 4, *"the gentleman,"* describing them as *"troubled,"* *"unfortunate,"* or *"pitiable."* Rather than identifying as the "vengeful victim" these co-victims were thereby transformed into the "forgiving mother" or "compassionate Catholic," for example. Similar to findings of previous work,[20] by cognitively reframing the situation, these co-victims were able to construct meaning that naturally engendered emotions aligned with their fundamental identity standards and self-sentiments. That is to say, these new interpretations of the offenders resulted in the co-victims feeling emotions that were better matched to their fundamental sense of self.

Such reframing of the situation was precipitated by a strong motivation within participants to change their emotional experiences. For many, their intense emotions paralyzed them and *"kept [them] from moving forward"* or *"stagnated."* Jeanne reflected upon a time when her anger and hatred were goading her into becoming someone she was not:

I'm not saying that everybody should be forgiving, that's their choice. But for me, I was becoming so angry and so mean. I was looking for kids to mess with me so I could, like, run them over with my car … I mean the hate [was] *starting to consume me. My health was getting bad and I'm thinking "I can't do this any more." And it took me a long time to get to that point … I felt that* [forgiving him] *was the right thing to do. The hatred was consuming me as a person.*

Emotions serve as a signal,[21] so when these co-victims felt emotions that were misaligned with their self-sentiments, they reasoned that the emotions signaled that something was not right. They felt as if something needed to change within themselves. These participants talked about how the anger and hatred they felt toward the offender were *"consuming"* them or *"weighing* [them] *down."* Barbara, who lost her daughter at the hands of a serial murderer, said, *"I wanted to be able to forgive him because I didn't want to live with anger … I didn't want that* [to have a] *hold over me."* Others shared how their thoughts of revenge frightened them. Jeanne said in regard to her intense feelings of vengefulness, *"*[It] *started to scare me after a while, like, what am I thinking? This is just not me!"*

These participants were describing the distress caused by deflection from their identities as, for example, peaceful or caring people. Their intense discomfort with the persistent experience of feeling emotions that diverged from fundamental identity standards illuminated their connection to the positive identities. These co-victims viewed their negative emotions as misaligned with their authentic selves and sought to resolve the incongruence. Correspondingly, viewing themselves within negative identities such as "revenge-seeker" clashed with their fundamental self-sentiments as good people. A shift in perspective was a means of changing the emotions these co-victims were feeling.

Many of these individuals discussed a point at which they made a conscious decision to shift their thinking toward cognitions more aligned with their true identities. During her first meeting of LOLB, Glenda talked about her conscious effort to get out of a *"loop of rumination"* by focusing on forgiveness and the offenders' basic humanity. And Diane felt that choosing to *"not harbor all this resentment"* would allow her not only to perceive the offender's humanity but to also *"hold on to* [her] *own humanity,"* which she believed resided within her connection to her true identity as a loving and peaceful person.

Forgiveness through Abstract Role-Taking and Redefinition of the ABO Event

These participants redefined the actor in the ABO event, coming to perceive the offender as more than solely a murderer. He or she was also viewed as a member of a shared humanity. References to this shared humanity included mention of people being *"in the same boat,"* referring to the offender as *"a victim too,"* and noting *"this common thing throughout all of us."* Their reorientation toward the offender was accompanied by a curiosity about the offender's circumstances, experiences, and state of mind. One participant explained that it was important for her to *"get to know* [the offender] *for more than his action of murder."* She said, *"That's the only way I knew him. So it was important for me to be able to see the man he is and like how he grew up."* Many participants discussed their certainty that the offender must have been suffering great turmoil in order to reach a state of being homicidal. Cathy referred to this reframing as a *"perceptual shift."* This shift allowed participants to become open to consideration of a shared humanity between self and other and to perceive, or imagine, the suffering of the offender, thereby leading to empathy and ultimately forgiveness by applying a victim label. In this way, participants were finding likeness between self and other, focusing on similarity rather than difference, despite great cultural distance. The victim status of the offender provided the moral claim for empathy, as the offender was seen as empathy-deserving due to his or her victimhood.

This reinterpretation was not based on direct or personal understandings of perspective. Instead, it was born from an ability to imagine the suffering of the other, despite his or her extreme actions, which remained beyond understanding. These individuals identified with general suffering and they reinterpreted the homicide as a result of such suffering based on the offenders' newly applied identity label. They described a belief that all people are capable of making mistakes or *"falling short."* Roger said, *"Basically, people are trying to do the best they can and sometimes they make some horrible, horrible decisions."* He called the robbery resulting in his grandfather's death *"a crime of circumstance"* and explained that we must *"avoid putting people into situations where they can't handle it."*

Often, these co-victims did not perceive the offenders' suffering directly and knew nothing of their experiences, but they were still able to engender feelings that confirmed their self-sentiments by imagining such suffering (by speculating). Reflecting back upon the definition of empathy employed here (*the ability to recognize, or cognitively construct, the emotional experience of another, understand that emotional experience, and subsequently experience parallel or reactive emotions*), these participants were able to *cognitively construct* the emotional experience of the other despite their inability to *recognize* it directly.[22] Even without direct knowledge, many of these forgiving participants speculated about the social environment in which the murder took place. Glenda said, *"The killers were acting according to the rules of their culture."* She viewed her brother's murder *"as part of this larger picture in which a wrong has been done to that whole community, into the core of our society."* She no longer felt anger toward the person who took her brother's life because he was *"probably trying to make his reputation."* She said:

> *I have not been with them face to face but I felt* [early on] *that there were a lot of causes and conditions, there was just a lot of complexity that went into this. The fact that we live in a society that gives unequal opportunity in education to poor kids, and the fact that families are getting destroyed by drug wars, the fact that this whole illegal drug trade has come up through the war on drugs, there are no jobs, and the health of these communities is just not there, and these kids do not have a lot of options. So, I was really aware of that and I did not feel a lot of personal animosity towards the alleged killers.*

Others also placed blame on society's larger injustices and inequities. Renee, whose nephew was murdered after breaking up a fight, referred to the saying *"forgive them because they know not what they do."* She said:

> *I think that* [saying] *is so true. I think that sometimes people really don't know what they're doing. They don't understand. Either through ignorance or who they are. They just don't get what the consequences are … I forgive because … he did the best he could with what he had.*

She described her reaction to seeing the offender's family:

> *The day when he was convicted, they were threatening us. I think that really sealed the deal. I can see how this* [murder] *happened! … 'Cause I saw his family, I saw how he was raised. And that's where I came to that conclusion: you do have to bring up people's pasts to make a judgment. People say you have free choice, and you do somewhat, but you don't have a choice over where you are dropped on this planet or who you are dropped with.*

In these cases, empathy and forgiveness were not obvious, expected, or normative responses. Existing empathy frames[23] did not endorse empathy, but participants were able to perform emotion management[24] in order to cognitively construct a situation in which situation-specific empathy rules[25] allowed for such a response.[26] This emotion management involved these co-victims redefining the situation in which the homicide occurred, thereby recasting the offender as someone deserving of empathy: a victim. As Candace Clark notes, "The more we view a person as a victim of impersonal systems, inexorable processes, or a blocked opportunity structure, the less their personal culpability, the greater the element of impersonal luck, and the more likely we are to sympathize."[27]

For other co-victims, redefinition of the offender occurred without any conscious thought or effort. There was a moment in time when they realized that the only way the action of homicide made sense was if the offender was, for example, mentally ill or under the influence of drugs at the time of the incident. During a meeting of LOLB, Barbara described a moment when her tears suddenly turned to laughter as she was leaving the prison where she had met with the man who had killed her daughter and several other young women in the area. She shared how she realized in that moment that she had entered the interaction with unrealistic expectations:

> *What did we expect? Of course he was not going to be remorseful! After what he'd done to all those girls—he's a sociopath. A person who does those things doesn't understand the harm they've caused. They're incapable* [of remorse].

Barbara and other co-victims like her speculated about the mental state of the offenders, constructing a reality that made sense by qualifying the identity labels of the offenders with states such as *"sociopathic," "high,"* or *"out of his mind."* Using the language of Affect Control Theory, these co-victims had redefined the actor in the ABO event.

These cases are illustrative of the imagination often involved in role-taking. When direct knowledge of the offender's social history was out of reach, participants often imagined the offender experiencing hardships, struggle, mental illness, or drug addiction, which could have led to murder. They cognitively restructured the situation, creating meaning by imagining a past that, in their minds, could lead to such a tragic moment. In doing so, they identified the offenders as proper empathy recipients.[28]

It is important to note that the understanding necessary for speculative empathy is that of the emotional experience. Therefore, empathy does not necessarily require development of an understanding of the act. If one can imagine possible circumstances of another, one can role-take, and therefore empathize through understanding of emotion. Role-taking is "an attempt by one individual to understand another by explicitly *imagining* the other's perspective."[29] One does not need to have meaningful interaction with the other or know details of his or her social experiences; role-taking only necessitates imagery. Similarly, empathy does not require interaction between parties.[30] Empathic imagination[31] is an interpretive process of developing understanding of another person by evoking similar emotions within oneself. If one can imagine suffering, one can empathize with such suffering. As one co-victim said, *"We've all suffered. Maybe not at that level, but I can understand how it feels to see red and be out of control. So I can imagine what* [the offender] *must've been going through."*

In this way, participants made sense of the murder of their loved ones, utilizing what little knowledge they had of the offenders' circumstances, constructing a world to which they knew how to respond. Such redefinition is made possible by focusing upon abstract similarities between self and other (in this case, the ability to suffer) rather than specific differences. These findings indicate that perceived similarity may be more consequential than actual similarity in regard to fostering empathy and forgiveness, at least in cases of extreme harm.

Participants who entered a state of empathy in this manner often spoke of the offender's victim status explicitly, whether it be as *"a victim of the streets,"* *"a victim of the system,"* or *"a victim of circumstance."* Roger said, *"Offenders, a lot of times, have a more compelling story than the victims … They have been victimized themselves."* Similarly, another forgiving co-victim justified violence by saying, *"Hurt people want to hurt."* These co-victims shared a belief that the fundamental reason people cause harm to others is that they have been harmed themselves, therefore, as one co-victim said during a self-help group meeting, *"We are all victims of victims."*

At times, these patterns of thought allowed co-victims to justify continued criminal behavior. For example, Carol maintained a sort of victim status for the 16-year-old her family had taken in, who subsequently shot and killed her husband and son. In her interview, Carol shared details of how the teen, now in his late 30s, had recently had his prison sentence extended because he had been *"caught with a shank."* I asked, *"So he's not making changes to the ways he's acting?"* to which Carol replied, *"Well, you gotta remember they need to protect themselves too. Let's face it, the weak are preyed upon."* Here it is clear that the offender's continued violent behavior is not defined by Carol as evidence of a pattern of anti-social choices or a criminal mindset. Rather, it is justified and defined as expected and appropriate, given the circumstances. In this way, Carol maintained the offender's victim status. This status allowed for judgment of empathy-worthiness, given the empathy rules she employed.

By altering or qualifying the offenders' identities, these co-victims were able to empathize and forgive, releasing their previously felt intense, negative, other-directed emotions, such as hatred, rage, and vengefulness. Instead, their new definitions of the situation engendered emotions that confirmed their self-sentiments, such as sympathy, peacefulness, hope, and care for the offender. As one participant explained, once she entered a state of empathy for the man who killed her mother, *"forgiveness was a natural progression."* Turning back again to the definition of empathy, these participants were experiencing reactive emotion (sympathy, care, etc.) in response to their understanding of the offenders' emotional experiences (suffering).

According to Affect Control Theory, if one experiences emotions that are misaligned with their fundamental identities, they will either redefine the situation and/or engage in emotion management in order to change the impression of self.[32] Here, participants were reframing the situation in order to change or qualify the identity label for the offender (redefining the actor within the ABO event). The perpetrators were often still seen in a negative light, but less so. They were often still held responsible for their acts, but their suffering was also considered. Because our emotional responses are based upon how we interpret events and the actors involved,[33] this reframing engendered emotions that were more aligned with participants' enduring positive self-concepts, such as peacefulness and compassion. These findings support previous research which shows that changing one's interpretation of the situation will change one's emotional response.[34]

Speculative Empathy in Cases of Close Cultural Proximity

It is interesting to note that the speculative empathic process was also present within the narratives of four other participants whose loved ones had been killed by a family member (close cultural proximity) but who defined the offenders' actions as falling outside acceptable standards of behavior. Based on a lack of direct understanding of the action (usually a fatal act of intimate-partner violence), the experiential empathic process, which is based on personal experiences of similar situations, was not available to these co-victims, despite shared cultures and social histories. They therefore found themselves in a similar situation as those standing at a greater cultural distance and underwent the same speculative empathic process to enter a state of forgiveness: redefining the actor in the ABO event in order to combat deflections caused by misalignment between situational and fundamental self-sentiments. For this group, the redefinition involved seeking commonality between self and other at a higher level of abstraction. In other words, when such individuals were unable to empathize based on role-taking associated with direct understanding of the offenders' actions, forgiveness remained possible through a more abstract redefinition of the actor as sharing a common identity as a member of humanity. By doing so, these participants were able to consider the offender's suffering, thereby applying a victim status.

Alex offered a prime example of this process. After over a decade of suffering with intense feelings of hatred and anger, Alex had come to forgive her father for taking her mother's life only after considering his suffering. In doing so she was able to construct a sense of similarity between herself and her father that had been lacking after his heinous act. She said:

> *Once* [I made] *the human connection, understanding that people are people, and we have some great things about us and some great things we do, and then we have some bad things we do, right then it shifted from right and wrong, good and bad, to "we're on the same team here." … Whereas before, you know, there was a lot of anger, a lot of mixed emotions. So, in retrospect, it was the idea of empathy and compassion to other people that got me to consider visiting him, but*

it was the actual human contact that sealed the deal for me. It's really changed my life … Before, I saw [forgiveness] as like a destination and something that was always out of reach. And it was just incredible how it became available after understanding and compassion was there.

Despite Alex's inability to understand his specific actions, she entered a state of forgiveness by considering her father's general humanity. In doing so, she said, *"forgiveness became possible."* Her previously felt negative emotions were replaced by sympathy, compassion, and renewed love. Such emotions were better aligned with Alex's fundamental self-sentiments, evidenced by her description of herself as *"generally, a very positive, peaceful, and loving person."* Forgiveness was accomplished through empathy, despite Alex's inability to understand the circumstances that led to her father's actions.

The four cases falling within this group indicate that this second pathway to forgiveness (through abstract role-taking and speculative empathy) remains available to those who are within close cultural proximity to the offender but do not forgive based on direct understanding. When considered in tandem, these two paths more clearly illuminate the processes involved in the emotional transformation of forgiveness (Figure 5.2).

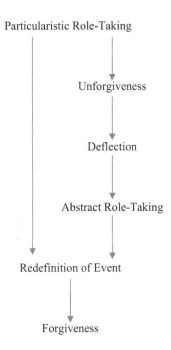

Figure 5.2 Forgiveness through experiential and speculative empathy (particularistic and abstract role-taking).

Lack of Empathy, Lack of Forgiveness

When participants did not enter a state of empathy, they described experiences of unforgiveness. Eight participants fell into this categorization, describing intense anger and prolonged feelings of hatred toward the offender. When asked if he ever felt vengeful, Vin said:

> *Yes, always. And I won't deny this: I've always fantasized about killing that individual … If I could get away with it, I think I'd probably do it…. There's a hatred towards him … Pure and simple.*

These participants often indicated a desire to inflict pain or punishment upon the offender and perceived the consequences of the crime as unjustly lenient, saying things like, *"The death penalty is not harsh enough"* or *"He shouldn't be in prison, he should be under the prison."* Rather than taking revenge, one participant felt justice was best served by the offender *"continuing to live and suffer with his crack habit,"* as more pain would come from such a fate.

One unforgiving co-victim understood the social context of the homicide but judged the offenders' actions as outside acceptable standards of behavior. Dawn, a 35-year-old, explained how her son's actions did not warrant the violence that ended his life. She said, *"My son never once raised his hand,"* describing how her son was calmly backing away from the altercation that ended his life, clearly communicating to the other teen that he did not want to fight. Since her son was not a threat, she felt the attack that claimed his life was unjustified and in violation of the rules of the street, which Dawn understood based on her own cultural experiences. For this reason, Dawn did not empathize with the offender and remained angry and vengeful. For Dawn, particularistic role-taking only solidified feelings related to unforgiveness, because she interpreted the behavior in the ABO event as not adhering to role expectations within the social context.

Other stories of participants falling within this category emphasized a lack of understanding based on the general senselessness of the act. When asked if he thought he would ever forgive the man who killed his uncle, Vin said, *"Forgiveness is not going to happen because it was something senseless, there was no meaning, no reason for it."* Rose offered a similar response:

> *I do not think I can forgive because, my God, how could you do that to somebody? I can see if by accident things happen, I could forgive those things, everyone makes mistakes. But to be intentional, it's really hard to forgive that.*

Here it is clear that participants were unable to effectively take on the role of the offender due to the nature of the offender's actions.[35] The role played by the offender was foreign to them and they had no context for understanding. This negated the opportunity for empathy based on such particularistic role-taking (experiential empathy).

Those co-victims who remained unforgiving also did not move to a higher level of abstraction to establish a sense of commonality with the offenders that could lead to speculative empathy. In fact, two participants placed themselves at such great social distance from the individuals who took the lives of their loved ones that the offenders were described as not belonging to the same general humanity as the participants. These individuals reduced the offender in a similar manner as those who inflict harm, whether it be in justification of genocide, rape, slavery, or the death penalty.[36] Dehumanization signifies exclusion from the "human family"[37] or one's moral community.[38] Here, the offenders' complexities as human beings with impactful histories were denied and they were viewed as solely bad. These co-victims spoke of their respective offenders as being *"a monster,"* *"uncivilized,"* and *"not normal."* Paul, a 57-year-old whose sister was brutally killed during a widely publicized series of cult murders, described the offenders as *"a step beyond being human."* He called the individual charged with his sister's death *"this thing,"* likening him to a *"wolf in the wild."* Paul explained that seeking understanding of the cult's actions was futile due to their lack of human nature:

> *There's nothing to understand ... It's so sick and so non-human, unhuman. I may as well go out in the wild and just talk to a pack of wolves ... If a wolf can talk in the wild, it's not going to explain to you why it ate its prey. It's because it's just an animal.*

Creating such distance between self and other allowed these individuals to maintain their intense, negative emotions while living peacefully and positively in other social contexts. In these cases, the emotions related to unforgiveness were aligned with participants' identities as co-victims (various co-victim identities are discussed in detail in the following chapter). They viewed themselves as individuals who could not, and would not, forgive such heinous crimes. By perceiving the offenders as standing in stark contrast to their own humanity, reduction of the offenders[39] allowed these individuals to maintain their identities as positive and loving people in contexts involving other members of a common humanity, but their feelings of anger and hostility were allowed to persist unabated in the context of murder, because the offenders were no longer characterized as belonging to that shared, moral humanity. Through construction of such distance, participants were able to preserve their fundamental self-sentiments without their interpretation of the homicide causing deflection. When their co-victim identities were socially relevant, the negative emotions toward the offenders were judged as appropriate and aligned with their identities.

In other contexts, when these individuals' co-victim identities were not relevant, the negative emotions were quelled and positive emotions, aligned with enduring, compensatory, positive identities, were felt. Mark, an unforgiving co-victim, exemplified this when he shared how, since his brother's murder, he had worked to generate a *"Zen calm"* in other areas of his life but held strong to the intensely negative emotions he felt toward those who killed his brother. When asked about social support, Mark said,

> *I don't really see the point of going to a counselor and finding that I have one ounce of hatred less for these three ... I don't ever wanna risk forgiving these three kids, and I don't ever wanna risk hating them less, and I don't ever wanna risk my justified rage.*

This construction and embodiment of a very positive, calm identity to balance the very negative, active emotions he associated with his co-victim identity illustrates Neil MacKinnon and David Heise's theory of self,[40] which grew out of Affect Control Theory. As they explain, when the affective meanings one associates with a recently enacted identity are misaligned with one's self-sentiments, the individual will act within a compensatory identity to bring self-conceptions back into alignment. Here, Mark is balancing his co-victim identity by acting within the identity of a Zen practitioner. In Affect Control Theory terminology, Mark is activating a highly positive and inactive identity (Zen practitioner) to offset his co-victim identity, to which he assigns affective meanings that are more negative and active than his fundamental self-sentiments. Doing so protects his self-conceptions from being impacted by the situation-specific emotions related to the identity of co-victim.

The distinction between co-victims who forgave through abstract role-taking and those who did not informs our understanding of the impact of the meanings one assigns to situational identities. The co-victim identity is not associated with widely shared affective meanings. For this reason, individuals experiencing comparable losses may associate vastly different emotions with their newly formed, or still developing, identities. The affective meanings each assigns to the co-victim identity will then determine whether or not their offender-directed emotions will cause deflection due to inconsistency with fundamental self-sentiments. For example, in my sample, some co-victims felt that hatred, rage, and vengefulness were emotions well aligned with their identities as "parents of murdered children" while others felt that compassion, sympathy, and pity were better suited for this identity. Since the former group would not experience deflection based on experiences of intense, negative emotions, they were not motivated to engage in the abstract role-taking necessary to redefine the ABO event in such a way as to temper those emotions. Consequently, they remained unforgiving.

Concluding Remarks

Based on previous research, we know that understanding[41] and similarity[42] lead to forgiveness in cases of minor and/or hypothetical offenses. We now know this is true in cases of extreme harm and have more precisely detailed this pathway to forgiveness. Chapter 4 shows that common group membership influences forgiveness by creating shared role expectations. If action is defined as adhering to these expectations, this path can lead to forgiveness. In such cases, the redefinition taking place is either a redefinition of the behavior (the act of killing) or the object person (the victim of the homicide).

The current chapter indicates that forgiveness is also possible when such understanding is not present and one, therefore, cannot redefine the behavior or object person in the event. In such cases, forgiveness remains possible by redefinition of the actor. In these cases, individuals consider similarity between self and other at a higher level of abstraction, regarding the offender's humanity as meaningful and empathizing with his or her suffering. By applying a victim label to the offender, participants in my sample redefined the offender as empathy-worthy and therefore entered a state of forgiveness.

These findings have practical applications for those who have lost loved ones to homicide. After homicide, a co-victim has a very limited amount of control. He or she cannot alter the circumstances of the murder. Also out of the co-victim's control are the thoughts, feelings, and actions of the perpetrator following the murder. Therefore, co-victims have no control over most of the factors that influence forgiveness, including severity and intentionality of the act; innocence of the victim; and offender acceptance of responsibility, expression of remorse, and pro-social change. If co-victims wish to shift their emotional states, the only factors allowing them such control are understanding and empathy. In other words, following homicide a co-victim's control is, in many ways, limited to his or her own interpretations of the event and the offender. And this work shows that such interpretations are malleable. Therefore, if co-victims choose to do so, focusing upon these two factors provides an opportunity for co-victims to transform their emotional responses. This knowledge has the potential to serve co-victims, as well as those who support co-victims, in that it calls attention to the pivotal factor in fostering emotional transformation: shifting one's narrative.

By more clearly explaining the process of forgiveness through abstract role-taking, this work both supports and extends previous work. It supports work showing that empathy is a key process involved in forgiveness,[43] that empathy is rooted in the ability to role-take,[44] and that empathy is largely dependent upon perceived similarities between self and other.[45] We now know that these claims are also true in cases of serious, real-life offenses.

Despite previous work showing that direct understanding,[46] shared group membership,[47] and the empathizer's ability to relate the situation of the other to one he or she has personally experienced[48] lead to empathy, we now have evidence that the generation of empathy does not necessitate these factors. Empathy remains possible when one engages in more abstract role-taking and perceives more general similarities between self and other. This indicates that perceptions of similarity may be more impactful than actual similarity and that there are different forms or types of empathy (experiential and speculative, for example). This also could be evidence that empathy functions differently in cases of varying levels of harm. Though previous work indicates correlation between similarity, understanding, empathy, and forgiveness, the analyses presented here propose a causal order and suggest the mechanisms through which these factors may promote forgiveness. With this knowledge, we can begin to construct testable hypotheses and predict individuals' emotional reactions to extreme harm and their resultant behavior.

Previous work on forgiveness has been largely descriptive, suggesting what factors make forgiveness more or less likely but failing to offer theoretically grounded explanation of the processes involved in emotional transformation or arguments for why some cases lead to forgiveness and others do not. The current analysis fills this gap by utilizing concepts from Affect Control Theory to propose explanatory arguments regarding how individuals forgive (or do not forgive). We now know that, at least in cases of extreme harm, there are two pathways to forgiveness, each involving role-taking and redefinition of the situation. The first depends upon the forgiver's ability to effectively adopt the role of the offender based upon direct understanding of the social environment. The second involves a more abstract form of role-taking in which the forgiver redefines the offender as a victim, thereby developing empathy and compassion, despite a lack of direct understanding. At present, the models presented here of forgiveness pathways through experiential and speculative empathy remain unpolished and incomplete. Future research should attempt to refine these models and determine if there are other pathways to forgiveness and, if so, how they are distinct from those described here.

This work contributes to the advancement of Affect Control Theory in several meaningful ways. Generally, it extends the limits of the theory by using it to explain qualitative data and observations of people in settings in which strong emotions arise naturally. As Jonathan Turner and Jan Stets suggested,[49] a focus upon the social setting in which emotions naturally arise allows for expansion of well-established theories of emotion. The potent negative emotions studied here fall at the far end of the emotional spectrum. Therefore, these analyses may drive theorists to expand the scope of Affect Control Theory to include emotions that are more intense than those previously studied in a laboratory or by exploring the experiences of undergraduate students, as is often the methodology employed for research of emotion generally and affect control in particular. Furthermore, it applies core theoretical arguments to real-world interactions, presenting instances of redefinition of the actor (offender), behavior (homicide), and object (victim), each resulting in reduction of inconsistency between transient impressions and fundamental sentiments. It also lends evidence to the assertion of affect control theorists that one's definitions are based on prior socialization by showing that many co-victims' definitions of the situation depended upon their prior experience within a violent environment.

This work demonstrates the usefulness of incorporating cultural proximity when modeling interaction and should provoke theorists to develop parameters to measure cultural distance. Identities are positional by definition and are, therefore, always relative within the social context when investigating phenomena of an interactional nature.[50] Therefore, their distance from one another could be quantified in terms of cultural markers. Theorists could develop methods similar to those used to rate identities, actions, and emotions along scales of evaluation, potency, and activity.[51] Identities could be classified as hierarchical and non-hierarchical, then we could ask individuals to organize identities along social hierarchies (for hierarchical identities) and by cultural similarity (for non-hierarchical identities), for example, in terms of values, attitudinal expectations, and behavioral norms. Through such work, we could theoretically establish the relative distance between identities relevant within various cultures (and subcultures), including when such distance is multidimensional. Future work could then include laboratory experiments incorporating a modifier of cultural distance to test predictions about when redefinition of actor, behavior, and/or object is most likely to occur, and to what end. Such research could both validate and expand upon analyses presented here, as it is interesting to note that all cases of forgiveness through abstract role-taking in the current sample involved redefinition of the actor within the ABO event, whereas redefinition of all three aspects of the ABO event was evidenced within cases of forgiveness based on direct, personal understanding.[52] This may be due to the fact that this project investigates events in which the actor is the least-understood aspect of the ABO event. In these cases, the object person (the loved one) is well known by definition, and the behavior is typically verified by witness accounts or police reports, but the actor was most commonly a stranger.

Utilizing controlled experiments to study the effects of cultural distance could substantiate this explanation or generate alternatives.

Affect control theorists are urged to also consider cases at the fringes of social experience, including acts that are less common and identities that are less familiar. For example, at present the algorithms used in Affect Control Theory can be run using myriad relevant identities and emotions, but it is impossible to capture the nuances differentiating various types of homicide. Affect control theorists have not yet quantified distinct killing actions. Therefore, though we could use current affect control models to quantify and form predictions for the event "gangster murders brother," we could not consider differences between similar but distinct events in which the killing action was a consequence of, for example, a jealous rage, an act of swift revenge, the result of a drug-induced frenzy, and a premeditated and heinous act involving torture and post-mortem mutilation. Undoubtedly, these nuances affect the resultant emotions of all parties involved. Given the usefulness of Affect Control Theory in explaining a host of emotional experiences, more work is needed to allow for quantitative application of the theory to actions, identities, and emotions at the fringes of typical experience. Alternatively, theorists could expand upon Affect Control Theory to allow for inclusion of additional qualifiers upon the actors and behavior. For example, it would be useful to quantify the differences between "husband murders wife," "jealous husband murders wife," "husband brutally murders wife," and "husband murders disabled wife." Such work may be especially useful in studies of jury behavior and sentencing outcomes as well as analyses of narrated experience.

The current findings also illustrate the need to include social context and prior social experience when considering emotional transformation and its connection to one's definition of the situation. Affect control processes cannot be removed from the contexts (and their respective situational definitions) within which they take place. Also, our understanding of context is constantly being negotiated in interaction; the meaning of the context shifts and transforms as we interact within it. When we interact with others, the way they describe their experiences and reactions influences not only the way we see the world in general but also the way we view our own social world, both internal and interactional. Future research should focus upon the way interaction with others influences our emotions by affecting the way we define ourselves, others, and our experiences within varying settings and culturally defined institutions. By engaging in more qualitative research, theorists can more directly investigate the shifting nature of definitions of situations as individuals move through their social worlds and interact with others whose experiences not only shape each interactant's worldview but also influence the way each interprets his or her own experiences, whether that be internal, emotional experiences or lived experiences.

Finally, though affect control theorists have explored reidentification of both the actor and the object person in an ABO event, they have not adequately investigated redefinition of the behavior itself as a means of reducing deflection. Here, I have demonstrated instances of redefinition of the actor (offender), behavior (homicide), and object person (victim), each resulting in reduction of inconsistency between transient impressions and fundamental sentiments. Future work expanding Affect Control Theory should include controlled laboratory experiments and quantitative studies that account for redefinition of all three aspects of the ABO event (as well as setting or relevant defining institution) in order to begin to make predictions about when each type of redefinition will occur, and to what end.

The current analysis indicates that the co-victim identity does not have culturally established cognitive or affective meanings. In other words, it has not been fully institutionalized, and those enacting the role do not necessarily agree on the attributes and meanings of the identity. This is not surprising, given that the word "co-victim" itself is used rarely and typically only within academic or similar domains. Those who have lost loved ones to homicide do not typically refer to themselves as "co-victims." In fact, the language they use to label themselves and each other is quite variable. It is clear that co-victims define their identities in varying ways, and the analyses presented in this chapter indicate that these differences are consequential in their social and emotional worlds. Based on previous work, we know that the character of one's emotions is in large part determined by the identities one assigns to one's self in the relevant social context.[53] That is to say, one's emotions are determined, and potentially altered, by the narrative he or she constructs about the self and how it fits within the social world, to make meaning of experience. Therefore, in order to understand co-victims' emotional experiences, we must better understand the co-victim identity itself. To this end, the next chapters of this book will explore various aspects of the co-victim identity (Chapter 6) as well as determine who is likely to adopt one set of meanings versus another (Chapter 7). Such work will aid in better understanding when co-victims will and will not forgive by engaging in higher-order levels of abstraction to generate empathy. Thus far, we have explored *when* and *how* co-victims forgiven; next we will explore *why*.

Questions for Further Discussion

1   How do you anticipate the forgiveness process would unfold in cases of serious harm in which the person who caused the harm and the harmed party are extremely close, such as husband and wife, siblings, or mother and child?

2   Do you believe there are other types of empathy (beyond experiential and speculative)? If so, do you believe the various types of empathy function differently with regard to fostering forgiveness?

3   What emotions, activities, and attitudes do you believe are fundamental to a co-victim identity?

4   What do you believe motivates some co-victims to forgive?

Notes

1   Sections of this and the previous chapter are based on a previous publication from this project: Hourigan, Kristen Lee. 2019. "'The gentleman who killed my daughter': Exploring the effects of cultural proximity on forgiveness after an extreme offense." *Journal of Ethnographic and Qualitative Research* 13:212–230.

2   Schneider has begun work in this vein, demonstrating the usefulness of Affect Control Theory in multicultural settings (see Schneider, Andreas, Linda E. Francis, and Herman W. Smith 2013. "Measuring cultural variations in the sacred and the profane." *Journal of Integrated Social Sciences* 3(1):130–156) and constructing an estimate for cultural intersubjectivity, a Culture Gender Ratio, which standardizes cultural differences through consideration of gender differences between cultures (see Schneider, Andreas. 2002. "Behavior prescriptions versus professional identities in multicultural corporations: A cross-cultural computer simulation." *Organization Studies* 23:105–131. https://doi.org/10.1177/017084060202300106)

3   Smith-Lovin, Lynn. 1990. "Emotions as the confirmation and disconfirmation of identity. An affect control model." Chapter 9 in *Research Agendas in the Sociology of Emotions,* edited by T. Kemper. Albany, NY: SUNY Press.

4   Hewitt, John P. 2003. *Self and Society: A Symbolic Interactionist Social Psychology.* Ninth edition. Boston, MA: Allyn and Bacon.

5   Heise, David. 2002. "Understanding social interaction with Affect Control Theory." pp. 17–40 in *New Directions in Contemporary Sociological Theory,* edited by Joseph Berger and Morris Zelditch. Washington, DC: Rowman and Littlefield.

6   Osgood, Charles E., W. H. May, and M. S. Miron. 1975. *Cross-Cultural Universals of Affective Meaning.* Urbana, IL: University of Illinois Press.

7   MacKinnon, Neil and David Heise. 2010. *Self, Identity, and Social Institutions.* London: Palgrave Macmillan.

8   Heise, David. 2002. "Understanding social interaction with Affect Control Theory." pp. 17–40 in *New Directions in Contemporary Sociological Theory,* edited by Joseph Berger and Morris Zelditch. Washington, DC: Rowman and Littlefield.

9   Smith-Lovin, Lynn. 1990. "Emotions as the confirmation and disconfirmation of identity. An affect control model." in *Research Agendas in the Sociology of Emotions,* edited by Theodore Kemper. Albany, NY: SUNY Press.

10 Smith-Lovin, Lynn. 1990. "Emotions as the confirmation and disconfirmation of identity. An affect control model." in *Research Agendas in the Sociology of Emotions,* edited by Theodore Kemper. Albany, NY: SUNY Press.

11 Thoits, Peggy. 1995. "Managing the emotions of others." *Symbolic Interaction* 19(2):85–109. https://doi.org/ 10.1525/si.1996.19.2.85

12 Heise, David. 2002. "Understanding social interaction with Affect Control Theory." pp. 17–40 in *New Directions in Contemporary Sociological Theory*, edited by Joseph Berger and Morris Zelditch. Washington, DC: Rowman and Littlefield.

13 Hochschild, Arlie R. and Anne Machung. 1989. *The Second Shift: Working Parents and the Revolution at Home.* New York, NY: Viking; Presser, Lois. 2013. *Why We Harm.* London: Rutgers University Press.

14 Francis, Linda E. 1997. "Ideology and interpersonal emotion management: Redefining identity in two support groups." *Social Psychology Quarterly* 60(2):153–171. https://doi.org/10.2307/2787102

15 For another example of use of Affect Control Theory to understand qualitative data, see Francis, Linda E., Kathryn J. Lively, Alexandra König, and Jesse Hoey. 2020. "The affective self: Perseverance of self-sentiments in late-life dementia." *Social Psychology Quarterly.* https://doi.org/10.1177/0190272519883910

16 Francis, Linda E. and Richard E. Adams. 2019. "Two faces of self and emotion in symbolic interactionism: From process to structure and culture—and back." *Symbolic Interaction* 42(2):250–277. https://doi.org/10.1002/symb.383

17 Hoffman, Martin L. 2000. *Empathy and Moral Development: Implications for Caring and Justice.* Cambridge, MA: Cambridge University Press.

18 McAuliffe, William H. B., Evan C. Carter, Juliana Berhane, Alexander C. Sniher, and Michael E. McCullough. 2019. "Is empathy the default response to suffering? A meta-analytic evaluation of perspective taking's effect on empathic concern." *Personality and Social Psychology Review* 24(2):141–162. https://doi.org/10.1177/1088868319887599

19 As described by Osgood, Charles E., W. H. May, and M. S. Miron. 1975. *Cross-Cultural Universals of Affective Meaning.* Urbana, IL: University of Illinois Press.

20 See Hochschild, Arlie R. and Anne Machung. 1989. *The Second Shift: Working Parents and the Revolution at Home.* New York, NY: Viking; Presser, Lois. 2013. *Why We Harm.* London: Rutgers University Press.

21 Hochschild, Arlie R. 1979. "Emotion work, feeling rules, and social structure." *American Journal of Sociology* 85(3):551–575.

22 This aligns well with the claims of other sociological inquiries into empathy, including Clark, Candace. 1997. *Misery and Company: Sympathy in Everyday Life.* Chicago, IL: University of Chicago Press; Cooley, Charles Horton. 1902. *Human Nature and the Social Order.* New York, NY: Scribner; Shott, Susan. 1979. "Emotion and social life: A symbolic interactionist analysis." *American Journal of Sociology* 84(6):1317–1334. https://doi.org/10.1086/226936; and Ruiz-Junco, Natalia. 2017. "Advancing the sociology of empathy." *Symbolic Interaction* 40(3):414–435. https://doi.org/10.1002/symb.306

23 Ruiz-Junco, Natalia. 2017. "Advancing the sociology of empathy." *Symbolic Interaction* 40(3):414–435. https://doi.org/10.1002/symb.306

24 For a review of literature on emotion management, see Lively, Kathryn J. and Emi A. Weed. 2014. "Emotion management: Sociological insight into what, how, why, and to what end?" *Emotion Review* 6:202–207. https://doi.org/10.1177/1754073914522864

25 Hochschild, Arlie R. 2016. *Strangers in their Own Land: Anger and Mourning on the American Right: A Journey to the Heart of Our Political Divide.* New York, NY: The New Press.

26 For another example of how emotion management is used in establishing empathy-worthiness, see Ruiz-Junco, Natalia. 2017. "Advancing the sociology of empathy." *Symbolic Interaction* 40(3):422. https://doi.org/10.1002/symb.306

27 Clark, Candace. 1997. *Misery and Company: Sympathy in Everyday Life.* Chicago, IL: University of Chicago Press.

28 Hochschild, Arlie Russel. 2016. *Strangers in their Own Land: Anger and Mourning on the American Right: A Journey to the Heart of Our Political Divide.* New York, NY: The New Press.

29 Davis, Mark. 2006. "Empathy." pp. 443–465 in *Handbook of the Sociology of Emotions*, edited by J. Stets and J. H. Turner. New York, NY: Springer (p. 446, italics added for emphasis).

30 Hoijer, Birgitta. 2004. "The discourse of global compassion: The audience and media reporting of human suffering." *Media, Culture & Society* 26:513–531. https://doi.org/10.1177/0163443704044215

31 For a discussion of how the concept of "empathic imagination" originated within discussions of "sympathetic knowledge" in the work of Cooley, see Ruiz-Junco, Natalia. 2017. "Advancing the sociology of empathy." *Symbolic Interaction* 40(3):414–435. https://doi.org/10.1002/symb.306

32 Heise, David. 2002. "Understanding social interaction with Affect Control Theory." pp. 17–40 in *New Directions in Contemporary Sociological Theory*, edited by Joseph Berger and Morris Zelditch. Washington, DC: Rowman and Littlefield; Smith-Lovin, Lynn. 1990. "Emotions as the confirmation and disconfirmation of identity. An affect control model." in *Research Agendas in the Sociology of Emotions*, edited by Theodore Kemper. Albany, NY: SUNY Press.

33 Smith-Lovin, Lynn. 1990. "Emotions as the confirmation and disconfirmation of identity. An affect control model." in *Research Agendas in the Sociology of Emotions*, edited by Theodore Kemper. Albany, NY: SUNY Press.

34 Thoits, Peggy. 1995. "Managing the emotions of others." *Symbolic Interaction* 19(2):85–109. https://doi.org/10.1525/si.1996.19.2.85

35 Goffman offers insight into the effects of interpretation of the "virtual offense" as beyond remediation: Goffman, Erving. 1971. *Relations in Public.* New York, NY: Harper & Row.

36 As described by Presser, Lois. 2013. *Why We Harm.* London: Rutgers University Press.

37 Kelman, Herhert. 1973. "Violence without moral restraint: Reflections on the dehumanization of victims and victimizers." *Journal of Social Issues* 29(4):25–61. https://doi.org/10.1111/j.1540-4560.1973.tb00102.x

38 Belanger-Vincent, Ariane. 2009. "Discourses that make torture possible: The Abu Ghraid case." *Explorations in Anthropology* 9(1):36–46.

39 As described by Presser, Lois. 2013. *Why We Harm.* London: Rutgers University Press.

40 MacKinnon, Neil and David Heise. 2010. *Self, Identity, and Social Institutions.* London: Palgrave Macmillan.

41 Zechmeister, Jeanne S. and Catherine Romero. 2002. "Victim and offender accounts of interpersonal conflict: Autobiographical narratives of forgiveness and unforgiveness." *Journal of Personality and Social Psychology* 82(4):675–686. https://doi.org/ 10.1037//0022-3514.82.4.675

42 Exline, Julie Juola, Roy F. Baumeister, Anne L. Zell, Amy J. Kraft, and Charlotte V. O. Witvliet. 2008. "Not so innocent: Does seeing one's own capability for wrongdoing predict forgiveness?" *Journal of Personality and Social Psychology* 94(3):495–515. https://doi.org/10.1037/0022-3514.94.3.495

43 Macaskill, Ann, John Maltby, and Liza Day. 2002. "Forgiveness of self and others and emotional empathy." *Journal of Social Psychology* 142(5):663–665. https://doi.org/10.1080/00224540209603925; Zechmeister, Jeanne S. and Catherine Romero. 2002. "Victim and offender accounts of interpersonal conflict: Autobiographical narratives of forgiveness and unforgiveness." *Journal of Personality and Social Psychology* 82(4):675–686. https://doi.org/ 10.1037// 0022-3514.82.4.675

44 Davis, Mark. 1996. *Empathy: A Social Psychological Approach.* Boulder, CO: Westview Press; Davis, Mark. 2006. "Empathy." pp. 443–465 in *Handbook of the Sociology of Emotions,* edited by J. Stets and J. H. Turner. New York, NY: Springer; Hoffman, Martin. L. 2000. *Empathy and Moral Development: Implications for Caring and Justice.* Cambridge, MA: Cambridge University Press.

45 Sturmer, Stefan, Mark Snyder, Alexandra Kropp, and Birte Siem. 2006. "Empathy-motivated helping: The moderating role of group membership." *Personality and Social Psychology Bulletin* 32(7):943–956. https://doi.org/10.1177/ 0146167206287363

46 Hakamsson, Jakob and Henry Montgomery. 2003. "Empathy as an interpersonal phenomenon." *Journal of Social and Personal Relationships* 20(3):267–284. https:// doi.org/10.1177/0265407503020003001

47 Sturmer, Stefan, Mark Snyder, Alexandra Kropp, and Birte Siem. 2006. "Empathy-motivated helping: The moderating role of group member-ship." *Personality and Social Psychology Bulletin* 32(7):943–956. https://doi.org/ 10.1177/0146167206287363; Tarrant, Mark, Sarah Dazeley, and Tom Cottom. 2009. "Social categorization and empathy for outgroup members." *British Journal of Social Psychology* 48:427–446. https://doi.org/10.1348/014466608X373589

48 Hoffman, Martin L. 2000. *Empathy and Moral Development: Implications for Caring and Justice.* Cambridge, MA: Cambridge University Press.

49 Turner, Jonathan H. and Jan E. Stets. 2005. *The Sociology of Emotions.* New York, NY: Cambridge University Press.

50 Schneider has demonstrated the usefulness of considering affect control processes in multicultural settings: Schneider, Andreas. 2002. "Behavior prescriptions versus professional identities in multicultural corporations: A cross-cultural com-puter simulation." *Organization Studies* 23:105–131. https://doi.org/10.1177/ 017084060202300106

51 See Osgood, Charles E., W. H. May, and M. S. Miron. 1975. *Cross-Cultural Universals of Affective Meaning*. Urbana, IL: University of Illinois Press.

52 For initial research into identifying which event component is most likely to be reidentified, see Nelson, Steven. 2006. "Redefining a bizarre situation: Relative concept stability in Affect Control Theory." *Social Psychology Quarterly* 69(3):215–234. https://doi.org/10.1177/019027250606900301

53 Averett, Christine and David R. Heise. 1987. "Modified social identities: Amalgamations, attributions and emotions." *Journal of Mathematical Sociology* 13:103–132. https://doi.org/10.1080/0022250X.1987.9990028

Chapter 6

Constructing Victim, Survivor, and Transcender Identities

It is a movement, from Chicago or down to Philly, and it is like a brotherhood in a sense, or sisterhood, where humanity is just looking at life on life's terms and realizing your life matters, my life matters, let us cease the fire. You know? ... I was once a part of the problem. I made a decision to change my life around and be a part of the solution.—J. R.

Her grace and confidence as she moves around the room are inspiring. All in attendance know the source of her motivation and have come dressed in their best: fine suits and sequined dresses. They greet one another as they peruse the goods upon the long tables lining the hall outside the gala: colorful scarves, silver jewelry, quilted handbags. A three-tiered table offers guests simple hors d'oeuvres: berries and grapes; hummus and pita triangles; orange and yellow cheeses aside crackers of various shapes and textures. The table nearest the entry to the night's main event is manned by two older women, large rolls of blue raffle tickets in hand: $1 per ticket, $20 for an arm's length. The theme of the gala changes from year to year, and each raises more money than the year prior, as more supporters join the coalition of people who have been inspired by Gloria's resilience and determination to help women like her late daughter to escape abusive relationships before it is too late.

At 6:00 p.m. sharp, the doors open to the main room and the guests flood in, moving toward their assigned seats. The table settings are impressive, despite their hand-crafted nature. Deep purples and greens flood the space, with beaded masks and handmade candles arranged into striking Mardi Gras centerpieces. Wine glasses and pure white dinnerware mark each attendee's position. A team of neatly dressed servers move through the space, filling water glasses and coffee cups. In the background, a PowerPoint flips through a list of organizations, families, and individuals who have contributed to this lavish event. As Gloria moves through the space, the emotional weight of the night becomes palpable, somber yet powerful. She takes the microphone upon the podium and lightheartedly welcomes everyone to the gala, her natural sense of humor poking through despite the sorrow that is clear under her chipper outward demeanor. Once all have been seated, the emotional energy of the night shifts as Gloria begins to speak of the motivation for this event, the death of her beloved daughter, whose life-sized picture adorns the stage to Gloria's left.

As I look around the room, I see several familiar faces, including co-victims I have met over the last two years, many of whom have shared their stories with me in one-on-one interviews. Gloria is connected to both Loved Ones Left Behind (LOLB) and Homicide Bereavement Circle (HBC) and takes on an active role in a variety of homicide memorial and victims' rights events each year. She uses her story not only to raise funds, but also to soften hearts, strengthen wills, align forces, and create change. While doing so, she has become a champion for my work, inviting me to events such as this night's gala and proudly introducing me to her friends, family, neighbors, and supporters.

It is because of people like Gloria, and events like her annual gala, that the data informing this work is so rich and robust. It was while in the presence of these inspiring folks, and while taking an active role in events so mean-ingful to each of them, that the ideas presented here were given the space to be born, develop, percolate, change, obtain validation, and solidify. One such idea is that of the emergence of various types of identities in the wake of tragic loss. Gloria's story will be used to demonstrate what I call a "survivor" identity, as compared to "victim" and "transcender" identities. In order to more fully understand the consequences of homicide upon co-victims, the next analysis in this work explores the construction of such co-victim iden-tities and how each identity relates to forgiveness.

In this chapter, I present the three co-victim identities that I found arise after loss to homicide. I compare each in terms of where co-victims focus their attention; the language they use to narrate their stories; what emotions correspond to their co-victim identities; what roles they adopt and the associated attitudinal and behavioral expectations; what groups they engage with; and the purpose they associate with the roles they play. More generally, this chapter is an exploration of how the co-victim identity manifests itself in co-victims' everyday lives. The three emergent identities are: (1) those formed around the individual's loss of a loved one (the victim identity); (2) those related to connections to other crime victims (the survivor iden-tity); and (3) those generated through an outward approach toward injustice and tragedy within society at large (the transcender identity). Table 6.1 lays out the main distinctions between these three identities. The following sections are designed to lead the reader through the intricacies of each

Table 6.1 Co-Victim Identity Typology

	Victim identity	Survivor identity	Transcender identity
Focus	Past, inward, singular/specific (self)	Present, outward, singular/specific (others)	Future, outward, plural/generalized (others)
Language	Negative	Neutral	Positive
Emotion	Anger, hatred, vengefulness (unforgiveness)	Neutrality, balance (non-benevolent forgiveness)	Acceptance, compassion, sympathy, hope (benevolent forgiveness)
Role expectations	To be supported and heard by others, maintain memory	To support and hear similar others	To promote broad change
Group memberships/ activities	Memorials, retributive justice	Victim-focused advocacy, charity (for similar others)	Restorative justice; offender-focused advocacy; anti-violence, first-time offender/at-risk youth programs

co-victim identity, demonstrating each area of distinction with the depth and nuance only qualitative methods such as those employed here can offer.[1]

Background

Literature emerging from within the symbolic interactionist perspective provides much insight into factors that influence one's identity. This school of thought informs our understanding of inter-personal relationships; the development and alteration of one's sense of self; and the processes by which one comes to hold (and alter) one's ideas and behaviors. According to symbolic interactionists,[2] people learn from one another how to perceive, interpret, and evaluate reality, and this prior learning determines the meaning they will assign to each aspect of that reality. Such social learning can lead to the construction of a new identity.[3] For this reason, the methods of semi-structured interviews coupled with participant observation of events at which individuals share their personal stories are well suited for an investigation into the development of a co-victim identity. Through these methods, I observed participants in interaction with various others, over extended periods, and within differing social contexts.

The self is rooted in symbolic interaction because individuals come to form a view of self (one's sense of who one is) from the standpoint of others, considering how they perceive they are viewed by others.[4] A person has an identity, or what Sheldon Stryker called an "internalized positional designation,"[5] for each role or position he or she holds in society. Each position one holds has a set of meanings and expectations associated with it. The identity is what it *means* to be within that position and serves as a standard or reference for the individual's behavior and attitudes. Identities provide individuals' lives with meaning, purpose, and structure.[6] By understanding the identities one holds, we can best understand social behavior. From this understanding, we can begin to generate meaningful theories and predict behavior.

Key Concepts in Identity Theory

Salience, Commitment, and Identity Verification

A few key concepts in Identity Theory[7] that are relevant to this analysis are salience, commitment, and identity verification. The salience of an identity is the likelihood that it will be invoked or activated in any situation, so that the more salient an identity, the more likely it is that it will be activated in the situation.[8] This is important in the analyses presented here, because participants' identities as co-victims were highly salient during all of the events I observed, given the nature of the events. In other contexts, which I was not privy to, participants' co-victim identities may have been less directly relevant to the interactions in which they engaged, and therefore less salient and less likely to be activated.

People also have different levels of commitment for each of their identities, and this commitment has both breadth and depth. As used in Identity Theory, commitment has two dimensions, which are known as "interactional commitment" and "affective commitment."[9] Interactional commitment to an identity refers to the extensiveness of social relationships in one's life that are based upon that identity. Affective commitment to an identity refers to the intensity of the social relationships tied to that identity. These types of commitment are distinct from one another and can therefore operate separately, leading an individual to simultaneously have a high level of interactional commitment to an identity and low level of affective commitment to that identity, or vice versa. For example, a woman may feel that the most important person in her life is her father, demonstrating a high level of affective commitment to her "daughter" identity. But, her level of interactional commitment to her "daughter" identity might be quite low if, for example, she only acts within her "daughter" identity during rare visits with her father and occasional phone calls with his doctor. In such a case, there are very few interactions in her life in which she invokes her "daughter" identity (low interactional commitment). At the same time, this woman may have a high level of interactional commitment to her "administrative assistant" identity, because she regularly interacts with a wide range of people through her work. But if she feels as if the ties to those people are not important (if, for example, she is unlikely to miss them if she were to quit her job), her level of affective commitment to her "administrative assistant" identity is quite low. Therefore, commitment can refer to either the importance or number of inter-personal relationships associated with an identity (or both). The level of commitment one has toward an identity is important because increased commitment leads to increased salience for that identity. The more commitment and salience attached to an identity, the more likely the individual is to activate that identity, engaging in role-related behaviors.[10]

When an identity is activated, it is attempting to verify itself through interpretation of the social meanings perceived within the social environment. If those meanings are compared to the identity and found to be in alignment, the identity is verified. Verification of identity leads to positive feelings, including authenticity when a person identity is verified, self-efficacy when a role identity is verified, and self-worth when a social identity is verified (person, role, and social identities are explained below). The more important an identity to an individual, the more important verification of that identity is.[11] Behavior is used to control perceptions related to the identity so that if an identity is not verified, then behavior will be altered until the identity is verified. The group meetings and events I participated in and observed provided the perfect vantage point from which to witness participants' co-victim identities being verified. According to symbolic interactionists, there are three types of identities that can be verified, each distinct yet intimately connected to the others. The three types are known as person, role, and social identities.[12]

Types of Identities

According to Identity Theory, there are three types of identities: person, role, and social identities.

Person Identities

One's person identity consists of the unique attributes that set him- or herself apart from others. It includes biographical characteristics, such as one's name or home town, and idiosyncratic characteristics that one uses to define oneself, such as personality traits, preferences, or worldviews. For example, one may place one's self within a person identity by saying "I am Janet," "I like living on the west coast," or "I am very generous."

Role Identities

A role identity is the set of internalized meanings and expectations connected to the roles one plays and can be based on both our culture and our own individual interpretation of the role. Many identity theorists have focused upon this aspect of identity by exploring how one categorizes oneself as an occupant of various roles within an overarching social structure, as well as the meanings one attaches to those roles and role performance. Role identities are individual-level identities in that they reference the self as an individual "me" and individuals identify themselves within a role, such as "I am a mother" or "I am a victim."

Role identities are created and maintained within interaction with other relevant roles, or counter-roles.[13] Therefore, the role cannot exist without the counter-role to which it is oriented. Each is defined in relation to the other. For example, the role of "husband" is formed within interaction with its counter-role of "wife." And this takes place within the group of "family," even if this family is a group of only two. Without the group, the role cannot exist because, by definition, roles are created and maintained within groups. Therefore, the roles are embedded within the group and the group is constituted of the relevant roles. Therefore, role and social identities, explained next, are interdependent. Since roles are related to counter-roles, identities are related to counter-identities, which are also formed and maintained within social groups.[14]

Social Identities

In contrast to role identities, social identities reference the self as belonging to the same category or social group as a set of others, for example, "We are victim advocates" or "We are the loved ones left behind." Social identities are therefore collective in nature. These collective-level identities categorize one within a group of like others. Self-meanings originating from one's social identity are based on a group or category one places oneself within and these self-meanings are shared with others in the group.[15]

Peggy Thoits and Lauren Virshup[16] point out that both role and social identities can be thought of as being *both* individual and collective because where there is a role there is a counter-role and, therefore, a group. Likewise, where there is a social group there are roles defined within the group and intragroup relations. Therefore one is acting within a role and as part of a social group simultaneously.[17]

Despite their interrelated nature, there are key differences between role and social identities. For example, role identities are defined by their counter-roles, so each role is *different* from its counter-role in ways that are essential to performing within the role in accordance with the counter-role (for example, I act as "teacher" within interaction with others acting as "students"), whereas the social identity is based on being similar to others within the same category or group, so here it is important that one is *like* the other (for example, my student-athletes may identify as "Eagles" while cheering on their classmates at a soccer game). Therefore, one's social identity links him or her to many similar others whereas one's role identity is linked to one, or a few, different others.[18] Therefore, what is important when considering a role identity is what one does, rather than what one is, which is key to the social identity.

Interplay between Person, Role, and Social Identities

Person, role, and social identities cannot be easily disentangled. The person identity is connected to both role and social identities in that one maintains a sense of who he or she is individually (person identity) while acting within roles and groups. Through what is known as "selective affiliation," individuals choose which others with whom they will interact, as well as within which situations they will place themselves, in order to ensure they are treated in a way that is consistent with their identities and given the opportunity to act out these identities with supportive others. As Peter Burke and Jan Stets point out, "[W]e prefer to associate with those who see us as we see ourselves."[19] Therefore, people will join groups and enter activities that maintain and support the identities that are most important to them.[20] In this way, certain identities are encouraged while others are discouraged, depending on the situation and the others present in the situation. For example, a co-victim may see him- or herself as resilient (a person identity), and act accordingly, while playing the role of parent (role identity) and interacting in a self-help group (social identity). This gives the person identity a high degree of salience, as it is continuously activated in a wide range of activities and interactions. Because it has such high salience, it operates like a master identity.[21] In this way, the person identity is more likely to influence one's choices about entering into role and social identities than vice versa. For example, if a person views him- or herself as a confident and outspoken individual, he or she may choose to take on roles such as leader or lobbyist. Likewise, he or she may choose to join groups that would benefit from his or her personal characteristics such as victims' rights networks.

The self is made up of all of these identities and the attitudinal and behavioral expectations attached to each. Despite their differences, the underlying operations are the same for each of these three types of identity. Because individuals are positioned within multiple roles and groups at any given point, individuals hold multiple identities throughout their lives and each identity is enacted at different times based on the relevance to the situation.

Relevance in this Research

After criminal victimization, individuals often feel a sense of uncertainty about the social world.[22] What was once seen as knowable and ordered is now volatile and unstable. Identity processes can alleviate some of this uncertainty by allowing for increased predictability. By categorizing self and others, one can anticipate attitudes, emotions, and behaviors likely to occur in social interaction.[23] This allows individuals to effectively navigate their social worlds by reducing uncertainty. When acting within groups, members guide one another's behavior and thus facilitate predictability within one's social environment. Individuals come to relate the expectations connected to their roles to those connected to other roles within an organized system.[24] Therefore, we learn what is expected of us, and what we can in turn expect from others, through interaction with those in our social spheres.

Such significant others and reference groups serve as a source of one's values, perceptions, and self-conceptions and root the self within the larger social world through identification and informal labeling.[25] Individuals have multiple significant others and reference groups at any point in time, including organized groups of generalized others, such as classmates and families, and individual significant others, such as teachers or specific peers. These relationships simultaneously enable and constrain individuals in their behavior depending on how others define what is desirable and appropriate in the immediate context.[26] Which groups are most influential in any given situation depends on several factors, "most important of which is the relevance of the group to the perceived problematic situation at hand."[27] In 1970, Nathan Hurvitz[28] studied groups similar to those I observed and recruited from within, and he showed that members become significant others for one another and the group becomes a new reference group for its members. This is not surprising, given that individuals drawn together due to personal tragedy and the resultant struggles are dealing with trauma that can be all-consuming. Therefore, such groups are likely to be viewed as quite relevant to the situation. Members are likely to feel that groups consisting of other co-victims are likely to have knowledge, life experience, and tools that could prove valuable to new or struggling members.

It has been shown that individuals will be more devoted to those groups consisting of members they believe share their feelings and less dedicated to groups in which they feel members' feelings are divergent.[29] This means that co-victims will be drawn to groups in which they sense a common emotional response to loss to homicide. As I will show, the power of a common emotional experience was a key factor in participants devoting themselves to certain groups and choosing not to return to others.

Victimization and Identity

Though a great deal of work has been conducted on identity generally and with various specific foci, little attention has been paid to the effects of victimization upon identity. Because social relationships and interactions have a powerful influence upon one's identity, it is crucial that we come to understand how threats to our sense of a safe, knowable social world affect our sense of self. After criminal offense, victims often feel the need to reassess the safety of their environments.[30] They are likely to feel increased levels of vulnerability, mistrust, anger, shame, or self-blame. This is especially true for those victimized within "unanticipated incidents in familiar or benign settings" and victims of highly intrusive crimes, since such crimes are typically the most stressful for victims.[31] These kind of offenses "upset the victim's balance in ways most central to self as well as the victim's sense of autonomy, order, control or predictability in ordinary activities central to the victim's identity."[32] Since effects upon identity are most substantial in cases of serious, unexpected crime that upsets the individual's sense of order and predictability in the world, research such as this, which focuses upon a crime most worthy of these characterizations, is invaluable. Here, I will explore what it means to an individual to be one who has lost a loved one to homicide. By speaking directly with co-victims and observing them within interaction with others, I examine participants' narrated identities. Through symbolic interaction, identities and selves are products of language. Therefore, investigation of narrated experience is inherently well suited for explorations of identity and self-processes.[33]

Co-Victim Identities: Victim, Survivor, and Transcender[34]

When someone loses a loved one to homicide, it may disturb his or her sense of reality and sense of self within the larger social world. As Howard Zehr eloquently noted, "[v]ictimization represents a profound crisis of identity and meaning, an attack on oneself as an autonomous but related individual in an orderly world ... so we must recover a redeeming narrative which reconstructs a sense of meaning and identity."[35] The data I gathered through interviews and observation showed that individuals who lose loved ones to violence construct identities to suit their new realities as co-victims, and these identities are used to begin to establish what many of my participants referred to as a *"new normal."*

Three distinct co-victim identities emerged from within this data. I have termed these the "victim," "survivor," and "transcender" identities. Eight participants in this sample displayed victim identities, eight displayed survivor identities, and 20 displayed transcender identities. These identities are distinct in terms of several aspects of one's internal and external social world, including one's focus, language, dominant emotions, attitudes, behavior, group memberships, and perceived purpose.

Below, I offer detailed descriptions of each of the three identities. Aspects of each of these identities could be classified as relating to one's person, role, or social identities and there is great interplay between the way each co-victim views and categorizes the self as a unique individual (person identity); the roles he or she plays (role identity); and the groups with which he or she identifies and within which he or she spends time acting (social identity). Depending on the depth of disruption of one's experiences of self, the identities that emerge may take the place of old ways of viewing the self or may develop as secondary identities that remain less the focal point of everyday life, but nonetheless remain personally meaningful and salient in various relevant contexts.

It should be noted that, although many co-victims use the terms "victim" or "survivor" to refer to themselves and others who have lost loved ones to homicide, as do many advocates, policy-makers, support persons, criminal justice personnel, and researchers, these terms are not accepted by all co-victims, including some from this sample. In fact, some co-victims intentionally avoid use of one or both of these terms. Some feel the term "victim" implies a direct victimization and therefore reserve use of the term for the person killed in the homicide. Others feel the word "victim" has negative connotations, implying a vulnerability and weakness that they do not identify with. The term "survivor" engenders similar criticism from some co-victims. Some feel that it implies that someone survived the incident. For example, Diane said during her interview, *"To me, 'surviving a homicide' seems like an oxymoron ... I never really like 'survivor' in the same sentence as 'homicide.' To me ['survivor'] goes with illness, like you're a breast cancer survivor, right? So you survived through breast cancer, that makes sense."* Others shared this view, indicating that they felt the word "survivor" typically indicates that a homicide attempt was unsuccessful and there was, therefore, a survivor of the attempted homicide. Because their loved ones died due to the fact that they were not survivors, the term "survivor" is emotionally distinct from anything they would connect to themselves and brings a negative emotional reaction.

With acknowledgment of these views, I respectfully use these terms to indicate the first and second group of co-victims discussed here. The majority of participants in this study who fell into these classifications identified with these terms and many used them in interactions with other co-victims. Those who identified themselves as "victims" felt the term was fitting because of the immense trauma they suffered due to the homicide. They felt as if the loved ones they had lost were not the only victims of the crimes. Rather, they too were victims in that the offenders' actions caused irrevocable devastation to their lives. The label of "victim" was therefore justified and fitting, in their opinions, and the word did not have negative connotations. Instead of implying continued weakness or vulnerability, the word acknowledged the pervasive and long-lasting effects of the crime upon the co-victim. Those who identified as "survivors" indicated that the term signified a unique sort of strength brought about through the trauma and their subsequent healing processes. The label also indicated a deep connection to the lost loved one and paid tribute to the ways in which the trauma forever altered their identities. I hope that through analysis and discussion of these identities, it will be clear as to why the terms "victim" and "survivor" capture the experiences of these individuals, despite disagreement on the most fitting labels.

Victim, Survivor, and Transcender as Person Identities

There were several qualities unique to each of the three co-victim identities that could be construed as aspects of one's person identity. Rather than being connected to a role or group membership, these differences surrounded such things as one's general focus, linguistic choices, and dominant emotions.

Focus

Victims

The first distinction that became obvious between the victim, survivor, and transcender identities was that of one's focus. In general, those displaying what I call a "victim" identity were inwardly focused. In other words, their focus was singular and specifically directed at self. The victim identity was constructed around the individual's loss of a loved one. These individuals often referred to themselves as "*victims*" and they remained focused upon the past. The majority of their stories, whether shared during interviews or within group settings with other co-victims, involved detailed descriptions of the original loss and the losses that resulted from the initial trauma. Bev, an 85-year-old mother of seven who lost her youngest daughter to murder, is a great example of a co-victim occupying a victim identity. Over the three years I engaged in participant observation, I listened to Bev narrate her story more than 40 times. Despite the fact that these narrations occurred in front of a variety of audiences during a range of events, each iteration of her story centered around the original tragedy. In this way, Bev's focus did not waver from its emphasis on the past and, therefore, Bev is a prime example of occupying a victim identity.

Survivors

Whereas those with a victim identity focused upon the murder as a part of their histories and a story to be shared from the past, other co-victims viewed the murder as motivation for helping others who have also lost in similar tragedies. For these individuals, the loss had become a catalyst for action toward healing the trauma that follows tragedies such as theirs. I adopted the term "survivor" for these individuals, as their focus was not the past but the present. They described themselves as having been changed by their experiences in the past. Their focus was still singular, in that it was aimed at specific others, but it had shifted from their personal loss outward, toward others who had lost in similar tragedies. They viewed their struggles as having been a learning journey from which they had gathered valuable knowledge and skills that they could now offer to others to aid them in their own personal journeys after loss and trauma. These individuals were present-focused in that they used their losses in the past to fuel the work in which they were involved in the present, as they dedicated their attention and energy toward the current suffering of others.

The survivor focus became clearest during self-help group meetings and interviews with regular self-help group members. During such interviews, I inquired about participants' experiences within group meetings and other events. Survivors often talked about *"being in that space with the person,"* and one survivor regularly said, *"It's important to meet them where they're at."* These comments make it clear that survivors are focused upon the present moment, rather than the past or the future. These co-victims saw the narration of aspects of their previous experiences as a tool to be used within a present moment with another suffering individual. They did not spend time contemplating the past, nor did they focus upon the future. They felt the most important moment was the present, and this was where they concentrated their attention.

During self-help group meetings, survivors were keen to share portions of their stories with newcomers or other members who were dealing with present challenges that the survivors had previously overcome. For example, survivors commonly shared aspects of their experiences with trials or appeal processes when other members came to meetings distraught, emotionally exhausted, or disheartened by the criminal justice system. In this way, survivors remained focused upon helping others in the present by using their prior experiences as a vehicle for establishing commonality and offering guidance and understanding.

Transcenders

I adopted the word "transcender" for those participants who discussed a surpassing or movement well beyond the shock and trauma associated with the loss of their loved ones to homicide. Therefore, the transcender identity refers to those individuals whose focus had become more forward-thinking. For transcenders, the boundary between self and other was blurred. Their focus also moved beyond helping other co-victims to helping society at large. The loss, for these individuals, had become a catalyst to do good in the future, to *"make a difference,"* and to ensure some positive effects came from the loss of their loved ones. There was a strong sense of the loss of life being given meaning by protecting others from harm or heightening the awareness of offenders so that they will not cause future harm. In this way, transcenders had what could be described as a plural focus, a more generalized interest in helping others and in reducing risk of future harm to all.

Often, the transcenders' drive to serve extended to offenders, not only in reducing potential harm within society by reducing criminal activity and combating trajectories toward crime, but also in lessening the trauma suffered by previous, current, and potential offenders. They sought to develop empathy and understanding of fellow co-victims and offenders alike. They often talked about how offenders are victims as well. It was not uncommon for transcenders to share stories of volunteering in prisons or juvenile offender programs in the hopes of utilizing their stories to offer potential future criminals a new perspective upon their actions and the associated consequences. At times, transcenders also aimed to reach out to families of offenders to help address their unique needs, especially if their loved ones were serving lengthy prison sentences and were, therefore, also lost to them in a similar but distinct fashion. In these ways, the focus of the transcender was outward, plural, and generalized. Alex, a transcender, spoke of the activities of others like her:

> *The fact that they get together and talk to kids is a healing process in itself for them and it just changed their life. Versus sitting at home, mourning your son, which, yeah, that's always going to be part of it, but it doesn't just have to be that.*

Here it is clear that, for Alex and other transcenders with whom she is acquainted, the outward, plural focus is personally fulfilling. Taking part in such activities does not negate the opportunity to mourn or grieve their losses, but for transcenders the outward focus is healing in and of itself.

In the next section, I demonstrate how co-victims' linguistic choices communicate their general focus and attitude, not only to myself as a researcher, but also to those they come into contact with on a regular basis.

Language

As I accumulated more and more narratives through interviews and observation, it became evident that the language individuals used to narrate their stories also differentiated victims, survivors, and transcenders. When narrating their unique histories of loss, victims' accounts gave a sense that what mattered most in the story was that "this happened to me," with a focus upon the personal impact of the loss. Survivors' language indicated a feeling that this is something that "happens to people," indicating a more general focus. And for transcenders there was a strong sense that "this could happen to anyone," not only generalizing the reality to others who have suffered similar losses, like survivors tended to do, but also generalizing beyond those who have lost to murder. This generalization stretched to offenders as well.

The language one uses is a type of inter-personal prompt[36] employed within interaction to elicit reactions from others that align with the speaker's identity within that situation. It is a means by which the speaker ensures others will treat him or her in a manner that is consistent with his or her identity. This in turn verifies the speaker's identity. Words chosen by co-victims in my sample situated the speaker within a victim, survivor, or transcender identity, and this language can serve as a window into what it means to identify as each sort of co-victim. Such language includes words used to describe the loss, the effects of the loss, the act of homicide itself, the offender, and the self.

Victims

Those displaying a victim identity used value-laden language that was often expressive of the strong negative emotion generated by the experience of loss to homicide. When describing their losses they often used words like *"traumatic"* or *"devastating"* and focused upon the negative effects to self, such as saying *"She was stolen from me"* or *"My daughter was ripped away from me."* When recounting the details of the homicide, they would use words such as *"heinous,"* *"slaughter,"* or *"brutally murdered."* And when speaking of the offender, they labeled the individual as *"murderer,"* *"killer,"* *"monster,"* or *"bastard."* This language is demonstrative of the individual's perspective in regard to the offender. The individual who took the life was seen only in the role of murderer. There was no show of empathy or understanding for the circumstances of the offender prior to or following the offense.

Survivors

Survivors, on the other hand, used more neutral language. When describing their losses they would say things like *"We lost our daughter"* or use words like *"death"* rather than *"murder."* Their words were much less emotionally charged than were victims'. When speaking of the offender, they used labels such as *"guy,"* *"person,"* or *"individual."* Often they focused their story upon their own *"survival"* or said things like *"Her death will not be in vain."* Compared to victims, survivors' language indicated an emotional distance from the personal trauma and the enormous effects on self. Their choice of words was very matter of fact and detached, relative to that of victims.

Transcenders

The language used by transcenders was also expressive of their focus and perspective. They would use words like *"hope"* and *"heal."* They spoke of wanting to *"create change"* and *"make a difference"* from their losses. When narrating their stories, the language used to describe the offender was free from negativity or judgment, often implying the person's vulnerability or similarity to self. For example, some transcenders called the individuals who killed their loved ones *"kid"* or referred to their *"humanity."* At times, the labels used by transcenders for the offenders was strikingly positive. For example, Barbara continually referred to the man who brutally killed her daughter and several other women as *"the gentleman."* These word choices indicate a respect for the offender that transcends the act of homicide as well as a genuine sense of compassion for the individual who took the lives of transcenders' loved ones. The outward focus that these linguistic choices communicates has a profound impact upon the emotional experiences of transcenders, as having an outward focus is a prerequisite for empathy.[37]

The words co-victims used gave meaning to their situations and are indicative of their foci, values, and coping mechanisms, as well as the emotions beneath the surface in the aftermath of tragedy. In the next section, I will describe the various emotional experiences of co-victims holding each of these co-victim identities. In coming chapters, this connection between focus, empathy, and emotion will serve as the foundation for understanding the processes involved in the transformation of emotion following extreme trauma.

Emotion and Forgiveness

The aspect of the co-victim identity that is most important to this work is the many emotions expressed and included within participants' self-narratives. Negative emotions emerging from this data included those related to unforgiveness, including bitterness, anger, hatred, avoidance, resentment, and vengefulness. Positive emotions include hope, acceptance, and feelings related to empathy and forgiveness, including sympathy, compassion, and a sense of sameness. The three co-victim identities were distinct in terms of the dominant and pervasive emotions connected to each, as I will outline next.

Victims

The victim identity was connected to negative emotions indicative of unforgiveness. These included a perpetual sense of loss, anger, bitterness, hatred, and resentment as well as a desire for revenge or to see the offender punished (these emotions are demonstrated with co-victim accounts in Chapter 2). The unforgiving nature of victims' emotional state makes sense because of victims' focus upon the past. As Trudy Govier points out, one of the requirements of forgiveness is "[t]he setting of wrongful deeds in the past."[38] Drawing upon the work of Margaret Walker,[39] she explains that, when forgiveness takes place, the past is not forgotten but is "regarded as past." It therefore does not dominate one's thoughts and social interactions, and it is not a defining factor as one imagines or plans for one's future. In this same vein, those who committed the harm are not narrowly defined by the act, identified only as "murderers," for example. Instead, they are "regarded as human beings who are potentially equal members of a decent society." In the case of victims, there is a clear focus upon the past; the past is ever-present in one's daily interactions and thoughts, and it is expected to continue to be influential in the future. And the perpetrator is, indeed, defined solely by his or her wrongful actions. Therefore, it follows that forgiveness would not occur in such cases.

It is important to note here that individuals not only *felt* these negative emotions, but they also related these emotions to their sense of selves. They said things like, *"I have become an angry person"* or *"Ever since the murder, I just can't trust people, I assume the worst."* Sue described how she had become *"protective"* and *"guarded"* in ways that she had never been previously and how she had developed *"trust issues"* related to both strangers and anyone who attempts to get close to her family. Another co-victim shared how she changed after losing her loved ones: *"I know I've changed a lot. I used to be so friggin' naïve. I believed in everybody. I believed in people. I still do to some point, but not like I used to."* She went on to explain that she had come to believe that *"there's bad at every door."* She said, *"There's no security any more … It's like, you can't trust anybody sometimes. And I never was that way* [before]."

Survivors

Unlike victims, survivors spoke of having released any negative, other-oriented emotions as well as having healed much of the pain and trauma resulting from their losses. Their emotions often indicated a sense of neutrality or balance. Paul said that he had come to believe that there was *"no value in being angry"* and that anger *"served no purpose."* Though survivors were forgiving, as conceptualized here, and therefore did not feel emotions such as hatred, vengefulness, or anger, their forgiveness was non-benevolent. They therefore did not describe positive, offender-directed emotions such as compassion or respect. They described a sense of emotional distance from the offender, often saying things like *"I don't really think of him," "I've put them out of my mind,"* or *"He's just not relevant for me."*

The outward focus of survivors (and transcenders) made forgiveness possible for these co-victims. Having an outward focus is a prerequisite for the development of empathy.[40] Since victims maintained an inward focus, and survivors and transcenders developed an outward focus, it follows that co-victims falling within these two categorizations would be likely to empathize with the offender and thereby forgive.

Transcenders

While taking part in events and groups they connected to their co-victim identities, as well as in interviews, transcenders spoke of positive, offender-directed emotions including acceptance, respect, pride, and love. Transcenders also spoke of feelings of sympathy and compassion for the offenders in their cases. Such emotional experiences make sense given transcenders' outward focus and the blurring of boundaries between self and other, as such emotions "tie us, at least momentarily, to that person."[41]

These co-victims spoke of developing a sense of hope in the future. This future was not solely their personal future, but that of the world in general, inclusive of those who commit harm. Transcenders reported that they had moved beyond their anger and bitterness and sought to develop an understanding of the offenders' circumstances and struggles. In many cases, they had also become interested in raising the awareness of the offenders who took the lives of their loved ones, to include a level of understanding of the harm caused, rather than seeking vengeance or punishment. Jeanne exemplified this when she said:

> *I felt that there was hope for* [the offender] *because he was going to get back out in the world* [when released from prison]. *And that's what I felt, if I could make an impression on him toward goodness, you know, he may want to go that way. And he does, I mean, at least at this point. I don't have a crystal ball that says. But I said, "I'm not going to sit here and stress it every day." You know? I mean, that's part of being forgiving. I had to let that go. What he chooses to do now with his life, it's all up to him. And I said to him, "You are so lucky, you have a chance at your life, you're young enough to get married, to have a child.* [My son] *will never have that. So now it's all up to you where you go from here."*

Jeanne makes it clear that she has hope for a positive, pro-social future for the man who took her son's life. Now that he has been released from prison, she remains in contact with him and is uplifted by the steps he has taken to live what she considers to be a *"good"* life.

Unlike victims, who identify with a *"justified rage,"* transcenders do not see value in remaining *"in anger"* and instead choose to *"put down the anger and bitterness"* so that they can make space for other, more positive, emotions. Alex said, *"For a lot of people 20 years can go by easily and they are still in the same place."* Unlike such individuals, Alex felt that she was able to *"move forward"* when she *"started considering love and understanding ... compassion and empathy."* She said, *"That's when the movement started happening."* Positive, offender-directed emotions described by transcenders are indicative of their forgiveness being distinct from survivors in its benevolent character.[42]

The positive emotions described by transcenders frequently stretched beyond those associated with the offender. Often, they spoke of the excitement they felt about the programs they were involved in (which are discussed in detail later in this chapter) and the changes they felt they were fostering in the world. They also spoke about involvement in such activities being a *"passion"* and were proud of their accomplishments in these areas of life. In these ways, transcenders' emotional worlds were generally positive and upbeat.

Victim, Survivor, and Transcender as Role Identities

Several roles emerged as meaningful for those displaying each of the three co-victim identities, including fundraiser, activist, advocate, and various roles defined within victim self-help groups or organizations, such as *"joiner,"* leader, founder, speaker, chairperson, or board member. Through these roles, co-victims created meaning grounded in action.[43] Attached to each role was a set of specific attitudinal and behavioral expectations upheld by the individual filling that role.

Attitudinal and Behavioral Expectations

The attitudinal and behavioral expectations participants associated with the roles they played served as clear examples of the differences between the three co-victim identities. Attitudes toward such things as the criminal justice system, victim-oriented groups, other co-victims, specific offenders, offenders in general, and society at large differed according to co-victim identity. By exploring the roles participants adopted, we can uncover their underlying values, seeing them demonstrated in the attitudinal and behavioral expectations connected to those roles. Through action associated with each role, the meanings co-victims associate with their identities are performed.

Victims

Victims often shared opinions regarding the ineffective, unsatisfying nature of the criminal justice system. Most offered strong opinions about the benefit of use of capital punishment and the elimination of inmate early release through parole. Victims often held negative, retaliatory attitudes toward the offender in their specific cases as well as offenders more generally. For many of these individuals, forgiveness was seen as an offensive word or concept and engendered anger and further pain. For these individuals, forgiveness was not only something they did not feel, it was something they did not view as a positive outcome and they were therefore uninterested in experiencing forgiveness.

The attitudinal expectations associated with the roles participants held led to differences in behaviors and chosen activities. Those with a victim identity often adopted a role as guardian of the memory of the lost loved one and therefore spent a large amount of time memorializing and honoring their loved ones, even several decades after their murders. For some, this was a very private activity involving maintenance of shrines in the home, scrapbooks, or celebrations on birthdays or "angelversaries" (anniversaries of a death). For others, this was a very public endeavor. These individuals placed a great deal of value upon public memorials such as brick dedications or planting flowers or trees in the name of lost loved ones. The plaques or nameplates associated with the dedication were often of great importance and viewed as extremely valuable. For example, Bev often spoke of *"leaving pieces"* of her loved one in meaningful locations, spread throughout the nation, and she encouraged other co-victims to do the same. Such activities were seen as a means of keeping the memory of the loved one alive. Some memorializing activities involved scholarship funds used to better the lives or circumstances of individuals who embody characteristics of those lost. These co-victims focused upon the characteristics of their lost loved ones that they felt were most noteworthy or personally meaningful and created opportunities to help others who displayed these same characteristics.

Victims' focus upon the past and their personal trauma led to behaviors surrounding the telling of their stories. They reported finding the narration process healing, because they felt heard and understood by others who had endured similar situations. These individuals regularly shared very detailed stories of their losses with various groups, thereby focusing on the loss and the resultant negative emotions and experiences.

Victims were also regularly involved in activities that supported their attitudes toward the criminal justice system. For example, some victims took an active role in the court cases surrounding the murder of their loved ones. They wrote letters, attended hearings, and *"kept tabs"* on the offenders during their prison stays. Many victims also took part in activities aimed at the criminal justice system more generally. Some lobbied for harsher sentences for violent crimes, and others fought to prevent parole releases of inmates.

Survivors

Contrarily, for survivors there was a sense of neutrality with regard to the criminal justice system and indifference toward offenders. They often shared feelings of disappointment with the system but did not harbor negative feelings regarding its shortcomings. They said things like *"it is what it is"* or *"it's not perfect but it's the system we are stuck with."* Their attitudes toward offenders were similarly dispassionate. Often during interviews, survivors had little to say in regard to the offenders in their cases and noted that they did not think of the offenders often, if ever.

Unlike victims, survivors were often involved in victim-focused advocacy. They spent a great deal of energy volunteering with other crime victims or raising funds for charities related to support services. These individuals often dedicated a large amount of time to fundraising endeavors with a specific focus upon other victims of crime.

Charitable activities became an informative example to illustrate the distinction in behavioral expectations between the victim identity and the survivor identity. Though both groups often developed scholarships in the name of their loved ones, victims set up scholarships to support people who were like their lost loved ones, whereas survivors raised funds for those touched by similar crimes. For example, Florence set up a scholarship to support young artists like her deceased son, and Bev founded a scholarship for aspiring female culinary students in honor of her deceased daughter. These women both fit the victim identity model and their activities in developing and delivering scholarships demonstrate their focus upon memorialization. On the other hand, Gloria, whose gala opened this chapter, displayed a survivor identity. She has dedicated much of her life to raising awareness and funds for survivors of intimate-partner violence, all in the name of her daughter who was killed by her abusive husband. This distinction in activities relates to the difference in focus between the two identities. Though victims and survivors were involved in similar activities, their efforts had different motivations and foci. In these examples, it was clear that the victims were attempting to keep the memory alive, thereby focusing on the past and the loved one's life, whereas the survivor was focused upon the present, helping others who have been similarly harmed. The expectation here goes beyond maintaining the individual's memory toward using his or her death as motivation to help others who have suffered in a similar manner.

Transcenders

Compared to victims and survivors, transcenders had more positive attitudes toward the criminal justice system and offenders. Their attitudes indicated a sense of powerfulness in that they believed their efforts could bring about change on both small and large scales. Transcenders described strongly held beliefs that healing is possible in all instances and that those who cause harm are equally capable of invoking change, given the right tools and support. Transcenders believed their behaviors could fuel such change, promoting peace, safety, and a stronger sense of community.

Transcenders dedicated their time and energy to activities that were future-focused and served the whole of society. Some used their stories to advance restorative justice initiatives and others focused on prevention of future crime by taking part in offender-focused programs within prisons; community-based anti-violence or reentry programs; or programs serving first-time offenders or at-risk youth. Here, it is clear that transcenders were focused upon the community at large and the future safety of all. Some transcenders had personally developed programs to bring about such positive change whereas others joined existing programs in hopes of advancing a mission they felt passionate about.

Though the specific roles co-victims adopted are too numerous to name, it is the attitudinal and behavioral expectations associated with those roles that demonstrate the similarities between co-victims falling into each identity category. It is interesting to note the parallel between the activities associated with each of the three co-victim identities and the themes identified in Marilyn Armour's discussion of the "intense pursuit of what matters"[44] that emerge in the wake of homicide. She explains that this pursuit is "a form of coping composed of intentional acts that have symbolic meaning" and describes three categories of action, which could be loosely tied to the victim, survivor, and transcender identities. First, *declarations of truth* "consist of pronouncements that define territories of insecurity and personal autonomy." This could be equated with the victim identity. As Armour points out, such declarations include recounting of personal injustice and justified anger. The second category, *fighting for what's right*, could be likened to the survivor identity. Armour describes meaning-making actions associated with this category as designed to respond to specific injustices. Given survivors' drive to serve others who have been harmed in similar tragedies, this category of meaning-making behavior is well aligned with the survivor identity. Finally, *living in ways that give purpose to the loved one's death* could be viewed as a manifestation of the transcender identity. As Armour says, this category encompasses acts that "transcend the negativity or senselessness of the loved one's violent death." She describes such acts as generative, life-affirming, proactive, and focused upon the benefit of others. Though these three themes are not seamlessly correlated to the three identities uncovered here, the association is unmistakable and justifies further investigation.

In the next section, I will illustrate the various social groups co-victims participated within and how each of these groups supported the identities, attitudes, foci, and emotional experiences of the co-victims within them.

Victim, Survivor, and Transcender as Social Identities

The three co-victim identities could also be viewed as social identities, as they relate to the social categories one places oneself within or the social networks of which one considers oneself a member. In my sample, it was apparent that participants' group membership choices were directly connected to their co-victim identities. Relevant groups included victim advocacy and memorial committees; self-help groups; charity organizations; anti-violence programs; restorative justice initiatives; community outreach and peace-building programs; offender reentry, awareness, and educational programs; and at-risk youth or youthful offender divergence programs. Given the complex interplay between the self and the social world within which the self develops, I will attempt to unravel the causal order of group membership and identity in Chapter 7. Before doing so, I will discuss the strength of bonds formed (the high level of affective commitment) within these groups as well as the purpose co-victims attached to their membership.

Connecting to Like-Minded Others

The participant observation I engaged in allowed for exploration of the relationships co-victims developed with one another within relevant social networks. The character and strength of these relationships were especially apparent within self-help groups in that members saw one another on a regular basis, allowing not only for prolonged contact but also for anticipation of continued interaction. Regular members sought to form mutually respecting bonds and to make positive impressions upon others in the group.

During meetings of all three self-help groups observed, members shared their stories with the group (although in varying degrees of detail and with different motivation). There was a sense of meaning-making within these repeated stories and they also situated the speaker within his or her healing process, current relationships, and sense of self. Long-standing members of victim self-help groups had a substantial amount of influence over newer members because of an implicit authority related to having lived through similar trauma and having *"made it out"* or *"survived."* Newer members listened intently to those who were further along in their healing processes to gain knowledge and understanding, and to be validated in their own sense of trauma and loss of control. Even outside of the formalized co-victim support networks, or in cases of relatively new members, there was a sense of shared experience between those who had lost loved ones to homicide. This shared experience bonded individuals and gave influential power to each.

Co-victims often indicated that they felt others who had not experienced a similar loss *"could not possibly understand"* their experiences, regardless of good intentions or strong emotional bonds.[45] They therefore found solace and acknowledgment within co-victim networks that they could not find elsewhere. At her first meeting, one new member said, *"I have no one to talk to."* She explained that she came to the meeting because *"I have no family left. It's not that they think it should be fine, but, it's been a year. They think I should be further along in the process."* She shared how she felt as if her family and friends did not know how to support her at this stage of her grieving. Other co-victims were the only people who she felt truly understood. In support of this new member's feelings, Dawn commiserated, saying, *"They don't know what we are going through. They just don't know."*[46]

This sense of connection increased the level of influence other co-victims had upon those similarly victimized. Therefore, co-victims who were meeting for the first time had intrinsic power to influence due to their having endured the experience of loss due to homicide. For some, co-victim networks became a primary reference group. Members came to proudly identify themselves as members of these groups and many referred to the members of the groups as *"family."* One participant even described the bond among group members as *"sacred,"* indicating a very high level of affective commitment among group members to their identities as members of this group.

The intensity of the bond felt between members was often immediate and mutual. For example, at one meeting of HBC, I was able to watch a relationship form between two members. The first was a new attendee who said very little during the initial aspects of the meeting. When he began to share his story during customary introductions, a more seasoned member spoke up, mirroring his struggle by sharing details of her own journey. There was a clear connection formed between these individuals. It was the likeness of experience that shaped this bond. By the end of the meeting, these two individuals seemed to have an ease about their relationship more common to those with a long-standing affiliation. Rather than being based on continued contact and rapport building, this bond was formed almost instantaneously when commonality in trauma was found.

Group Attitudinal and Behavioral Expectations

Victims, survivors, and transcenders joined groups that held attitudinal and behavioral expectations similar to their own. For example, victims joined groups which held retributive attitudes and/or focused upon memorialization or grief. Many victims took part in annual homicide victim memorials and remembrance events during National Crime Victims' Rights Week. Some victims took on leadership roles at these events, acting as coordinators, speakers, or ambassadors. For example, since the death of her daughter 28 years earlier, Bev had been a regular speaker at the National Day of Remembrance events for homicide victims in her area.

During group events or meetings, behavioral expectations among members were also similar. For example, in monthly meetings of HBC, which consisted predominantly of individuals with a victim identity, discussion of each offender's sentence length was expected. Whether sharing their own stories of loss, mentioning another co-victim they had met, or discussing current events in the local or national news, members of this group consistently referenced the number of years the offender received in the case. In fact, at the start of every meeting, during which everyone present would share his or her story, every member included the sentence length within their story.

One meeting in particular stood out as demonstrative of the behavioral expectations of HBC, because a new member was present: Dawn. I was present at Dawn's first meetings at both HBC and LOLB and was struck by how the narration of her story was influenced by the inter-personal dynamics of these two self-help groups. At HBC, Dawn's initial narration of the story of the death of her son did not include details of the sentence length received by the offender. As soon as Dawn finished detailing her experience, Bev, the leader of the group, asked Dawn directly about the length of the offender's sentence. Bev then turned to Sue, a long-standing group member, and asked her about the sentence in her case. What struck me as interesting was the fact that Bev had heard Sue's story countless times, as they had both been a part of the group, as well as its advisory board, for several years. Bev knew the details of Sue's case quite well. So by asking Sue for this information, Bev was reinforcing the normalcy of including such details in one's story, thereby communicating group expectations to Dawn. Later in the meeting, when another first-time attendee spoke, Gloria, the vice president of HBC, asked her what the sentence was for the offender in her case. This is evidence that the behavioral expectations within HBC involved inclusion of sentence details within one's narrative of loss. This makes sense, given the proportion of HBC members with victim identities. The inclusion of details of the punishment in the case demonstrated the membership's collective identity by highlighting the focus and the associated retributive attitudes that constitute the victim identity.

On the contrary, in monthly meetings of LOLB, which is predominantly made up of transcenders, such details were not expected within one's narrative. It was interesting to note that the first time Dawn attended a meeting of LOLB, she did not include the details of the sentence received by the offender in her case, nor did such details arise in the telling of others' stories that night. In fact, during the years that I attended meetings of LOLB, never did I hear a member ask another member what the sentence was in their case. The outward and future focus of the transcenders in LOLB did not align with recitations of sentences handed out in the past. In fact, many transcenders' stories did not include mention of the offender at all and, if he or she was mentioned, it was only as a secondary character in the narrative.

Participants demonstrating each of the three co-victim identities often spoke of the like-mindedness of those within the groups to which they belonged. During her interview, Bev described other members of the group in which she was a leader as united in thought. On several occasions, she said of her fellow HBC members, "[They] *fall into my camp.*" Such similarity in attitude eased group processes and made group decisions uncomplicated, as members were unified in their ideas and viewpoints. One demonstrative example occurred when a decision needed to be made regarding HBC's newsletter. Traditionally, the newsletter had a page dedicated to a list of loved ones' birthdays and "angelversaries" (anniversaries of their deaths), but as more homicides occurred and the group grew, group members were faced with a decision regarding saving space. They realized they would need to have either birthdays or angelversaries moving forward, rather than both. The group quickly decided to remove birthdays and preserve angelversaries. No discussion or negotiation was required to reach this decision. I found this choice surprising, as my naïve perspective as someone who has never lost a loved one to homicide led me to believe that birthdays would be the more treasured of the two dates, especially considering the fact that almost everyone in attendance was a parent to their respective lost loved ones. When asked about this decision-making process in an interview following this particular group meeting, Bev, the long-time leader of HBC, said, *"I suggested we cut out the dates of birth, 'cause the dates of death are really more meaningful (chuckling) in this organization."* It was clear that group members share similar sentiments in regard to such things, and that leaders within the organization expect such uniformity in attitudes among group members.

J. R., a 37-year-old transcender who is heavily involved in anti-violence advocacy in the inner city in which his sister was murdered, shared similar sentiments in regard to the like-mindedness of the national organization in which he was involved. He said,

> For the most part, everyone can relate. It is a movement, from Chicago or down to Philly, and it is like a brotherhood in a sense, or sisterhood, where humanity is just looking at life on life's terms and realizing your life matters, my life matters, let us cease the fire, you know? Let us make some noise. Then of course you have the younger men that have not fully been bought into it entirely or cannot grasp the mission and model of it. So, at times, it is challenging.

J. R.'s words demonstrate that he not only sees individuals in his organization as like-minded, but he also views newcomers as less than fully initiated into such a mindset. He referenced the *"mission"* and the *"model"* several times throughout our conversations and made it clear that these were firmly established ways of approaching violence and disrupting cycles of retribution within communities. He shared how these attitudes were not inherent in new members, but if new members chose to remain with the group they would be effectively oriented toward this new outlook by more seasoned members.

Members' Purpose

Co-victims differed in the purpose they attached to their memberships within various groups and their dedication to various activities, and such differences related to their identities as victims, survivors, or transcenders.

Victims

For victims, the purpose of activities and group membership was most commonly to *"be heard"* and supported in their suffering. For these participants, time was spent within such groups in order to garner support in their personal healing processes and to be validated in their experiences and emotions. Therefore, their roles within the groups were that of a victim in need of support provided by others within the group. Other roles adopted by victims had a purpose of keeping the memory of their loved ones alive and/or to ensure that the offenders were not allowed to *"get away with"* crime. For example, many victims in HBC sought vengeance as activists by distributing petitions or writing letters in attempts to block the early release of inmates eligible for parole.

Survivors

Survivors, on the other hand, felt their purpose was to support others who have lost. They felt they had an obligation to help others who had survived similar tragedies and to share their wisdom learned through experience. Therefore, they dedicated much of their time to using their stories as tools for raising awareness of social problems that led to the deaths of their loved ones, such as intimate-partner violence or driving under the influence.

Unlike victims, survivors who took part in self-help groups focused their attention upon others in the group who had lost. They believed their roles in self-help group meetings revolved around supporting other co-victims and helping them to cope. Many survivors reported that they go to meetings to support others and to offer their perspectives and wisdom to people who are early in their healing processes or *"just coming along."* They found personal satisfaction in easing others through their pain by offering a sympathetic ear to those who felt unheard, unstable, and out of control. Survivors showed pride in their own progress toward healing and offered it as a ray of hope for others to consider when struggling in the present moment. One survivor said, *"I can laugh today, and that gives hope to others who are feelings as if there is no hope of a normal life, of laughing, and living, in the future."* When sharing their stories, survivors often focused on the aspects that were directly relevant to the current situation of the newcomers. For example, if a new member was struggling with the emotions resulting from the appeal process, survivors would focus the narration of their stories upon their experiences of appeal processes and the ways their feelings during that time mirrored the present emotional state of the newcomer.

Transcenders

Transcenders saw their purpose as more broad, often joining groups whose focus was restorative or community-based. Many transcenders dedicated their time to prison or youthful-offender programs with the aim of using their experiences as fuel to bring about future change in the lives of others. Other transcenders engaged in activism groups focused upon anti-violence or peace building. Transcenders sought to foster healing in all realms, including for those who have caused harm or may potentially cause harm in the future. For example, Jeanne had been volunteering at youth court for over 12 years when we spoke, sharing her story in hopes of altering the trajectory for troubled youth in the local area. She said:

> I look at it as: if I can change the mindset of one kid and possibly save a life, it's worth spilling my guts, 'cause I still cry with talking about it to a group, when

I'm sitting there in front of a group of kids [who have been] *doing the same things* [the individual who killed my son] *did, I think, "get your act together, kid." You know?*

Jeanne found purpose in her work within youth court, which she said was *"the one thing I do every year,"* and she was inspired by the impact she was able to imagine and, at times, witness. She said,

I feel passionate about helping a teenager to change their mind about something .... One time, after I spoke, one kid went up to his teacher with a knife in his pocket, gave her the knife ... I always say that, if I could save one, it's worth it.

Jeanne also spoke of the commonality of experience she sometimes found between herself and youthful offenders she referred to as *"hardcore kids from* [the city]." She said, *"A lot of these kids had went through* [loss to homicide], *with their father's being murdered, their mother's being murdered."* Jeanne spoke of the mutual healing that took place when she shared her story with these youths,

To see them, and how this heals them, with their lives, you know? And they were young. That was very healing for me, you know, to make a difference ... I just found ways to try to heal my heart and, like I said, one of them is talking to kids.

Other transcenders felt a broader commonality of experience with offenders, which they believed placed them at a unique vantage point from which they could help others change their paths. For example, J. R. shared how he felt the need to become *"part of a bigger picture."* He said, *"I was once a part of the problem. I made a decision to change my life around and be a part of the solution."* This decision led him to become involved in the anti-violence program within his community, of which he soon became the director and dedicated much of his time and energy to developing, marketing, and broadening. Letishia also felt connected to the inner city in which her loved one was killed, and she had become highly motivated to bring about change. She said enthusiastically during her interview:

I'm on a mission ... I want to make a change, I wanna help guide the underdogs. The underdogs are the people that have a sort of disadvantage. Doesn't matter what color, what background, religion you come from ... They just need that good, caring, empathetic, strong female to go out there, show them the way ... They has to have that respect, the morals and the values. You know, that spirituality. I'm here to bring that to them and show them that they can defeat the odds 'cause look at me! I came in the same, I came up in the same environment as [they] *did ... I have family members that went to jail or whatever, have family members that was on drugs, you know, and I also have family members that achieved the higher things in life. We are a mixture! I made it, and I'm still making it and you can too. This is my passion, being an advocate and a server of humanity. This is something that I wanna die doing ... I just wanna show them the way. I wanna show them that they can do it. They cannot think that, you know, they life, everyday waking up just hanging, hanging on the porch, drinking and laughing and dancing out on the street ... There's no future in that!*

She felt she was especially well suited because of her experience surviving in the same community within which she advocated for more peaceful solutions. She said:

I'm showing 'em, that they could do it too. You know, you don't have to be a superman or superwoman ... I let them know, you can do it. If I could do it, you can do it. Even though the odds were against you ... I say that a lot of people out here that are in that same situation ... You living in poverty, you barely know how to read and write and stuff like that and, oh, woe is me, whatever. [They] could defeat those odds, they just need somebody that's reputable, that could show them how ... These people out here, they gonna know if you for real or not. You sincere or not. They gonna read that on you. You know what I'm saying? No faking a funk, 'cause they gonna see you coming.

Such passion for sparking change in others was a hallmark of the transcender identity.

Like victims and survivors, some transcenders also took part in self-help groups. However, transcenders viewed the self-help group as a platform to do wider good for the larger community or world. They used the group to network and form relationships with like-minded others who could join forces in endeavors beyond those focused upon co-victims of homicide. In this way, transcenders were often involved in multiple groups with overlapping memberships. Time would be spent during group meetings to discuss happenings in other venues as well as to share news of upcoming opportunities, accomplishments, and current social crises in need of attention.

Clearly, though victims, survivors, and transcenders often took part in the same groups, the roles they adopted and the purpose they felt they served within such groups varied according to their co-victim identities. In this way, the co-victims' identities were simultaneously role and social identities. They were also person identities in that the purposes co-victims felt they served within roles and groups were well aligned with their unique characteristics, such as being troubled, indifferent, passionate, or altruistic. This is clear evidence that all three forms of identity operate simultaneously in situations, because roles are enacted, defined, and verified within groups and the actors playing those roles each have their own unique personal qualities that they bring to the role.

Concluding Remarks

The findings related to the three emergent co-victim identities are demonstrative of various aspects of Identity Theory. First, groups demonstrated uniformity of thought and action. Observational data indicated that there were attitudinal and behavioral expectations within groups that were passed from current members to newcomers. In the absence of a normative structure or established identity standard available to co-victims, such groups provided guidance and support for co-victims who were still discerning the appropriate response to their losses. Participants learned from others within the groups how to behave, what to feel, how to express that emotion, and what attitudes to hold.

Co-victims' choices about group membership and activities were clear evidence of "selective affiliation," as co-victims chose which groups to join and with which others to engage. This ensured participants were treated in a manner consistent with their co-victim identities and that they had the frequent opportunity to act out these identities with supportive others. The self as co-victim was one of the identities participants saw as meaningful in their lives and they therefore were drawn to activities and groups that would verify that identity. Concurrently, their co-victim identities were verified within the same groups and thereby strengthened. In this way, co-victims' identities and the groups they joined were mutually reinforcing.

By joining multiple groups and engaging in multiple activities that verified their co-victim identities, participants were also demonstrating high levels of both interactional and affective commitment[47] to these identities (the number of individuals with whom they interact on the basis of these identities was high, as was the relative significance of those relationships). In many cases, participants had formed meaningful relationships with countless others based upon their identities as co-victims.

As Richard Serpe and Sheldon Stryker[48] point out, individuals will engage in activities and join groups that maintain those identities which are most important to them. In this manner, participants demonstrated the importance of their co-victim identities. For many, activities and groups related to their co-victim identities had become a large part of their lives and consumed a considerable portion of their time and energy. Co-victims surrounded themselves with others who viewed them the way they viewed themselves, who expected from them attitudes and behavior they expected from self, and who engaged in groups comprised of like-minded others.

Due to the shared experience of losing a loved one to homicide, many participants reported feeling especially connected to other co-victims within their social networks. For many, groups like self-help groups took on the qualities of a primary reference group. Members had great influence over one another and often reported intense bonds. The allegiance to such groups was strong and the bonds between members was often immediate. Participants regularly referred to other co-victims as *"family"* and felt they could share aspects of themselves and their experiences with other co-victims that they could not share in other social circles, including biological family members and close friends. They often spoke of such groups being the only spaces within which they could be open and true to the full range of their emotions. Participants in this sample were especially devoted to the groups with which they identified due to the shared feelings within the membership, demonstrating the idea that individuals are more devoted to groups within which they find members with similar feelings than groups within which such similarity is not present.[49] Perhaps one reason people turn to others with similar victimization histories is that their identities can be verified in those circles when they cannot be verified elsewhere.

A final quality of the three co-victim identities warrants mention here, and that is their nature as obligatory versus voluntary. Peggy Thoits[50] differentiates between voluntary and obligatory identities, suggesting that voluntary identities (those one freely chooses to take on and those one can choose to exit at any point) lead to less stress and inner conflict because of their voluntary nature. Because people can leave voluntary identities at any point, those that people maintain are often those that provide much personal benefit to the individual. People acting within an identity they chose often feel as if they have greater control over their situation as compared to those acting within obligatory identities. Obligatory identities are more difficult to exit, such as parent or manager. These identities are often the source of distress and conflict. Because they are difficult to exit, those who have many obligatory identities often feel a lack of control over their lives.

In my sample, it was clear that those displaying a victim identity felt they had less control over their lives, in particular the long-term consequences of their losses to homicide, than those who had adopted survivor or transcender identities. This makes sense, given that the victim identity is more focused upon the loss and resultant trauma, which the co-victim did not freely choose. Therefore the victim identity could be thought of as an obligatory identity, as it was forced upon the co-victim. As expected with obligatory identities, the victim identity is a source of distress for co-victims.

Contrarily, the survivor and transcender identities are characterized by a sense of agency and power to create change. Survivors' and transcenders' focus is not upon the loss itself. Instead co-victims with these identities take control and create positive outcomes from the trauma, whether that be in service of other crime victims, as seen in survivor identities, or in service of bringing about positive change more generally, as seen in transcender identities. In building survivor and transcender identities, such co-victims are creating voluntary identities, which give the co-victims a sense of empowerment and control over their lives more generally. The survivor and transcender identities can also be exited freely. For example, a survivor may decide to stop attending self-help groups in support of others or a transcender may decide to withdraw from commitments to engage in peace talks. In this way, acting within the roles associated with the survivor or transcender identity is voluntary. The survivor and transcender identities, therefore, do not generate the same level of distress in co-victims as victim identities.

Therefore, an alternative way to consider the character of the victim, survivor, and transcender identities is that all co-victims have access to a victim identity, in which they can acknowledge and respect the devastation that resulted from their violent loss. Each is forced into this identity at the time of his or her loss and cannot exit the identity entirely (although they can choose not to act within it and thereby disallow its verification). However, some co-victims have constructed additional identities, namely survivor or transcender identities. In such cases, co-victims may choose to act within these alternative identities and surround themselves with others who view them as survivors or transcenders. In doing so, the survivor or transcender identity is verified and strengthened. Simultaneously, the victim identity is weakened, as such co-victims distance themselves from the emotions, attitudes, and behaviors that characterize a victim identity.

In 2002, Paul Rock asked a series of questions with relation to the process of becoming a victim (meant in his work as a person harmed by a criminal act). His words are relevant here, as they highlight the variety of avenues not yet fully explored with regard to the co-victim experience. He asks:

> [H]ow do these selves interplay with the wider biography of the victim and with retrospective and prospective readings of his or her identity; how much are they stereotyped and how much the result of reflective consideration and remodelling by the victim himself or herself; ... how do they sit with beliefs about fate and agency in human affairs; what practical, existential and moral consequences flow from the acquisition of victim selves; what parts do others play in formulating those interpretations; when and how would a victim seek their support, take action or call upon outsiders ...; and when, most importantly, is victimisation an enduring signifier?[51]

Given the potential impact of the finding of three distinct identities constructed in the wake of extreme loss, future research should aim to answer these questions with respect to the victim, survivor, and transcender identities and determine if these identities emerge following other types of losses or traumas, the extent of their potentially fluid nature, and the scope of their consequences. The current work is just the beginning of what could become an entirely new way of understanding victimization and trauma.

Based on this work, we know that the three co-victim identities that emerge after loss to homicide have considerable consequences in terms of felt emotion. We therefore know why some co-victims forgive and others do not; the answer lies in which co-victim identity each adopts. Co-victims who maintain a victim identity do not forgive, whereas those who transition into a survivor or transcender identity do forgive. And those who remain within a survivor identity will demonstrate non-benevolent forgiveness, whereas the experience of forgiveness for those who develop a transcender identity will be benevolent. But this leads us to ask yet another question: why do some co-victims develop survivor or transcender identities while others maintain a victim identity after loss to homicide? The next chapter will tackle this difficult question, wrapping up our exploration of *when, how,* and *why* forgiveness occurs after extreme harm.

Questions for Further Discussion

1   Given the inherent interconnectedness of person, role, and social identities, is it useful to distinguish between them? Why (not)?
2   How might a marriage be affected if each spouse adopts a different co-victim identity? For example, following the loss of their son to murder, what might be the consequence of a husband adopting a transcender identity while his wife maintains a victim identity?
3   Is it useful to differentiate between the voluntary and obligatory nature of co-victim identities? Why (not)?
4   How would you anticipate social positions (i.e., age, gender, racial identity, social class) affect the likelihood of a co-victim developing each type of co-victim identity?

Notes

1   Sections of this chapter are based on a forthcoming publication from this project: Discola, Kristen Lee. (forthcoming) "Emerging narratives in the wake of homicide: Victim, survivor, and transcender." *Journal of Victimology and Victim Justice.*
2   Blumer, Herbert. 1969. *Symbolic Interactionism: Perspective and Methods.* Upper Saddle River, NJ: Prentice-Hall; McIntyre, Lisa J. 2011. *The Practical Skeptic: Core Concepts in Sociology.* 5th edition. New York, NY: McGraw Hill; Stryker, Sheldon. 1980[2002]. *Symbolic Interactionism: A Social Structured Version.* Caldwell, NJ: Blackburn Press.

3 Burke, Peter J. and Jan E. Stets. 2009. *Identity Theory*. New York, NY: Oxford University Press.

4 Matsueda, Ross L. 1992. "Reflected appraisals, parental labeling, and delinquency: Specifying a symbolic interactionist theory." *American Journal of Sociology* 6:1577–1611. https://doi.org/10.1086/229940; Mead, George H. 1934. *Mind, Self and Society*. Chicago, IL: University of Chicago Press.

5 Stryker, Sheldon. 1980[2002]. *Symbolic Interactionism: A Social Structured Version*. Caldwell, NJ: Blackburn Press.

6 Burke, Peter J. and Jan E. Stets. 2009. *Identity Theory*. New York, NY: Oxford University Press.

7 Burke, Peter J. and Jan E. Stets. 2009. *Identity Theory*. New York, NY: Oxford University Press.

8 Serpe, Richard T. and Stryker, Sheldon. 1987. "The construction of self and the reconstruction of social relationships." pp. 41–82 in *Advances in Group Processes: Theory and Research*, Volume 4, edited by E. J. Lawler and B. Markovsky. Greenwich, CT: JAI Press.

9 Stryker, Sheldon. 1980[2002]. *Symbolic Interactionism: A Social Structured Version*. Caldwell, NJ: Blackburn Press.

10 Stryker, Sheldon and Richard T. Serpe. 1982 "Commitment, identity salience, and role behavior: Theory and research example." Pp 199–218 in *Personality, Roles, and Social Behavior,* edited by W. Ickes and E. S. Knowles. Springer Series in Social Psychology. New York, NY: Springer.

11 Burke, Peter J. and Jan E. Stets. 2009. *Identity Theory*. New York, NY: Oxford University Press.

12 For in-depth explanations of person, role, and social identities, see Burke, Peter. 1980. "The self: Measurement requirements from an interactionist perspective." *Social Psychology Quarterly* 43:18–30. https://doi.org/10.2307/3033745; McCall, George J. and J. L. Simmons. 1978. *Identities and interactions: An examination of human associations in everyday life*. New York, NY: Free Press; Stryker, Sheldon. 1980[2002]. *Symbolic Interactionism: A Social Structured Version*. Caldwell, NJ: Blackburn Press; Thoits, Peggy A. and Lauren K. Virshup. "Me's and we's: Forms and functions of social identities." pp. 106–133 in *Self and Identity: Fundamental Issues,* Volume I, edited by Richard D. Ashmore and Lee Jussim. New York, NY: Oxford University Press.

13 Turner, Ralph H. 1962. "Role-taking: Process versus conformity." pp. 20–40 in *Human Behavior and Social Processes,* edited by A. M. Rose. Boston, MA: Houghton Mifflin.

14 Burke, Peter. 1980. "The self: Measurement requirements from an interactionist perspective." *Social Psychology Quarterly* 43:18–30. https://doi.org/10.2307/3033745

15 Stets, Jan E. and Peter J. Burke. 2000. "Identity theory and social identity theory." *Social Psychology Quarterly* 63:224–237. https://doi.org/10.2307/2695870

16 Thoits, Peggy A. and Lauren K. Virshup. "Me's and we's: Forms and functions of social identities." pp. 106–133 in *Self and Identity: Fundamental Issues,* Volume I, edited by Richard D. Ashmore and Lee Jussim. New York, NY: Oxford University Press.

17 Thoits and Virshup believe that a distinction should not be drawn between the role and social identities. Burke and Stets maintain that the difference is mainly analytical and suggest that, in order to establish a complete understanding of societal processes, researchers must incorporate both the role and group orientations toward identity.

18 Burke, Peter J. and Jan E. Stets. 2009. *Identity Theory*. New York, NY: Oxford University Press.

19 Burke, Peter J. and Jan E. Stets. 2009. *Identity Theory*. New York, NY: Oxford University Press (p. 74).

20 Serpe, R. T. and S. Stryker. 1987. "The construction of self and the reconstruction of social relationships." pp. 41–82 in *Advances In Group Processes: Theory and Research*, Volume 4; edited by E. J. Lawler and B. Markovsky. Greenwich, CT: JAI Press.

21 Burke, Peter J. 2004. "Identities and social structure: The 2003 Cooley-Mead award address." *Social Psychology Quarterly* 64:5–15. https://doi.org/10.1177/019027250406700103

22 Gottfredson, Michael. 1989. "Experiences of violent and serious victimization." pp. 202–237 in *Pathways to Criminal Violence*, edited by Neil A. Weiner and Marvin E. Wolfgang. Thousand Oaks, CA: Sage Publications; Strang, Heather. 2002. *Repair or Revenge: Victims and Restorative Justice*. Oxford: Oxford University Press; Zehr, Howard. 2001. *Transcending: Reflections of Crime Victims*. Intercourse, PA: Good Books.

23 Burke, Peter and Jan Stets. 2009. *Identity Theory*. Oxford: Oxford University Press.

24 Mead, George. 1934. *Mind, Self and Society*. Chicago, IL: University of Chicago Press.

25 Bartusch, Dawn Jeglum and Ross L. Matsueda. 1996. "Gender, reflected appraisals, and labeling: A cross-group test of an interactionist theory of delinquency." *Social Forces* 75(1):145–176. https://doi.org/10.2307/2580760

26 Hurvitz, Nathan. 1970. "Peer self-help psychotherapy groups and their implications for psychotherapy." *Psychotherapy: Theory, Research & Practice* 7(1):41–49 (p. 46). https://doi.org/ 10.1037/h0086549

27 Matsueda, Ross L. 1992. "Reflected appraisals, parental labeling, and delinquency: Specifying a symbolic interactionist theory." *American Journal of Sociology* 6:1577–1611. https://doi.org/10.1086/229940

28 Hurvitz, N. 1970. "Peer self-help psychotherapy groups and their implications for psychotherapy." *Psychotherapy: Theory, Research & Practice* 7(1):41–49. https://doi.org/10.1037/h0086549

29 Stryker, Sheldon. 2004. "Integrating emotion into Identity Theory." *Advances in Group Processes* 21:1–23. https://doi.org/10.1016/S0882-6145(04)21001-3

30 Strang, Heather. 2002. *Repair or Revenge: Victims and Restorative Justice*. Oxford: Oxford University Press.

31 Strang, Heather. 2002. *Repair or Revenge: Victims and Restorative Justice*. Oxford: Oxford University Press (pp. 18–19).

32 Gottfredson, Michael. 1989. "Experiences of violent and serious victimization." pp. 202–237 in *Pathways to Criminal Violence*, edited by Neil A. Weiner and Marvin E. Wolfgang. Thousand Oaks, CA: Sage Publications (pp. 221–222).

33 For a detailed examination of the processes involved in creating meaning through narrative following loss of a loved one, see Neimeyer, R. A. and Anderson, A. 2002. "Meaning reconstruction theory." pp. 45–64 in *Loss and Grief*, edited by N. Thompson. New York, NY: Palgrave.

34 Discussion of these identities as narratives has been developed elsewhere: Hourigan, Kristen Lee. 2019. "Narrative victimology: Speaker, audience, timing." pp. 259–277 in *The Emerald Handbook of Narrative Criminology*. Edited by Jennifer Fleetwood, Lois Presser, Sveinung Sandberg, and Thomas Ugelvik. https://doi/org/10.1108/978-1-78769-005-920191024

35 Zehr, Howard. 2001. *Transcending: Reflections of Crime Victims*. Intercourse, PA: Good Books (pp. 189–190).

36 Burke, Peter and Jan Stets. 2009. *Identity Theory*. Oxford: Oxford University Press.

37 Turner, Jonathan H. and Jan E. Stets. 2005. *The Sociology of Emotions*. New York, NY: Cambridge University Press (p. 175).

38 Govier, Trudy. 2012. "Public forgiveness: A modest defense." pp. 25–36 in *Public Forgiveness in Post-Conflict Contexts*, edited by B. Van Stokkom, N. Doorn, and P. Van Tongeren. Antwerp: Intersentia (p. 26).

39 Walker, Margaret. 2006. *Moral Repair*. Cambridge, MA: Cambridge University Press.

40 Turner, Jonathan H. and Jan E. Stets. 2005. *The Sociology of Emotions*. New York, NY: Cambridge University Press (p. 175).

41 Shott, Susan. 1979. "Emotion and social life: A symbolic interactionist analysis." *American Journal of Sociology* 84(6):1317–1334 (p. 1326).

42 The experience of transcenders in this sample can serve as an empirical example of Ruiz-Junco's "self-transcendent path" to empathy: Ruiz-Junco, Natalia. 2017. "Advancing the sociology of empathy." *Symbolic Interaction* 40(3):414–435. https://doi.org/10.1002/symb.306

43 Armor, Marilyn. 2003. "Meaning making in the aftermath of homicide." *Death Studies* 27:519–540. https://doi.org/10.1080/07481180302884

44 Armour, Marilyn. 2003. "Meaning making in the aftermath of homicide." *Death Studies* 27:519–540 (p. 534). https://doi.org/10.1080/07481180302884

45 Previous research focused on bereavement has shown that potential supporters who have not experienced similar grief may be ill prepared to effectively support those who have lost a loved one. See Goodrum, Sarah. 2008. "When the management of grief becomes everyday life: The aftermath of murder." *Symbolic Interaction* 31(4):422–442. https://doi.org/10.1525/si.2008.31.4.422

46 It should be noted that such statements were solely heard from white co-victims. Participants who self-identified as black indicated that they had an abundance of people they could turn to who understood their plight. Further research is needed, as this could be indicating cultural or structural differences, given the overlap between race and social class in the current sample. Perhaps there is a difference in culture in terms of individualistic versus community-oriented ideologies. Or, perhaps the white participants in this sample have few people to turn to because homicide is an atypical occurrence in their middle- and upper-middle-class neighborhoods and the experience is therefore quite foreign.

Concurrently, the black participants in the sample may have family, friends, and neighbors who have experienced loss to homicide because of experiences related not to race, but to the harsh realities of surviving within or near impoverished neighborhoods where violence is more commonplace. Research with a more diverse sample is needed to untangle these issues.

47 Stryker, Sheldon and Richard T. Serpe. 1982 "Commitment, identity salience, and role behavior: Theory and research example." pp. 199–218 in *Personality, Roles, and Social Behavior* edited by W. Ickes and E. S. Knowles. Springer Series in Social Psychology. New York, NY: Springer.

48 Serpe, Richard T. and Stryker, Sheldon. 1987. "The construction of self and the reconstruction of social relationships." pp. 41–82 in *Advances in Group Processes: Theory and Research* Volume 4, edited by E. J. Lawler and B. Markovsky. Greenwich, CT: JAI Press.

49 Stryker, Sheldon. 2004. "Integrating emotion into identity theory." *Advances in Group Processes* 21:1–23. https://doi.org/10.1016/S0882-6145(04)21001-3

50 Thoits, Peggy A. 2003. "Personal agency in the accumulation of multiple role identities." pp. 179–194 in *Advances in Identity Theory and Research*, edited by P. J. Burke, T. J. Owens, R. T. Serpe, and P. A. Thoits. New York, NY: Kluwer Academic/Plenum.

51 Rock, Paul. 2002. "On becoming a victim" pp. 1–22 in *New Visions of Crime Victims,* edited by Carolyn Hoyle and Richard Young. Oxford: Hart Publishing (p. 19).

Chapter 7

Unraveling Causal Order

Because of the insight I've gained of my own mental health, I've been able to look at other people in a different and more forgiving light. Working through the trauma to be in the place where I am now has changed my entire spirit. I would have to say, I will probably never think of myself as fully forgiving Rick for his actions, but I have a lot more empathy for maybe why he did what he did, and I regard him in a softer way than before.—Lauren

As I listen to Barbara share her story with two young college students who have come to this self-help group meeting to gain a new level of insight into their studies of grief, I reflect back to 2012, before this research study was born, when I met another woman, Bev. I remember the first time I met Bev. She was sharing her story at a local university and I was within the small audience of criminal justice students, captivated by her tale and heartbroken for her loss. Now, a year later, I sit beside Barbara who has an uncanny resemblance to Bev. As she speaks, I think about how Barbara's story also shares several key elements with Bev's, yet remains fundamentally distinct. As I listen, I begin to wonder about the causal direction of experience and emotion.

What intrigues me is the similarity between these women's social positions, coupled with the unmistakable differences between their current emotional states. Both are white, Roman Catholic, American women in their 80s. They are both retired from similar jobs, currently unwed, and enjoy a middle-class lifestyle. They grew up in similar areas in the northeastern United States, and each currently lives in the same town. They both lost a daughter to murder more than two decades ago, and the offender in each of their cases is a black male who was an acquaintance of their daughters but who these women had never met or learned about until the men were caught for their daughters' murders. Both offenders were convicted of the murders and are still in prison. Both Bev and Barbara are heavily involved in self-help groups, memorial events, and advocating for change to the criminal justice system. In fact, they have each attended monthly meetings of two of the same self-help groups for those who have lost loved ones to homicide. However, their emotional experiences are vastly different. This includes their feelings toward the offenders in their cases, toward offenders in general, and toward our criminal justice system and society at large.

Bev's emotional experience includes hatred, intense anger, and prolonged feelings of vengefulness. She is generally unforgiving of the man who killed her daughter and she spends time lobbying for harsher punishments generally and denial of parole in specific cases of violent offenses. Barbara, on the other hand, displays sympathy, compassion, and a general sense of benevolence toward not only the man who killed her daughter but also other men in prison for similar crimes, with whom she often meets to share her story.

As I listen to Barbara, and reflect on Bev, I begin to wonder, what factors or forces led each woman down these distinct emotional paths? Demographically, they are remarkably similar. From a sociological standpoint, we may expect that the way they would experience loss to homicide would therefore also be remarkably similar. But their experiences have been, in fact, vastly different.

It was from this intrigue that this research project developed. I decided to investigate the experiences of these two women, and others like them, to determine what factors play a role in determining one's emotional experiences after a traumatic loss, such as homicide. Through this process, I discovered that Bev had what could be described as a "victim" identity, and Barbara exhibited all the hallmarks of a "transcender" identity. Therefore, Bev and Barbara were on opposite ends of the spectrum in terms of forgiveness. Bev expressed unforgiveness and Barbara displayed a benevolent forgiveness. But why? Did each woman's co-victim identity draw her to groups that shared in her attitudes and behavioral expectations, or did their experiences within these groups, surrounded by other co-victims who had established victim or transcender identities, push each woman in one direction versus the other? And, if the former were true, why did Bev develop a victim identity while Barbara developed a transcender identity, given their demographic and social similarities?

As a sociologist with a focus on social psychological processes, the first place I am trained to search for causation is within various aspects of social interaction. Two factors in particular summoned my attention as I began my search for an answer to this puzzle: group interactions and social positions. The group interactions most relevant to this study are those occurring within the various groups participants engaged within and connected to their identities as co-victims. Did participants' interactions within these groups influence their identity development? For example, were those who initially became connected to Loved Ones Left Behind (LOLB) more likely than those who were first introduced to Homicide Bereavement Circle (HBC) to develop transcender identities? Or did participants' developing identities as co-victims compel them to seek out groups that supported and mirrored these identities? This is one puzzle that will be pieced together in this chapter.

I will then turn to an investigation of variation by social position to determine if demographics, and the social experiences related to such factors, are relevant to answering the question of why co-victims develop victim, survivor, or transcender identities after loss to homicide. As sociologists, we are taught that social interaction can often be better understood by comparing and contrasting the experiences of those falling into various demographic categories or social positions, such as race, class, and gender. Therefore, the final step of this analysis will do just that. I will explore whether or not individuals' prior social experiences, based on social position, influence the likelihood of developing a victim, survivor, or transcender identity after violent loss.

I will end the chapter with potential explanations for the patterns uncovered. I will draw upon the strengths of both theories used in previous chapters by using the concepts of fundamental self-sentiments from Affect Control Theory and the concepts of attitudinal and behavioral expectations, commitment, identity verification, and identity salience from Identity Theory. Here, I engage with the question of causation, offering arguments as to why prior social experiences may be the driving force for the transition away from a victim identity and/or into a transcender identity. Before diving into the question of cause, I present two cases from my sample that demonstrate the transitional process as co-victims move between victim, survivor, and transcender identities.

Omarr's Transition from Victim to Transcender

Several interviewees shared memories of being filled with rage and motivations to seek revenge and contrasted this to their current states. This was especially common in conversations with transcenders, as the difference between their current mental states and their initial emotional reactions to the loss of their loved ones was tremendous. Omarr's is a representative case and offers powerful insights into the transition from victim to transcender.

Soon after his cousin was killed, Omarr's anger and vengefulness were intense. He described his reaction to the impact of his cousin's death upon his cousin's younger siblings, to whom Omarr was very close. He said, *"It infuriated me to the point of wanting revenge ... What I desired as the outcome was revenge, you know, to avenge the death of my cousin."* When he brought the news of his cousin's death to his aunt, Omarr communicated his intention to retaliate and his willingness to take the life of the man who killed his cousin. He said to his aunt, *"You just let me know how you want it handled. And you don't have to worry about anything else. If you want it taken care of, it'll be taken care of, and it'll be done."* Omarr soon learned through the police investigation process that his cousin may have been shot because he was defending Omarr. He told me:

> [The police] *were turning up different statements from whoever they were talking to and my cousin was killed as a result of him trying to defend me from some adversaries or rivalries … This revealed a dark thing that we didn't know about, which was that someone actually had put a contract on my life. That someone, you know, had basically looked for an opportunity for me to be executed … My anger and rage went probably off the meter two or three times over … The anger was so intense, I pulled in some of my security team, people from out of the state who had no identity and who knew no one* [in the area].

Omarr continued, describing what he now considered an *"irrational"* mindset that was a necessary element of violent retaliation:

> *It's difficult to look someone in the eyes or to harm someone that you're familiar with. But when there's no connection and no relationship, it's just business, you know? So that was my reaction. And my response was to bring my security team into play. I wore a bulletproof outfit 24–7, feeling safe but at the same time, in the brief seconds of sanity that I would have, it was also stressful, ya know? To know that at 19 and 18 this is how I had to exist day to day, covered in Teflon and walking with security that the president would be envious of. So it started getting frustrating and stressful from that standpoint. There was a young lady that I had been involved with who also had made me aware by this point in time that she was carrying my child, which compounded the problem even more because it's a matter of, "Am I gonna live to see the birth of my child? Is someone gonna harm her knowing that she's carrying my child?" A whole bunch of different factors* [were] *in play and me wanting to make sure that everyone that I cared about would be safe.*

Omarr shared how another individual who knew his cousin *"from the streets"* also felt vengeful. He said this young man *"was going through the same thing"* as Omarr:

> *He wanted to do a revenge, he had everything set, a plan in motion. One night, he was at a party, a Jamaican party. And the person who had caused the death of my cousin was at the party and he saw the individual. And his emotions stirred*

up in him so intensely that he actually tried to kill him. He shot him. I think like maybe five times. But the person, he survived it. No vital organs were hit, and he went into a two-day surgery and he survived it. But he was the only other person that I had that kind of an interaction and contact with that were going through them revenge feelings.

Omarr's story then took an unexpected twist, as he described how he had decided to leave the state but was *"picked up"* on outstanding charges across state lines, for which he was convicted and sentenced to 20 years in prison. He explained how his time *"in the system"* contributed to his change in mindset. He said:

Seeing the young people coming into the system, younger and younger each year; reading the newspapers and calling home and hearing about obituaries of 16, 17, 18-year-olds and, two times zones over; turning on the news to see a homicide in [his hometown] *make the news in Texas, you know, these are the things that contributed to affecting me into the mindset to who I am now, to be more of an asset to society, rather than a liability.*

Omarr gave an eloquent description of his identity reconstruction process:

It's an evolution, a metamorphosis, that I went through to understand that I'm leaving something and someone behind, that something new and greater is coming out. A new life, so to say. So where I am now is definitely in a better place, a brighter place, a positive place. My passion and my every effort in community upliftment and empowerment is what and who I am.

He described how he fights for *"the underdog," "the weak,"* and *"those who are not able to fend and deal with themselves and take care of themselves, whether it's through disability, whether it's through overwhelm, whatever it is that has them in that place, or ignorance even, lack of information or knowledge."* He said:

I've committed myself and, you know, the rest of my life and journey, (1) to my family, and (2) very close behind that one, to helping to make sure that reasonable choices and options are out there for the community and for the youth in particular. That they don't have to make uninformed decisions or make decisions and choices out of ignorance. You could say, "Well, you have options," but if a person doesn't know the depth of those options, if they only see options A and B as an option, then because they don't know there's a C, D, and E, because they can't understand the script or whatever the case may be, then, yeah, they're gonna go with option A or B. You know, one or the other. So my thing is to make sure that they do understand there's three more letters, you know, in their options …

I came out [of prison] *with the primary concern and interest to be* [working in] *reentry, and it evolved into youth involvement and gang involvement. And that went to systems of government and agencies, based on the needs of the youth and those who are in different predicaments.*

Omarr's transformation from a rageful, vengeful adversary to a compassionate, dedicated advocate is a prime example of the transformation from a victim identity to a transcender identity. When we met, Omarr was a pillar in the community, standing at the helm of several large projects aimed at supporting and uplifting at-risk youth in the community. He used his *"street cred"* to create a safe space for wayward youth (and adults) to consider alternatives to a life *"hustling on the streets."* The outward, plural focus Omarr displayed at this stage of his life, coupled with the associated activities he dedicated himself to, typifies the cornerstones of the transcender identity.

Lauren's Transition from Victim to Survivor

I later had the unique experience of witnessing one participant's transition between victim and survivor identities that was also demonstrative. Lauren had found both of her primary parents dead when she was a teenager, after her step-father killed her mother and then himself. I first met Lauren when she was an interviewee for this research. We had become connected through another co-victim who told her about my research and suggested she reach out to share her story. Lauren's was my 20th interview for this project, and I was therefore already formulating ideas around the patterns emerging from the data with regard to the three identity classifications. After her interview, I teetered with which category Lauren fell within. Her case challenged me to reconsider the boundaries between the three identities and to question whether they are best thought of as distinct or as falling along a continuum. The two identities that Lauren seemed to be straddling were that of a victim and that of a survivor. I decided to postpone the classification of Lauren's case and attempt to reconnect with Lauren for a follow-up conversation after my data collection had been completed.

At the conclusion of her interview, Lauren said that she hoped to remain in contact and wanted to read any works that came from this project. Therefore, I sent her the first publication that arose from this work. This communication was well received and she seemed interested in maintaining open lines of communication. Nearly three years after her initial interview, I emailed Lauren again, saying that I was thinking of her and just wanted to check in. Her response conveyed that she was genuinely happy to hear from me. A few weeks later, we met for lunch, and our conversation lasted for just over one hour. During that conversation, it became clear that Lauren had been within a transition period, between identities, when we first spoke. The field notes I wrote after that follow-up conversation are demonstrative of the process Lauren underwent as she moved from victim to survivor:

> *Lauren was very excited to share with me all the changes she had made since our interview. She said she was "in a completely different space than when we first met." She reflected back to the date of our interview and said that that was a bad time during which she was still struggling, having "just begun truly healing." Now, she is back in school at* [the local university], *has what she considers a "better job," and is looking forward to moving out of her grandmother's house soon. She has been in counseling for a while now and has made great progress toward healing … She said she was "in a different place in her mind" when we met before … Before, she had a lack of motivation and now she's highly motivated: "I'm in school, and it feels so good!"*

At the point of our follow-up lunch, Lauren was not sure what she wanted to do with her degree when she graduated, but she knew she wanted her career to focus on post-traumatic stress disorder (PTSD), and she said this was due to her personal experiences suffering from the disorder after her mother's murder. She shared how she had realized that *"it's so intricate of a disorder"* and affects so many aspects of life, *"not just behavioral, but also physiological."* My field notes continued:

> *Lauren's high level of motivation to do positive in her life, her daughter's life, and the world was palpable. She shared that when she went to career counseling, she realized that she needed to figure out her own emotions first, before figuring out her future in terms of a career, so she began counseling for her PTSD. That process led her to want to dedicate her career to helping others who suffer with the disorder.*

Lauren had nearly finished her bachelor's degree when she lost her mother at the hands of her step-father, and she had soon become addicted to drugs. She had shared with me her experiences of drowning her pain with both drugs and alcohol. In her initial interview, she said, *"I didn't have reason to go on."* Such feelings eventually motivated Lauren to shift her definition of the situation and ultimately forgive her step-father. My field notes from our follow-up continue:

> *Lauren said, "Since I started working on the core of my issues, I have no desire to use drugs at all … It makes me so sad that maybe if I had took care of things earlier, I never would have been in that position." She talked about how those experiences led her to where she is now, saying her struggles made her stronger*

and more knowledgeable. She said, "I didn't read this in a book. And that's the biggest reason why I want to do this [earn her degree] because it took a third of my life away. It's crazy … So I really just don't want that to be the downfall of anybody else when there's a way to reverse that and heal!"

As is characteristic of survivors, Lauren was motivated to help others whose suffering was similar to hers. For Lauren, this plural, specific focus was directed toward the struggles associated with PTSD.

Lauren's emotional state from the initial interview to the follow-up was also indicative of a transition from victim to survivor. The anger and vengefulness she felt toward her step-father the first time we spoke were no longer present at this follow up. My field notes from the follow-up relayed Lauren's response to having read the first publication from this project:

> *She said she had read the paper, so I asked "Did it resonate?" and she scrunched up her face, as if not wanting to quite say "no," then said, "It's difficult because the feelings about our situation aren't always concrete." I asked what she meant and she said she recognized her own case in the publication and she found her quotes "interesting." She said, "So what I told you a few years ago, I might not feel the same way now. I read what I'd said and I can totally see myself saying that then. That sounds like something I would say. But I wouldn't say that now … That stuff doesn't affect me daily, like it used to, which is very freeing."*

Here it is clear that Lauren had moved into a survivor identity, as she demonstrates a sort of detachment from, or indifference toward, the events. She no longer feels the intense, negative emotions that she once felt regarding her mother's murder.

The following week, I emailed Lauren and asked her directly about her statements during her initial interview. I wrote:

> *When I asked you about forgiveness (what forgiveness means, whether or not you forgave your step-dad, and what factors make it harder/easier to forgive), you said: "Really the only time that I would be able to forgive somebody is if I can say in my mind 'it's really not that bad' and 'they needed to do that.' Then I can understand and it's okay with me." You said that for this reason you really couldn't forgive your step-dad for his actions. Now that you're in a different place, can I ask how you'd respond to the same types of questions now?*

Lauren responded:

> *Because of the insight I've gained of my own mental health, I've been able to look at other people in a different and more forgiving light. Working through the*

trauma to be in the place where I am now has changed my entire spirit. I would have to say I will probably never think of myself as fully forgiving Rick for his actions, but I have a lot more empathy for maybe why he did what he did, and I regard him in a softer way than before.

Based on her original interview, I know that Lauren defines forgiveness differently than I define it in this book. She believes that to say you forgive a person indicates that you are condoning his or her act. Lauren will never condone her step-father's actions. However, based on the definition used in this book, she has moved into a state of non-benevolent forgiveness (the release of negative, other-directed emotions that resulted from harm caused by prior actions of the other which are not replaced by positive, other-directed emotion). This, too, typifies the survivor identity.

The distance between the emotional experience of victims and survivors, and between survivors and transcenders, is shorter than the distance between the emotional experience of victims and transcenders. It is easier to transition between similar emotions than to move across vastly dissimilar emotions. For example, the rage and vengefulness felt by victims are closer to the indifference and balance felt by survivors than to the compassion and sympathy felt by transcenders. Therefore, the survivor identity, and its accompanying emotional states, may serve as an "emotional segue"[1] between the victim and transcender identities. With the current data, this idea is not easily investigated. Future research should expand upon the insights offered here in order to determine if adopting the survivor identity is a necessary step in moving between the victim and transcender identities.

Exploring Causation

Having presented evidence of the existence of three distinct co-victim identities and explicitly connecting these to the emotional transformation of forgiveness, I will now turn to an exploration of causality. From where do these identities stem? First, I will explore the connection (or lack thereof) between the development of these identities and time. Then, I will attempt to further elucidate the connection between co-victim identities and social networks. Finally, I will explore variation in co-victim identity based on demographic categories and social experience. This investigation will bring us full circle, answering the question of *why* some co-victims forgive and others do not.

Passage of Time

As shown in Table 7.1,[2] the association between the passage of time and the development of victim, survivor, and transcender identities was not

Table 7.1 Co-Victim Identities by the Passage of Time since the Loss (*n* = 36)[1]

Co-victim identity	Passage of time		
	Less than 15 years since loss	15–30 years since loss	More than 30 years since loss
Victim identity	4 (27%)	2 (17%)	2 (22%)
Survivor identity	6 (40%)	2 (17%)	0 (0%)
Transcender identity	5 (33%)	8 (67%)	7 (78%)
Total	15 (100%)	12 (101%)[2]	9 (100%)

Chi-square test's *p*-value = 0.136.

1 Despite some small expected frequencies, Chi-square tests were performed on relevant analyses presented in this book. Corresponding *p*-values indicate levels of statistical significance. An effect is reported as significant if *p* < 0.05. Such statistics should not be interpreted as results of tests of predetermined hypotheses but rather used to bolster the qualitative analyses presented here. Future analyses with larger sample sizes are needed to verify findings related to variability across categories presented here.

2 Totals do not equal 100% due to rounding.

statistically significant (*p* = 0.136). That is to say, those whose losses were more recent did not necessarily display victim identities, and those whose losses had occurred many decades prior were not necessarily transcenders. For example, Rose demonstrated a victim identity even though she had lost her daughter over 39 years prior to our interview. On the other end of the spectrum, Glenda had lost her brother just over one year prior to our initial conversation, yet she already demonstrated characteristics of a transcender identity. And Carol and Camila both held survivor identities, but Carol had lost her husband and son over 20 years earlier while Camila's cousins had been slain just months before our interview. Therefore, it is clear that movement from a victim identity into a survivor identity, or from a survivor identity into a transcender identity, does not necessarily become more likely with the passage of time, and not all co-victims undergo such a transition between identities. Some clearly remain within victim or survivor identities throughout their lives.

Group Interaction: Which Comes First, the Co-Victim Group or the Co-Victim Identity?

For several years, one question continually presented itself as I collected and analyzed my data: do co-victims with established identity types join groups because of the like-mindedness they perceive within the member-ship, or do a co-victim's experiences within a certain group influence which co-victim identity he or she develops? In other words, which comes first, the co-victim group or the co-victim identity? For example, do transcenders seek out groups with foci, attitudes, and behavioral expectations similar to their own? Or do individuals' experiences within future-focused, restora-tive, compassionate groups of co-victims steer them toward development of a transcender identity? The next section of this chapter ventures to answer such questions.

Some readers may feel that this analysis creates a tautology. That is to say, investigating the existence of a link between the co-victim identities and the groups co-victims engage within creates an irrefutable stance, since the identity categories were created, in part, by considering what groups co-victims engaged within. I agree that this could be viewed as tautological reasoning, but I maintain that such an investigation remains valuable and interesting for three reasons. First, the three co-victim identities were constructed around *several* distinct factors, only one of which is the groups within which the person engages or classifies him- or herself. Second, as you will see in later sections, not all co-victims take part in groups rele-vant to their co-victim identities. Some are not active members of any such groups, for various reasons, such as the demands of work schedules or young children. Therefore, individuals can maintain a co-victim iden-tity without actively engaging in groups that are directly relevant to that identity. Finally, several co-victims, within this sample (including Bev and Barbara, whose similarities and differences opened this chapter) reported having spent time engaging in multiple groups with differing foci or ideologies. These co-victims eventually came to choose which groups to spend their time and energy engaging within on an ongoing basis. Such a choice indicates that the co-victim identity can exist separately from one's group affiliation, a point that will become the crux of the penultimate argument of this book.

Group Participation

Given the number and variety of groups participants took part in, it was necessary that I establish meaningful categories to explore the connection between identity and group membership. The first distinction to be drawn was between those participants who were and were not active members of groups related to the loss to homicide or the circumstances or consequences of that loss. Therefore, the first category (not active) indicates all participants who were not regular[3] participants in group events or activities surrounding issues relevant, directly or indirectly, to their losses to homicide.

The most meaningful data surrounding participants' participation in group events came from observation and the narration of participants' stories at the outset of interviews. Most participants (29 out of 36, or over 80%) were classified as being active within at least one group directly or indirectly relevant to their losses to homicide. Such group events were, at times, where I initially met participants. Other groups were salient aspects of participants' stories but I did not have the opportunity to participate in those groups and therefore based my understanding of those groups upon the participants' descriptions.

Upon further consideration, it became clear that the types of groups participants connected to their co-victim identities and took part in regularly could be separated into two categories. The first category consists of those groups that are focused upon crimes committed and their consequences upon others (meaning everyone other than the person who committed the crime). The foci of these groups' activities and missions surrounded events occurring in the past (the original crime) and the current state of affairs with regard to the effects of the commission of the crime. For example, memorial committees, all of which fell within this group classification, focused upon maintenance of the memory of loved ones lost to homicide. This could be considered a past focus or a present focus, depending upon which aspect of the mission is emphasized: the life lost (the past) or the continual mainten-ance of the memory (the present). Other examples of groups falling into this classification include Crime Victims' Rights Week planning committees and HBC.

Distinguishing between past-focused and present-focused groups is not a meaningful task, in my opinion. As a sociological social psychologist, I believe there is a strong and indelible link between the past and the pre-sent, as the past is only known as it exists in our minds and interactions in the present moment, and the present only takes form as interpretation of experience which is based on our past interactions and experiences. I there-fore do not attempt to separate groups within this category by past versus present focus, as the placement of groups into categories of past and present focus would be arguable in all cases. This leaves us with three categories of participants: (1) those who were not active members of groups related to their co-victim identities; (2) those who were active members of predomin-antly, or entirely, past/present-focused groups; and (3) those who were active members of predominantly, or entirely, future-focused groups. The final cat-egory, "future-focused," includes all participants who regularly took part in group activities that focused upon the future and upon taking steps to tackle larger societal problems, including the suffering of offenders. Such activities included anti-violence programs, restorative justice initiatives, at-risk youth programs, peace-building events, and some reentry programs.[4]

Upon reflection after completion of data collection, it was interesting to note that the majority of group events and activities participants spoke of were what I came to refer to as "future-focused," despite the fact that my data collection methods created a bias toward discovering connection to past/present-focused groups for two reasons. First, the majority of the events I observed were past/present-focused. This was in part due to the fact that the future-focused events were often only indirectly connected to loss to homicide, and I was therefore less likely to come upon information about such events, given my research topic. Second, the only question included in my interview script that asks directly about group participation was: "Have you ever attended any sort of victim groups or events?" At the time of construction of my interview instrument, I was not aware of the meaningful distinction that would later come to light between groups and events focused directly upon crime victims and those focused upon broader social problems. Given these biasing realities, one would anticipate that the data generated from this project would be likely to indicate participants' regular participation in past/present-focused groups. On the contrary, the majority of participants in this sample discussed their active participation in future-focused groups and events, many of which I had not taken part in. These participants' candor about these future-focused groups and events opened up opportunities for me to consider and, in some cases, observe groups and events I would not have otherwise thought to include within my analyses.

Though it created small cell sizes, in Table 7.2 I display the relationship between co-victim identity type and group participation category.[5] By doing so, this table indicates what percentage of all those falling into each co-victim identity category regularly engaged with each type of group. For example, in the first cell, the 50% indicates that 50% of all those with a victim identity were "not active" in groups relevant to their losses.

Table 7.2 Group Participation by Co-Victim Identities (*n* = 36)

Group participation	Co-victim identity		
	Victim	Survivor	Transcender
Not active	4	2	1
	(50%)	(25%)	(5%)
Past/present-focused	4	4	0
	(50%)	(50%)	(0%)
Future-focused	0	2	19
	(0%)	(25%)	(95%)
Total	8	8	20
	(100%)	(100%)	(100%)

Chi-square test's *p*-value < 0.001.

The differences displayed here are statistically significant (p-value < 0.001), despite small cell sizes. This suggests that there is an association between these two variables in the current sample. Only half of victims participated in relevant groups, but those who did were drawn to groups with a past/present focus. Survivors were more evenly spread among the group categories. And all but one transcender took part in future-focused group activities.

It is interesting to note that the deviant transcender case (the one case of a transcender not taking an active role in future-focused groups) was Cleavon, a 31-year-old who had not yet had the time to become actively involved in such pursuits but who expressed a desire to do so. Cleavon had been released from prison less than two months before I met him, after spending nearly half of his life behind bars. At 16 years old, Cleavon had been sentenced to 20 years' imprisonment for murder. After serving 16 years, he had recently been released. I met Cleavon at a local anti-violence program, to which he had been invited a few days prior. During his interview, Cleavon explained that he had *"bumped into J. R. across the street."* He had served time in prison with J. R. and, when they began talking earlier that week, Cleavon became interested in the program J. R. was running in the neighborhood. I asked Cleavon if he saw himself becoming a part of the anti-violence program. He said: *"Maybe. I could do this. I could go and talk to these kids."* He explained that his current focus was himself and his immediate family, as his recent reentry came with immediate challenges he needed to focus his attention upon, such as setting up employment and strengthening crucial familial bonds. I asked Cleavon if he thought he would get involved with the program some day. He said:

CLEAVON: *I wouldn't mind, if given the opportunity, I wouldn't mind coming and speaking to the kids, just giving them a broader scope of things. [Telling them] "It's fun right now, but this is what can happen (gesturing to himself)."*

I: *Do you believe sharing your story would be helpful to those kids?*

C: *Yeah. I believe so, because no one shared it with me, and I didn't think that it could've happened like that. Looking back, had I known the things then that I know now, I wouldn't have been in the situation, running in gangs.*

I: *Is that something that you'd want, the opportunity to pass that knowledge on?*

C: *I would love to! It would also mean that my time served wasn't in vain. I could be someone else's shining light. Like, "Look, I'm the light, that's where [gangs] are going to lead you to."*

Unfortunately, reconnecting with Cleavon to see if he ever became a part of the anti-violence program is not possible, as he chose not to share any contact information with me after our time together. However, I believe that if

I were to return to that program today, it is likely that I would find Cleavon, using his story to lead at-risk youth away from the harsh consequences of violence and toward a more pro-social path.

Choosing a Group

Though there is no question that group participation verified and supported co-victims' identities, it was clear that many participants chose which groups to engage with based on how the group expectations, emotion norms, and ideologies paralleled those they connected to their fundamental self-sentiments (in cases in which the participant had not fully established a co-victim identity) or their co-victim identities (in cases in which the participant had established a co-victim identity). Such participants shared stories of attending meetings of multiple groups and joining the group that had the *"right focus."* Participants talked about getting a sense of which groups *"fit"* or *"worked"* for them, where they *"like what* [the members] *are doing."*

Several participants who had lost a daughter or son to homicide had attended meetings of local support groups for bereaved parents but had quickly come to realize that within such groups they were unable to find the depth of support they were seeking. They described feeling as if the other attendees could only understand a portion of their experience, as their loss was *"different."* Most parents who attended such meetings had lost children to illness. Co-victims explained that these parents were able to support them in their grief, hopelessness, and general sense of injustice. However, loss to homicide resulted in a host of other emotions that parents who had lost to natural causes *"could not possibly understand."* Therefore, in order to make sense of their loss and the resulting experiences, these co-victims sought others who had not only lost a child but lost a child to homicide. Such individuals were the only others who offered the opportunity for true understanding and fellowship, who could help these individuals construct and verify their co-victim identities.

Many interviewees shared experiences of attending multiple co-victimization groups and finding dissimilar attitudinal and behavioral expectations within various groups. They described how quickly it became apparent which groups did or did not fit with their own expectations of self. Such realizations led to concrete choices as to where to dedicate their time and energy and, in turn, with whom to spend their time. Since criminal victimization is often accompanied by feelings of disempowerment and loss of control, choosing to engage with groups within which one could anticipate the attitudes and behaviors of others offered the opportunity for co-victims to reestablish a sense of control over their environment.

Some participants who had found that local co-victim groups were not aligned with their personally held ideologies decided to establish new groups to connect with others who shared their viewpoints. One participant attended several meetings of two local groups, concluding that each was not a fit, and decided to create a new group. Through this group, she was able to connect with like-minded individuals and take part in activities that aligned with her viewpoints. Another participant, a transcender, spoke of attending a group which focused upon the past and the self. She explained how members of this group offered a great deal of detail when relaying their stories each month, often *"dwelling on the past."* She said in regard to the focus on self, *"It's just a way of getting to be in the middle of the circle for a moment or whatever, and it's a way of people really all of a sudden paying attention to you."* She shared how she preferred to be a part of a group with a focus upon new members and their current situations in order to help them heal and envision a brighter future. She felt that new members were *"in need of support of others who know what* [they're] *going through."* She said, *"*[They] *should be able to get that without having to hear all the details of what* [others] *went through."* She felt that offering such detail was *"counterproductive"* because first-time attendees were looking for other members to be *"on the other side,"* so that they would *"know that there's going to be some sense of a new normal and life goes on."* Rather than continue attending this group, this participant chose to dedicate her time to a more future-focused group, aligned with her own attitudes and behaviors. In the absence of such a group in her area, she founded an organization *"to work with families of homicide victims but also to work with families of people who had committed crime."* She said, *"*One of the things that I saw was that there was a lot of commonality. So there was families that were losing their children because they had committed homicide and there were families who were losing their children to murder."* She said she began to see *"where the needs were similar"* and she felt it was important to figure out *"how you roll out the welcome mat for all to be able to share and to be able to grow and to be able to really examine* [their ideas] *in a non-pressure way."* This example demonstrates the power of one's identity and its corresponding focus, emotions, attitudes, and behavioral expectations to affect what groups one chooses to become a part of. If a group that verifies the meanings one associates with their co-victim identity is not available, a new group may be created to satisfy that need. In this case, a co-victim with a transcender identity was keen to surround herself with others who shared her broader focus and belief that offenders and offenders' families were also in need of attention, compassion, and support.

Others moved outside of victim-centered networks to connect with like-minded others. For example, Alex, who developed very strong beliefs about the benefit of compassion and empathy, joined an international group dedicated to the promotion of peace. Examples such as these demonstrate the importance of group attitudes aligning with those of potential new members. Without such alignment, individuals may not be motivated to continue to associate with that group.

These stories serve as evidence that participants' co-victim identities developed independently from the group experience. Several participants attended multiple groups and then chose to continue taking an active role in one group, or one type of group. Others sought out groups that fit their needs or founded new groups when they were unable to find an established group that suited them well. Such evidence supports the claim that, though groups supported and verified co-victim identities, the groups did not precede the identities. As demonstrated next, in this sample such decisions about group participation were demonstrated in cases in which participants had, and had not, established co-victim identities.

Choosing a Group that "Fits" Prior to Establishing a Co-Victim Identity

When I met Glenda, she had been a co-victim for a relatively short amount of time: just over one year. At the time, she was actively seeking out a group that she felt would be supportive of her emotional journey. Glenda viewed herself as a compassionate, peaceful person, who was quite dedicated to her Buddhist practice. She had never known anyone who had lost to homicide, and therefore did not have a firmly established sense of what it meant to be a co-victim. Therefore, she aimed to connect to folks who would support her in maintaining her fundamental self-sentiments, despite her new role as a co-victim. Glenda told me that there were regular meetings of a local support network taking place within her neighborhood, but she said that she feared interactions within that group would *"lead [her] into a victim identity"* and cause her to focus more heavily on negative emotion than she was comfortable with. She believed that such negative emotions would not align with those emotions she felt were foundational to her general sense of self. She said that she did not want to *"keep repeating the story and focusing on the pain and dwelling there,"* which she believed she would be expected to do during meetings of that group. Glenda therefore chose to drive quite a distance to engage with LOLB, after she spoke to two regular members of the group. From those conversations, she said she got the sense that the membership would be able to understand how she felt (compassionate and empathetic) and that they may have had similar emotional experiences following their losses. Each month, this emotional commonality among members served as motivation for Glenda to endure the inconvenience of traveling the long distance between her home and the LOLB meetings. It is within this supportive community that Glenda was able to solidify her identity as a co-victim, as other members verified the emotions, attitudes, and behaviors

Glenda attached to her fundamental sense of self, confirming that these remained appropriate and expected after loss to homicide as she developed her co-victim identity.

Glenda is a prime example of a co-victim who chose which groups to engage with based on how the group expectations, emotion norms, and ideologies paralleled those she connected to her fundamental self-sentiments. Viewing herself as a generally positive, compassionate, forward-thinking individual, Glenda sought a group consisting of folks who had developed co-victim identities that reinforced such fundamental self-sentiments.

Choosing a Group that "Fits" After Establishing a Co-Victim Identity

Carol also had the experience of feeling drawn toward some groups and away from others. However, unlike Glenda, Carol had a well-established co-victim identity, which she spent years enacting in a variety of venues and while taking on multiple roles. She said that over time she had gotten *"burnt out"* from interactions with a few of the groups and activities she had been involved in, which did not align well with her co-victim identity. She said:

> I remember looking at people and thinking, "Nobody's changing, nobody's going anywhere. It's like we're staying in this rut. Nothing is going beyond, nothing is trying to do more, to open up more, to connect more." I like [the people]. But things weren't changing. And even when I come back, it's really not changed. There's new faces. Some of the old faces have died or gotten sick, but it's not changed a lot.

Carol continued to visit with the members of the group she speaks of here, but she came to focus her time and energy upon groups that were better aligned with her own attitudes and ways of seeing the world. As a transcender, she was uninterested in reflecting upon the past and she did not feel the need to be heard. Rather, she sought opportunities to bring about larger changes to the world, to use her experience to positively affect the lives of a wide array of others, including at-risk youth and currently imprisoned offenders. Such activities, therefore, became those to which she dedicated her time and attention. Having become a consistent, leading force in a group dedicated to organizing and engaging in such activities, her transcender identity was continually verified, as others expected from Carol the same attitudes, emotions, and behaviors she expected from herself. The identity standard Carol had developed around her co-victim identity was, therefore, consistently confirmed through the appraisals of those with whom she surrounded herself. That is to say, Carol's own self-meanings matched the meanings others attached to her co-victim identity.

Carol is an archetypal case of a co-victim who chose which groups to engage within based on how the relevant group expectations, emotion norms, and ideologies paralleled those she connected to her established co-victim identity. With countless connections to co-victims in her area, she made intentional decisions about where to devote her limited time and energy. Those groups with which she consistently engaged were those that most effectually verified her transcender identity.

Feelings of Group Rejection

Some participants spoke of experiencing a feeling of subtle rejection when their attitudes, behaviors, and/or emotions did not mirror those of group members. One co-victim, a survivor, said he felt that one particular group was *"not really a good place for anyone to voice a different opinion."* When asked about this group's reaction when she shared her story of forgiveness, another co-victim said, *"Not good, no. Everybody was not happy about that. I think it was kind of like I was a leper at that time, you know? 'Cause like* [they] *had hate in* [their] *hearts, and that's just the way it is."* She felt her story of for-giveness caused *"tension"* within the group. Though she enjoyed visiting with members of this group at annual events, she chose to spend her time throughout the year focused upon using her story to engender compas-sion and interrupting trajectories toward crime for at-risk youth. Another transcender shared a similar story about feeling that she could not openly share her experiences surrounding forgiveness with one particular group. When asked if forgiveness typically comes up at group events, she said that forgiveness was not discussed and that one could sense that group members were unforgiving. She said:

PARTICIPANT: *You just sense it, or something is said like, "I'm never gonna forgive him. And he can rot in hell."*

INTERVIEWER: *How does the group react when you share your story* [of forgiveness]?

P: *They don't like it! ... That's probably another reason why I've stopped going too, because I feel like the outsider.*

I: *Because you've forgiven?*

P: *Yeah, yeah. And for a long time I wouldn't even talk about it (laughing), because I thought I was gonna be thrown out or something.*

Here we can see that a mismatch between personal and group attitudes and emotion norms is consequential in that it leads to explicit choices about with whom co-victims will spend time engaging and therefore with which groups they will identify.

As I considered my interviewees' recollections of feeling subtle rejection when they expressed clashing viewpoints with members of these groups, my observation of one group meeting in particular stood out as especially informative, as it echoed the experiences described above. On this night, two new members were in attendance. At the start of the meeting, everyone began sharing their stories of loss with the group, by way of introduction. The first new member to share was Curtis. He spoke about his rage and hatred for the man who killed his youngest son. As he spoke, all eyes were fixed upon him and regular members nodded and offered short remarks in agreement. After his story reached its conclusion, a few regular members shared stories of having had similar experiences and emotions. Eventually, the group returned to the process of moving around the room with introductions and stories, and soon it was Martin's turn. Martin was also new to the group on this night, but his story elicited a much different reaction from regular members. Early in his story, he began to speak of his forgiveness process and how he had come to generate acceptance toward the man who had murdered his daughter. There were no agreeing nods from the membership and no one offered similar experiences. A few members began holding quiet side conversations as he spoke. Others fiddled in their purses or ruffled through papers. When his story was complete, the next person in line to share did so quickly and without acknowledgment of Martin's story. Martin did not speak throughout the remainder of the meeting, yet Curtis was regularly encouraged to engage.

At the end of the meeting, everyone stood and began saying their goodbyes. Gloria wrapped Curtis in a bear hug, which was followed by another hug from Sue. Bev then approached and said to Curtis, *"You have to get a hug from everyone!"* as she embraced him. Martin stood off to the side, looking on. Jeanne (who happened to be the only regular member present at this meeting with a transcender identity) approached Martin and embraced him as she wished him well. Others did not follow.

Elena then brought a blank form to Curtis, explaining to him that they were collecting information for folks who wished to dedicate a brick in the name of their loved ones, to become a part of a homicide victims' memorial being constructed along the edge of the local rose garden. Gloria also shared details with Curtis of an upcoming event which many of the members attended annually and where Bev would be a speaker. Bev asked Curtis several times if he had given them his contact information, eager to add him to the group's mailing list. As Bev turned back to check the sign-in sheet for the information, she took notice of Martin standing nearby and said, *"Oh, well, would you like to give us your address as well?"* Follow-up with each new member was also conflicting. At the next group board meeting, Curtis's name was raised several times with regard to the need to get information to him about upcoming events. Martin was not mentioned.

Undoubtedly unintended, the effects of the discrepancy between the interactions had by each new member on this night were likely consequential with regard to these two co-victims' future choices about attendance of such meetings. It was therefore no surprise when Curtis attended a future meeting of this group as well as a memorial event in town. Martin was not seen again.

Similar subtle rejection was felt by members who did not participate in activities directly related to the behavioral expectations of the group. One participant, who had attended meetings and events connected to several victim-centered networks, shared her experience of feeling disapproval from group members when she chose not to take part in behavior associated with strongly held group ideologies. This particular group regularly took part in organized efforts to prevent inmate parole releases, and this participant had chosen not to take part. She said, *"I got these looks. Like 'Who do you think you are? You're so much better than we are?' or something. But I couldn't sign those* [petitions] *without knowing what the circumstances* [of the cases] *were."* This is a clear example of group ideology leading to behavioral expectations for members. This individual did not share in the group ideology regarding parole release and therefore did not submit to the corresponding behavioral expectations. When she failed to take part, the group members' reactions served as a subtle reminder that her actions, and thereby her attitudes, were not aligned with the group's. In these examples, individuals' co-victim identities, and the meanings they associated with those identities, were not verified. These co-victims were then likely to seek such verification elsewhere, in groups of more like-minded others.

Commitment to Groups

When co-victims found harmony between personal and group attitudes and emotions, the result was quite powerful in that it led to strong ties between group members (a high level of "affective commitment"[6]) as well as a sense of allegiance to that group. Such similarity in attitude was comforting to participants. Tanya, a transcender, spoke of her *"way of life"* being supported by people *"in* [her] *circle."* She said she appreciated *"being a part of a group of people that thought the same way that* [she] *thought."* She continued:

> It's no different than just being in a study group where you all think the same or being a part of a women's group. We all think the same. It's just a different group of people who do the same things. So now I'm in a smaller circle. My circle got smaller and my vision got bigger … So the people that I am around now, we think the same, you know?

Tanya had previously been involved in a religion that she felt kept her *"stagnated."* She said, *"*[It] *kept me to where I couldn't ask questions and I could only see things one way."* She shared how helpful it was to her healing process to *"connect"* with others with whom she could share, and be accepted for, her perspectives. Here we see evidence of a co-victim abandoning a group to which she previously belonged and seeking out a new group that nurtured the attitudes she had come to develop as she healed from the loss of her son. As her ideas changed, so did those she chose to associate with. And as she settled into this new group, her levels of both interactional and affective commitment increased. Tanya spent a great deal of time engaging with various members of what she lovingly referred to as her *"circle"* (demonstrating high levels of interactional commitment) and developed a strong sense of attachment, loyalty, and positive affect toward those in the group (demonstrating high levels of affective commitment).

When participants, such as Tanya, connected to groups within which they developed high levels of commitment to their co-victim identities, these identities became increasingly salient. Their co-victim identities therefore became more likely to be invoked or activated in any situation.[7] With each instance of activation, there was another opportunity for the identity to be verified within interaction and therefore strengthened. This cyclical process presents a powerful demonstration of the foundation of Identity Theory.

In this section, I have presented evidence that social interactions taking place within groups relevant to the co-victim identity are not responsible for determining which co-victim identity will develop for each co-victim. Instead the co-victim identity (or fundamental self-sentiments, in cases in which a co-victim identity has not yet been established) influences with which groups co-victims will choose to regularly engage. Next, I will explore the prospect that one's social positions are consequential in developing a victim, survivor, or transcender identity.

Social Position: Are Certain Types of People More Likely to Develop each Co-Victim Identity?

Thus far, I have established that co-victim identities are supported and verified within relevant social networks, but these networks are not responsible for establishing which co-victims will come to adopt each of the three co-victim identities. This leads me to the final analysis of this book: an examination of variation in co-victim identities by social position. Here, I will explore educational level, age, gender, religion, social class, and race to determine if these social positions affect the likelihood of co-victims becoming victims, survivors, or transcenders. First, a warning of sorts is in order.

This research is qualitative in nature, which means it pursues depth, nuance, and complexity by utilizing in-depth analyses of a relatively small number of cases, as compared to generalizable, quantitative work which uses large samples in order to allow for generalization. Readers should therefore take care when utilizing the analyses, interpretations, and explanations presented here, so that the current findings are not assumed to be generalizable to all co-victims or all subgroups of co-victims. This is important to note before entering into an exploration of variation based on demographic categories, such as gender and race. Because the sample used here is too small for use of advanced quantitative statistical processes, the findings presented in the following sections should be used to raise questions and pique curiosity about future lines of investigation and possible explanations for variation rather than being viewed as tests of predetermined hypotheses. That said, the final sections of this chapter will draw attention to potential explanations for the variation uncovered between participants with a range of demographic characteristics and social histories.

Level of Education

As shown in Table 7.3, when co-victims were categorized by level of education, the variation between categories did not indicate concrete patterns. Though it seemed as if co-victims were less likely to be within a victim identity and more likely to be within a transcender identity as education level increased, the variation was not statistically significant (p-value = 0.297). This remained true when the category of "BA/BS or more" was separated into two categories, those holding a BA/BS degree and those with a graduate-level education, despite the fact that those co-victims holding a master's degrees or in the final stages of completing doctorate degrees (a total of five participants) displayed transcender identities (not shown in table).

Table 7.3 Co-Victim Identities by Level of Education (n = 36)

Co-victim identity	Level of education		
	High school diploma or equivalent	Some college, associates, or technical/trade	BA/BS or more
Victim identity	4 (50%)	3 (18%)	1 (9%)
Survivor identity	1 (13%)	4 (24%)	3 (27%)
Transcender identity	3 (38%)	10 (59%)	7 (64%)
Total	8 (101%)[1]	17 (100%)	11 (100%)

Chi-square test's p-value = 0.297.

1 Totals do not equal 100% due to rounding.

One may expect co-victims with higher levels of education to be substantially more likely to have developed survivor and transcender identities than those falling within the lowest category of education, given that one may expect those with higher levels of education to have wider worldviews and therefore be more likely to take on a more plural focus, as seen within the transcender identity. One may also expect participants with higher levels of education to be more likely to be future-focused (also telltale of the transcender identity) than those with lower levels of education, as those with a future focus may be more likely to establish advanced educational goals than those with a focus upon the past or present. However, the current sample cannot substantiate these claims. Further work is needed with larger samples to determine if any reliable patterns exist.

Age

As shown in Table 7.4,[8] the differences in co-victim identity classifications between participants of various ages were not statistically significant (p-value = 0.398). Despite the statistical insignificance of the variation seen in this sample, it is interesting to note that participants 60 years of age and older were evenly spread among the three identity classifications. One may expect older individuals to be more likely to develop transcender identities because, as compared to younger individuals, they may have a more expansive worldview and be more empathetic, having had more numerous life experiences. However, this was not the case in the current sample, as difference based on age was not statistically significant.

The findings surrounding co-victim identities and time (age and passage of time, discussed in an earlier section of this chapter) were surprising. One

Table 7.4 Co-Victim Identities by Age (n = 36)

Co-victim identity	Age		
	Under 40 years old	40–59 years old	60 years old or older
Victim identity	1	3	4
	(10%)	(21%)	(33%)
Survivor identity	2	2	4
	(20%)	(14%)	(33%)
Transcender identity	7	9	4
	(70%)	(64%)	(33%)
Total	10	14	12
	(100%)	(99%)[1]	(99%)

Chi-square test's p-value = 0.398.

1 Totals do not equal 100% due to rounding.

might expect that older individuals would have a higher likelihood of being within a transcender identity simply by consequence of the passage of time or based on an increase in education level. Analyses discussed earlier indicate that the passage of time and education level do not significantly affect the likelihood of shedding a victim identity or developing a survivor or transcender identity. Future research with larger samples may be warranted to determine if these variables influence the likelihood of a co-victim developing a victim, survivor, or transcender identity.

More work is also needed to explore potential generational differences in attitudes toward offenders and inter-racial harm. The majority of older participants in this sample were white and had lost their loved ones at the hands of a black offender. Racial biases and intolerance learned earlier in life may result in a higher likelihood of persistent feelings of anger, hatred, or vengefulness toward minorities in general, and offenders in particular, in cases of older co-victims. Larger sample sizes are needed in order to clearly tease out possible connections between co-victim identities, age/generation, and the race of the co-victim and the offender.

Gender

Co-victims' identities also did not vary remarkably by gender. As shown in Table 7.5, the differences between males and females were not statistically significant (p-value = 0.274). This means that males were no more likely, and no less likely, to demonstrate a victim, survivor, or transcender identity, as compared to females.

This lack of substantial difference between the genders is notable, as this suggests that the development of victim, survivor, or transcender co-victim

Table 7.5 Co-Victim Identities by Gender (n = 36)

Co-victim identity	Gender	
	Male	Female
Victim identity	4 (33%)	4 (17%)
Survivor identity	1 (8%)	7 (29%)
Transcender identity	7 (58%)	13 (54%)
Total	12 (99%)[1]	24 (100%)

Chi-square test's p-value = 0.274.

1 Totals do not equal 100% due to rounding.

identities is not related to one's gender. This is interesting given the differences in emotions associated with the three co-victim identities. For example, research has shown that women are generally more forgiving than men,[9] so one may expect women to be more likely to adopt transcender identities than men, given the transcenders' association with benevolent forgiveness. But, in the current sample, this is not the case. Similarly, one may expect men to be substantially more likely than women to maintain a victim identity due to gender norms associated with hostility or vengefulness. But, in this sample, men are statistically no more likely than women to do so.

One possible explanation for these findings relates to the gravity of loss to homicide. An identity constructed around such a life-altering event could take on a quality and intensity that are capable of overshadowing one's gender identity. The co-victim identity may take on the qualities of a sort of "master" status. Everett Hughes first developed the concept of a master status in 1945, noting that such an identity "tends to overpower, in most crucial situations, any other characteristics which might run counter to it."[10] The emotions resulting from the untimely, violent death of a child, for example, may challenge parents of both genders to establish a new set of meanings surrounding their roles as parents and to wrestle with a series of emotions more intense and consequential than any they have felt previously. Qualitative research that focuses more squarely upon the effects of loss to homicide upon one's previously held identities, such as parent identities, is needed to determine if this explanation is valid. Further research should also utilize generalizable samples to determine if the lack of variation by gender seen here is evidence of a reliable pattern or is a result of sampling biases.

Religion

When religion was broken down into denominational categories and distributed among co-victim identities, cell sizes were too small to make meaningful comparisons. However, a few noteworthy patterns emerged. First, all co-victims who self-identified as Muslim were transcenders (not shown in tables). On the other hand, those who self-identified as Christian were fairly evenly spread among all three identity categories.

The majority of religious interviewees were Christian, therefore, in Table 7.6, I compare Christian interviewees' identities to those who self-identified as spiritual but not religious or identified as religious but not Christian (these included interviewees who were Muslim, Jewish, Buddhist, and Santerían). The differences shown here between participants who self-identified as Christian and those who identified as spiritual but not religious or as religious but not Christian were not statistically significant (p-value = 0.113). Given the sample size, we cannot determine if these

Table 7.6 Co-Victim Identities by Religion (*n* = 28)

Co-victim identity	Religion	
	Christian	Spiritual/Religious Non-Christian
Victim identity	4	2
	(24%)	(18%)
Survivor identity	7	1
	(41%)	(9%)
Transcender identity	6	8
	(35%)	(73%)
Total	17	11
	(100%)	(100%)

Chi-square test's *p*-value = 0.113.

This table utilizes a subsample that consists of those participants who spoke of themselves as either spiritual or religious. The cell sizes of those who did not specify or those who consider themselves neither spiritual nor religious were too small to draw meaningful conclusions.

findings are indicative of a true lack of difference between individuals with various religious backgrounds or result from a lack of focus upon the salience of participants' religious identities. Future research investigating co-victim identities should not only inquire about interviewees' religious affiliations but also their strength of belief, level of participation in religious endeavors, and the size and closeness of their religious networks. This is especially true given the effects of one's "interactional" and "affective" commitment to an identity (the number and importance, respectively, of inter-personal relationships associated with that identity). Though religious categorization led to cell sizes that negated detailed investigation, findings here should act as a catalyst for future work considering the effects of religion upon construction of a co-victim identity.[11]

Social Class

Due to disagreement in the literature as to how many social classes exist in the United States and how each should be defined and delineated, for my purposes I created a simple dichotomy to explore social class. This allowed me to compare the experiences of two groups: (1) those co-victims who lived within areas labeled as *"the inner city"* and who described their environments as, for example, *"poor," "dangerous," "violent,"* or *"gang-infested,"* and (2) those co-victims who lived within areas labeled as *"suburbia"* or *"rural America"* and who described their environments as *"privileged," "very safe,"* and *"sheltered."* It is useful to think of this distinction as between areas of concentrated disadvantage and concentrated advantage.

Table 7.7 Co-Victim Identities by Social Class (*n* = 36)

Co-victim identity	Social class	
	Disadvantaged	Advantaged
Victim identity	1	7
	(8%)	(30%)
Survivor identity	0	8
	(0%)	(35%)
Transcender identity	12	8
	(92%)	(35%)
Total	13	23
	(100%)	(100%)

Chi-square test's *p*-value = 0.003.

A striking difference arose when comparing the identities of participants from these two social classes, and this difference was statistically significant (p-value = 0.003). As shown in Table 7.7, those co-victims who lived in areas of concentrated advantage were fairly evenly spread among the three identity categories. In contrast, all but one of the participants who lived within areas of concentrated disadvantage displayed transcender identities. Interestingly, this deviant case in regard to class was also deviant with regard to race; whereas all transcenders within impoverished areas in the inner city were people of color (ten black and two Latino/a), the one victim living in this area was white.

Those who have experienced the violence often found within areas of concentrated disadvantage may not expect to lose a loved one to homicide, but if such an event occurs it is within the realm of typical day-to-day existence, as most individuals in poverty-stricken areas in which homicide is a regular occurrence have friends, family members, or neighbors who have lost loved ones in this manner. Therefore, experiencing such a loss is relatively normative for individuals living in these areas.

For co-victims living in areas of concentrated advantage, the loss of a loved one to homicide is typically an exogenous shock that is separate and distinct from other aspects of one's life and identity. For those who have never lived within high-crime areas or known anyone who has endured such tragedy, coping with such a loss may be especially difficult. This may explain why participants within privileged areas had substantially more variability in their co-victim identities than those within disadvantaged areas. Again, in order to determine which explanations hold true, more research is needed that focuses on investigating the interplay between race and class (and religion).

Table 7.8 Co-Victim Identities by Race (*n* = 36)

Co-victim identity	Race		
	White	*Black*	*Latino/a*
Victim identity	7	0	1
	(33%)	(0%)	(20%)
Survivor identity	6	0	2
	(29%)	(0%)	(40%)
Transcender identity	8	10	2
	(38%)	(100%)	(40%)
Total	21	10	5
	(100%)	(100%)	(100%)

Chi-square test's *p*-value = 0.020.

Race

A few noteworthy findings emerged with regard to variation in co-victims' identities by racial category, shown in Table 7.8. Most striking was that co-victims who self-identified as black invariably displayed transcender identities, whereas more variation existed between those who self-identified as white or Latino/a (these differences were statistically significant; *p*-value = 0.020). White and Latino/a co-victims were very similar in their variation among categories, although cell sizes were very small for Latino/a co-victims.

The fact that white and Latino/a co-victims in this sample were similar in their variation among identities, yet all co-victims who self-identified as black held transcender identities, coupled with the fact that all Muslim participants and nearly all participants from areas of concentrated disadvantage were transcenders as well, leads to questions regarding the basis of this identity. Because all Muslim participants in this sample self-identified as black, and the majority of participants who resided in areas of concentrated disadvantage were also black, it cannot yet be determined if the transcender identity is generated through culture or structure. Are these co-victims more likely to develop a transcender identity because of previous experiences struggling with the realities of poverty or unequal opportunities, thereby supporting a structural explanation? Or is the culture of black Americans so distinct from that of Latino/a or white Americans that it leads to this high proportion of transcenders, supporting a cultural explanation? Or perhaps it is religion that affects the development of the co-victim identity. On the other hand, these findings could also be the result of sample biases based on recruitment methods, as snowball sampling may have led to an overwhelming number of like-minded black participants. In the concluding sections of this chapter and the next, I offer potential explanations for the patterns revealed here, to initiate the more extensive conversation that is necessary to fully understand the connection between, and causal direction among, identity, experience, and emotion.

Concluding Remarks

The experiences of the co-victims in this sample suggest that a co-victim's social interactions within groups directly relevant to the co-victim identity are not solely responsible for determining which co-victim identity will develop in the wake of that co-victim's loss. Rather, one's prior experience, based in large part on one's social positions, seems to have more influence. As discussed below, this may be due to the establishment and development of fundamental self-sentiments that become further realized through the process of constructing a co-victim identity.

Although there are limitations for generalization imposed by the sampling and recruitment methods employed here, the findings related to the association between identity development and social position are striking and therefore worthy of discussion and consideration in future research. Especially notable are the associations noted here between the three identities, social class, and race. In order to further tease out these issues and gain a better understanding of the origin of the three identities found to emerge after loss to homicide, further research is needed that aims to incorporate a wider variety of experiences. For example, in order to explore if variation is structurally based or culturally based, future work should purposively recruit black individuals from the middle, upper-middle, or upper class;[12] white participants who have experienced the social realities of poverty and concentrated disadvantage; and Muslim participants who are not black.

I expect that future findings of such research will indicate that it is the intersection of race and social class that brings about a strong likelihood of poor, black co-victims developing a transcender identity. Minority racial groups, black Americans in particular, have endured unique challenges and daily struggles due to unequal opportunities and differential treatment in a variety of social realms over the course of their lifetime and generationally. This includes a higher proportion of losses than white or Latino/a groups, whether due to natural deaths, exposure to violence, or loss to incarceration. The struggles these individuals and communities face are often magnified by their social class positions. The effects of such overlapping struggles are known to be cumulative and complex (Kimberlé Crenshaw refers to this concept as "intersectionality"[13]). Having survived such challenges, these individuals may be in a unique position to adopt a transcender identity because of the fundamental self-sentiments that developed through the transcendence they have undergone elsewhere in life. They may view struggle as motivation to rise up and grow stronger, loss as a catalyst for uniting as a community, and violence as an indicator of a larger problem requiring a refocusing toward maintaining strong community ties and a sense of interdependence. Such worldviews and self-sentiments may also be passed down generationally within these groups and may therefore constitute cultural meta-narratives. Conversely, individuals who have not overcome such difficulties, personally or generationally, namely those who are not racial minorities and/or have never experienced concentrated disadvantage, may be less likely to overcome tragedy in a transcendent manner. This explanation is at least tentatively supported by earlier findings from this project, in which I investigated the sources of people's ideas about forgiveness.[14] When asked where their ideas about forgiveness came from, participants invariably noted family or religion. This may be evidence that it is within close social groups that people are primed to respond to extreme trauma in culturally scripted ways.

This explanation may also help us to come full circle with the puzzle that served as the catalyst for this research: the varying emotional experiences of Bev and Barbara. Though Bev and Barbara had remarkably similar social positions, their prior social experiences were distinct in ways that may explain the difference between their emotional experiences following the losses of their daughters to homicide, despite their parallel social positions. Although I did not ask directly about trauma and suffering outside of loss to homicide, Barbara spontaneously included details in her interview regarding a variety of traumas she had suffered over the past several decades. These included Barbara caring for an unwell husband, who suffered from five heart attacks before he passed away, leaving her as a *"single mom"*; Barbara's youngest daughter had become addicted to drugs and alcohol, suffering with the addiction for 11 years, at times *"disappearing for months at a time"*; and Barbara had personally suffered from a host of illnesses, including cancer. Despite her relatively advantageous social positions, perhaps the suffering Barbara endured prior to her loss to homicide bred compassion. By definition, one cannot have compassion without first understanding suffering through experience. Therefore, those who have suffered most may be most likely to view the self as fundamentally compassionate despite the source of that suffering, whether it be structural, cultural, or personal. And this belief about the self may then be verified and realized through the development and maintenance of a transcender identity following traumatic loss.

The differing worldviews, that arise from divergent social experiences, may also establish differing empathy rules and empathy maps.[15] As Arlie Hochschild explains, empathy maps are a means of organizing the social world to determine who is most, and least, deserving of empathy. Such maps are built in interaction, as people assign empathy-worthiness to others both individually and collectively. The collective and interactional nature of the development of empathy maps may, in part, explain why the current sample indicates that individuals who have experienced hardships, individually and collectively, are more likely to develop transcender identities, with their characteristic elements of benevolent forgiveness and outward focus. Over time, individuals who have endured greater challenges, or who are immersed within the recurrent cultural patterns resulting from such challenge, may develop different empathy paths[16] than those who have experienced relatively less tribulation.

Lynn Smith-Lovin[17] has shown that individuals with more resources, a higher level of education, or who are higher up the status structure of a society have more identities available to them than those with fewer resources, less education, or who are lower in status. This could also explain why those in the lower social classes are more likely to adopt a positive, transcender identity than those within more privileged social classes. Tragedy such as loss of a loved one to homicide may result in a feeling of isolation and vulnerability, and holding on to the negative emotions associated with a victim identity may be especially unappealing to individuals who have endured great suffering in other realms of life or who occupy social positions that are lower on social hierarchies. For example, those who have endured poverty and racism may find a transcender's outlook especially appealing. Rather than adding another negative identity to their self-construct, co-victims who already have less socially desirable labels connected to their identities may be drawn to the opportunity to add a positive, pro-social identity to their repertoire, especially given the transcender identity's attributed sense of empowerment and associated hope for a better future for all. This may be why those in the lower social classes and in marginalized racial groups are more likely than white co-victims in privileged areas to adopt a transcender identity.

Similarly, those with less power tend to role-take more extensively and thus develop greater role-taking skills than those with more powerful social positions. Many studies have found that less powerful people, such as women and African Americans, have better role-taking abilities than more powerful people, such as those who are male and white.[18] This suggests that role-taking is a skill and one's effectiveness at taking on the roles of others is related to one's social position. This may explain the variation shown here, as those with less powerful positions in existing social hierarchies, such as racial minorities or those living in concentrated disadvantage, may be more adept at role-taking and therefore more likely to adopt an other-directed orientation and empathize with people more easily.

Although drawing firm conclusions based on this work would be premature, the insight gained here can help us to better understand the experiences of individuals who have lost loved ones to violence as well as those who have dealt with other forms of loss and trauma. It is my hope that this work, and the questions it raises, will serve as a catalyst for broader investigations that approach these powerful topics with varied perspectives and methodological strategies.

Questions for Further Discussion

1   Given the arguments outlined above, who would you anticipate would be more likely to develop a *transcender* identity after loss of a loved one to homicide—someone who suffers from a visible physical disability or someone who suffers from an invisible cognitive disability? Why?
2   Beyond what is discussed here, how might the development, expression, and maintenance of a *victim* identity affect one's social relationships and evaluations of self?
3   Do you believe the survivor identity is separate and distinct from the other two identities, or is it better conceptualized as a transitional stage between the victim and transcender identities?
4   How might conflicting meta-narratives influence the self-narratives co-victims construct in the wake of homicide?

Notes

1   Kathryn J. Lively and David R. Heise. 2004. "Sociological realms of emotional experience." *American Journal of Sociology* 109(5):1109–1136. https://doi.org/10.1086/381915
2   Several ranges were used to construct meaningful categories of the passage of time, including 5-, 10- and 15-year ranges. The emerging patterns were similar in each.
3   "Regularly" here is measured by attendance of at least one event annually.
4   This is not to say that all activities that could be labeled as anti-violence programs, restorative justice initiatives, at-risk youth programs, etc. are "future-focused." Classification of groups/events that participants described, but that I was not present for, was based on the participant's description of the group's mission, values, activities, etc.
5   In the Appendix, I present the cross-tabulation between the identity and group type variables in the opposite direction, to allow the reader to consider alternative causal theories. Though my data do not support the causal order indicating group membership affected identity type, the biased nature of my sample creates the need to remain open to alternative explanations and findings as this research area expands to include greater breadth and depth.
6   Stryker, Sheldon. 1980[2002]. *Symbolic Interactionism: A Social Structured Version.* Caldwell, NJ: Blackburn Press.

7 Stryker, Sheldon. 1980[2002]. *Symbolic Interactionism: A Social Structured Version.* Caldwell, NJ: Blackburn Press.

8 Utilization of 10- and 15-year ranges resulted in cell sizes that were too small for meaningful comparison.

9 Exline, Julie Juola, Roy F. Baumeister, Anne L. Zell, Amy J. Kraft, and Charlotte V. O. Witvliet. 2008. "Not so innocent: Does seeing one's own capability for wrongdoing predict forgiveness?" *Journal of Personality and Social Psychology* 94(3):495–515. https://doi.org/10.1037/0022-3514.94.3.495

10 Hughes, Everett. 1945. "Dilemmas and contradictions of status." *American Journal of Sociology* 50(5):353–359 (p. 357). https://doi.org/10.1086/219652

11 Zahorcova and colleagues recently found religious identification to influence the correlation between forgiveness and adjustment after loss of a child generally: Zahorcova, Lucia, Peter Halama, and Robert D. Enright. 2019. "Forgiveness as a factor of adjustment in bereaved parents." *Journal of Loss and Trauma* 25(2):188–203. https://doi.org/10.1080/15325024.2019.1664786

12 To date, nine additional interviews with black individuals from the middle or upper middle class have been added to this project. I therefore anticipate being better able to explain variation in coming publications.

13 Crenshaw, Kimberlé. 1989. "Demarginalizing the intersection of race and sex: A Black feminist critique of antidiscrimination doctrine, feminist theory and anti-racist politics." *The University of Chicago Legal Forum* 1(8):139–167.

14 Hourigan, Kristen Lee. 2016. "Homicide survivors' definitions of forgiveness: Intrapersonal, interpersonal, and extrapersonal orientations." *Violence and Victims* 31(5):869–887. https://doi.org/10.1891/0886-6708.VV-D-15-00015

15 Hochschild, Arlie R. 2013. "Empathy maps." pp. 32–44 in *So How's the Family? And Other Essays,* edited by Arlie R. Hochschild. Berkeley and Los Angeles, CA: University of California Press.

16 Ruiz-Junco, Natalia. 2017. "Advancing the sociology of empathy." *Symbolic Interaction* 40(3):414–435. https://doi.org/10.1002/symb.306

17 Smith-Lovin, Lynn. 2003. "Self, identity, and interaction in an ecology of identities." pp. 167–178 in *Advances in Identity Theory and Research,* edited by P. J. Burke, T. J. Owen, P. A. Thoits, and R. T. Serpe. New York, NY: Plenum.

18 Karp, David A., and William C. Yoels. 1986. *Sociology of Everyday Life.* Itasca, IL: F. E. Peacock.

Chapter 8

Conclusions and Future Directions

Sometimes we construct the language so much that we desensitize what's really occurring ... and sometimes we can put enough words together to make a certain amount of sense.—Diane

The findings of this work and its implications are many. In this final chapter, I will summarize the main conclusions, proposing avenues for future research to build upon the ideas presented here, and conclude with a few final thoughts, suggesting further questions raised by this work.

Summary of Main Conclusions and Avenues for Future Work

Forgiveness and Empathy

This work increases the scope of previous research into forgiveness and empathy and raises our level of awareness of possible differences between the processes involved in emotional transformation following different levels of inter-personal harm. It expands upon current understandings of forgiveness and the factors that both foster and impede forgiveness, including empathy, understanding, and perceived similarity. Though we knew previously that these factors were correlated to forgiveness, the analyses presented here substantiate the causal order of these variables as well as the mechanisms through which each promotes forgiveness. It would be worthwhile in future endeavors to include various measures of personality, religiosity/spirituality, and previous victimization to explore possible correlations between these factors and both forgiveness-related feeling rules and lived experience. The current findings may spark researchers to challenge the causal order often utilized by psychologists that assumes forgiveness leads to healing. Perhaps it is the healing that leads to forgiveness. Maybe traumatized individuals reach a point at which they are motivated to release intense feelings that they feel are holding them back from living a life they desire, and it is the way they see themselves (their specific identities or their fundamental self-sentiments) that propels them toward forgiveness.

Though both pathways to forgiveness discussed here involved role-taking and redefinition of the situation, the mechanisms through which individuals came to forgive were distinct. Those in close social proximity engaged in role-taking based on direct understanding of circumstance, resulting in redefinition of the situation that led to forgiveness. In the absence of direct understanding, those in distant social proximity engaged in role-taking at a higher level of abstraction to generate empathy, leading to forgiveness. This process was done through application of a victim status to the offender.

As mentioned previously, much of the prior research investigating forgiveness utilizes imagined or hypothetical scenarios or focuses upon relatively minor offenses or non-criminal acts. This is often the case for studies of empathy as well. Therefore, future work should continue to focus upon significant, real-life events to better explicate the two empathic pathways to forgiveness discussed here and determine if there are other pathways as yet unexplored. Victims of criminal violence experience much higher levels of emotional harm than victims of more minor offenses.[1] Therefore, investigation of the experiences of victims of serious, violent offenses, and the more intensely negative, highly active emotions associated with such harm, will lead us toward a more complete understanding of the empathic processes leading to forgiveness.

There is more to be learned about the cognitive and interactional processes involved in emotional change, and this research should serve as a springboard for such work. Those who study forgiveness and empathy may read these analyses and reapproach their conceptualizations and/or the scope and methodologies of their projects, utilizing qualitative methods, investigating cases of more severe harm, and considering new or more complex sociological processes in their theoretical backings. Comparative research should aim to uncover possible differences between forgiveness of extreme harm and lesser harm. Previous work has shown that expectations surrounding feeling rules may not be congruent with lived experiences of grief[2] and such discrepancies can become barriers to eliciting effective social support after the loss of a loved one.[3] Therefore, this work expands on prior knowledge by investigating emotions beyond grief, including hatred, anger, and vengefulness, as well as sympathy, compassion, and love. Future research should expand upon this with the aim of determining the generalizability of the current findings, utilizing larger samples that are representative of all co-victims of homicide. Longitudinal studies should also be constructed to more clearly explicate the development, transformation, and maintenance of emotion and its reciprocal effects upon identity. By continuing this line of investigation, we can increase the validity of future research and the scope of theory by developing a more accurate understanding of the forgiveness process, relevant feeling rules, and the interplay between the two. We can also bolster the sensitivity of those in support services and criminal justice realms and better equip them to assist those affected by various types of inter-personal harm.

Social interaction inevitably includes conflict, at times rising to the level of inter-personal harm and criminal offense. Given the role empathy played in creating a platform for forgiveness to take place after homicide in the cases studied here, future work should expand upon the current study to investigate the power of empathy to bridge difference. This work offers clear evidence that empathy has the potential to foster forgiveness, despite level and type of harm, by creating a framework for understanding. Given that empathic emotions can motivate pro-social behavior, it is reasonable to believe that empathy has the potential to spark social change by enabling the transformation of emotion through forgiveness. If we were to investigate emotion as an independent variable, we may uncover a variety of implications of the emotional transformation of forgiveness upon inter-personal relations, ranging from individual-scale disputes within marriages or workplaces to large-scale conflicts among nations or religious factions.

Identity and Affect Control

The theories drawn upon here, Identity Theory and Affect Control Theory, have been described as two stems emerging from the same root.[4] In 2019, Linda Francis and Richard Adams emphasized the usefulness of naturalistic research to enrich these theories and dive more deeply into understanding human behavior than is possible using strictly quantitative deduction.[5] It was my intention here to do just that, using these theories in concert to spark inductive insights. In doing so, avenues for future work emerged for both identity theorists and affect control theorists.

The current exploration highlights the benefit of considering both structural and cultural factors in concert, thereby drawing upon the strengths of Identity Theory and Affect Control Theory simultaneously to more fully understand complex interactional processes. It has the means to spur identity theorists to more directly consider the connection between culturally defined meanings related to emotion and the construction and loss of identity. Likewise, it may prompt affect control theorists to expand upon current models to more directly consider cultural distance between actors (which is often structurally based), more varied identity qualifiers, and more intense, nuanced emotions.

Future research should also continue in the current line of inquiry to investigate emotion as a multidimensional phenomenon. For example, theorists typically discuss emotions as falling along a continuum from negative to positive, with little consideration of which specific negative or positive emotions a person is feeling.[6] The focus typically falls upon the basic valence of the emotions felt in the situation (whether individuals feel good or feel bad; whether the emotion itself has an intrinsic character of being either attractive or aversive). It is my hope that this investigation will prompt affect control theorists to consider a fourth dimension of emotion within the EPA (Evaluation, Potency, Activity) model:[7] direction. By this I mean whether the emotion is inwardly or outwardly directed and, if outwardly directed, aimed at a specific other, or others, or generalized. Current models of Affect Control Theory may predict an emotion that falls at a certain place within the EPA space, but such space may have another dimension that has been ignored. I suggest that theorists expand upon the current model to encompass the direction of emotion (offender-directed, self-directed, other-directed, generalized). By considering if an emotion is directed outwardly, inwardly, or generally, we may improve the predictive value of affect control models.

Also, given the finding that cultural distance is consequential in the forgiveness process, future research should focus upon co-victims who lost at the hands of someone known. Having a previous relationship adds another opportunity for direct understanding and possible motivation for reparation through forgiveness. Such personal connection may therefore affect the paths through which individuals come to forgive.

Finally, identities assigned to individuals within any event are most impactful when considered in relation to other contextual identities. Recognition of similarity between self and other has important social consequences, including promoting opportunities for understanding. But perceptions of dissimilarity are also consequential in that the relevance of identities assigned to individuals may be heightened when juxtaposed to other, dissimilar identities, especially if the differences are multidimensional. That is to say, both the social positions themselves and the distance between positions are impactful. The importance of cultural distance may be especially significant in regard to the effects upon one's perceived ability to effectively role-take. More work is needed with such a focus.

The finding that social position influenced the likelihood of co-victims developing victim, survivor, or transcender identities should further prompt affect control theorists to consider the origin of one's pre-existing self-sentiments. From where do one's fundamental self-sentiments originate and do they change with experience? Such a line of inquiry could include both structural and cultural factors, and longitudinal studies could be particularly useful in illuminating the source of self-sentiments.

Victim, Survivor, and Transcender Identities

Through this research, I uncovered three distinct co-victim identities: victim, survivor, and transcender. Each is distinct in terms of its focus; corresponding language and emotion; attitudinal and behavioral expectations; and effects upon group membership as well as the associated purpose and roles played within such groups. My data showed that co-victims who assumed a victim identity were inwardly focused and spent a great deal of time concentrating on the past and their personal tragedies. They displayed negative, other-directed emotions, such as anger, hatred, and vengefulness and were, there-fore, unforgiving, as defined here. Victims engaged in activities that surround memorialization, story-telling, and seeking change in what they often viewed as a dissatisfying criminal justice system. They often joined groups to be supported and heard, such as self-help groups, as well as groups focused upon memorializing those lost to homicide.

Survivors, on the other hand, focused upon others who have been simi-larly harmed. Their focus was in the present and they reported emotions that were more neutral than those of victims. Survivors had released any negative, offender-directed emotions that they previously felt, but their forgiveness was non-benevolent, meaning they did not display posi-tive offender-directed emotions. They commonly engaged in activities surrounding supporting other victims of crime, co-victims of homicide in particular. Within groups, survivors saw their roles and purpose as pro-viding support to similar others. They often surrounded themselves with other co-victims and used their personal experiences to help others who were struggling with aspects of their losses that the survivors had already braved. For this reason, survivors often joined self-help groups with the goal of using their experiences to support others enduring similar struggles.

Like survivors, transcenders were also outwardly focused, but their focus was more generalized than survivors. Transcenders aimed to bring about larger change to what they viewed as grand social problems which lead to crime and tragedy such as homicide. They were forgiving of the offenders in their cases and this forgiveness was benevolent; they displayed emotions such as sympathy, respect, hope, compassion, and love for offenders, both those who took the lives of their loved ones and offenders more gener-ally. They often joined groups with a restorative approach toward criminal justice and dedicated their time and energy to programs that aim to divert at-risk youth from criminal paths or raise the awareness of offenders within prisons. Transcenders saw their roles and purpose as serving as a catalyst for larger change.

The three co-victim identities uncovered here could be considered person, role or social identities. That is, there are aspects of the co-victim identities' structures that arguably relate to their victimization stories through unique characteristics (person identity); roles played and associated expectations (role identity); and group memberships (social identity). The overlap between these structures is mutually reinforcing. For example, transcenders viewed themselves as peaceful, compassionate, and committed to social change, seeking to understand the offender's perspective (person identity); they therefore took part in groups consisting of like-minded others, such as restorative justice initiatives, victim impact panels, and reentry programs (social identity); and within these groups they adopted roles that verified these characteristics such as advocate or mentor (role identity). In this example, it is clear that the person, role, and social identity of the transcender are interconnected and each reinforces the other. That is, how transcenders viewed themselves led them to adopt roles that upheld the characteristics of their identities and joined groups that reinforced their ideas, attitudes, and emotions. This held true for survivors and victims as well. In this way, the co-victim identities were continually verified in relevant social contexts.

It is reasonable to believe that other inter-personal harm may result in effects to identity that parallel those uncovered here. That is to say, the victim, survivor, and transcender identities may also emerge after lesser crimes and more normative trauma circumstances. This may include trauma that is not inter-personal, such as loss of ability due to illness or injury and loss of possessions due to nature's wrath. They may also emerge after other forms of violent loss of a loved one, such as loss to suicide and accident. More work is needed to determine if these identities are unique to co-victims, or perhaps unique to individuals acclimatizing to what I call a "traumatic identity," such as those dealing with the aftermath of extreme trauma, or if they are likely to emerge in other circumstances.

I would speculate that there are likely a host of other "traumatic identities" that individuals find themselves struggling to accept and construct meaning around. By "traumatic identity" I mean an identity that is suddenly assigned to a person, against his or her will, and that is deeply distressing. Examples of other "traumatic identities" would include amputees and those who are falsely convicted. It is a relatively rare occurrence when an individual assumes an entirely new identity for which he or she had no desire, no intention of adopting. Typically, we move into and out of identities in a normative manner. For example, we expect to take on the role of student early in life, to modify this role as we transition through stages, and to shed this role when our final graduation ceremony concludes. We anticipate moving into identities related to roles we may play in life as we form relationships, including spouse, parent, and grandparent. We anticipate joining groups of various sorts as we move through life stages. We go to great lengths to construct identities around our careers, hobbies, and talents. But what happens when a new, unwanted identity is forced upon us by an event or interaction outside of our control? Co-victims' experiences offer us insight into one such "traumatic identity," but more work is needed to see if co-victims' experiences are similar to others who have had other such identities forced upon them. This is especially true in light of the finding that one's general self-sentiments, potentially stemming from previous experiences of struggle, trauma, or disadvantage, may be influential in the development of transcender identities. We know that one's general self-sentiments have powerful effects and that they can act as a catalyst for emotional transformation, as was shown here with regard to forgiveness after extreme trauma. More research is needed to understand the full depth and breadth of effects of one's self-sentiments as well as the narratives that one constructs to make sense of experience.

Given the findings of the analyses presented here, it is important that we also develop future research that utilizes larger samples as well as quantitative processes in order to determine the generalizability and scope of the patterns uncovered here. For example, in this sample, the majority of co-victims were transcenders and the minority were victims. This should not be construed as evidence that co-victims at large are more likely to display transcenders identities than victim identities. The recruitment methods applied here led to a disproportionate number of people who had considered forgiveness or felt as if they had forgiven. Therefore, it is not surprising that the majority of interviewees were transcenders. Future research with generalizable samples would have the potential to better determine the likelihood of co-victims developing a victim, survivor, or transcender identity.

Criminal victimization, and loss to homicide in particular, can leave individuals with a sense of uncertainty about, and vulnerability within, the social world.[8] By understanding the identity processes that shape co-victims' post-loss identities, we can better serve and support them and others who have endured great loss or victimization. As we move forward with research and service focused upon inter-personal transgressions of all types, we should do so with the knowledge of the various identities available to individuals after trauma. Undoubtedly, such identities are not restricted to those who have lost to homicide. With future work building upon the knowledge gained here, we can support and understand innumerable individuals as they seek to reestablish a sense of predictability in their social worlds after crime or tragic loss.

Final Thoughts

Losing a loved one is an inevitable aspect of life, but the circumstances of that loss can have a significant impact upon the way a person experiences that event and its aftermath. Making sense of one's experience of loss is particularly difficult if the loss is the result of violence. Therefore, co-victims of homicide have more difficulty creating meaning from their experiences than individuals who have lost loved ones to natural causes or accidents.[9] This leads co-victims to have a higher chance of suffering from complicated grief[10] (bereavement marked by persistent and elevated separation distress, severe impairment of functioning, etc.) than those who have lost loved ones in more normative ways.[11] We know that meaning-making is an essential component of the healing process following trauma.[12] Therefore, it is crucial that we continue this line of investigation to bolster our understanding of the sense-making processes discussed here.

Though the process of forgiveness within the population under investigation here may be unique in several meaningful ways, this study is relevant far beyond forgiveness after loss due to homicide. The analyses discussed in this book could be used to inform other investigations into the experiences of those affected in a variety of ways by violent loss, inter-personal harm, and criminal victimization. Forgiveness is an ideal within many religions and, some believe, a cornerstone of restorative justice practices. It is applicable to situations ranging from minor transgressions between individuals to major life-altering experiences or conflicts between groups. Therefore, the current findings should drive sociologists to study these concepts systematically with the aim of constructing robust, verifiable theories of both forgiveness and empathy. We can then test hypotheses regarding the effect of individuals' beliefs and experiences upon their emotional reactions and transformations.

Although my main aim with this research was to *answer* questions about when, how, and why co-victims of homicide forgive, it is my hope that these analyses have piqued even more questions than they have answered. Forgiveness is a complex, multidimensional phenomenon and cannot be easily explained or disentangled from the social contexts in which it occurs. Although the feeling rules surrounding loss to homicide have not been firmly established, forgiveness and empathy in general are a part of our moral code. As Peiro Ferrucci[13] points out, "Empathy is a prerequisite for communication, collaboration and social cohesion." Therefore, establishing a deeper understanding of the processes involved in the generation of empathy, and the consequences of those processes, may increase our ability to break down systems of inequality; minimize the likelihood and effects of conflict; and construct more tightly bonded societies in future generations. In order to reach such levels of understanding, we must create opportunities for deep conversation and remain open to considering perspectives other than our own. The purpose of this book is to create a catalyst for such open conversation. As Diane eloquently stated in the opening quote for this chapter, *"Sometimes we construct the language so much that we desensitize what's really occurring ... and sometimes we can put enough words together to make a certain amount of sense."* It is my hope that readers feel this book is an instance of the latter case and that it will be used to initiate dialogue across difference.

Notes

1   Strang, Heather. 2002. *Repair or Revenge: Victims and Restorative Justice.* Oxford: Oxford University Press.

2   Thoits, Peggy. 1990. "Emotional deviance: Research agendas." pp. 180–203 in *Research Agendas in the Sociology of Emotions*, edited by T. D. Kemper. Albany, NY: SUNY Press.

3   Goodrum, Sarah. 2008. "When the management of grief becomes everyday life: The aftermath of murder." *Symbolic Interaction* 31(4):422–442. https://doi.org/10.1525/si.2008.31.4.422; Riches, Gordon and Pam Dawson. 1998. "Spoiled memories: Problems of grief resolution in families bereaved through murder." *Mortality* 3(2):143–159. https://doi.org/10.1080/713685897

4   Francis, Linda E. and Richard E. Adams. 2019. "Two faces of self and emotion in symbolic interactionism: From process to structure and culture—and back." *Symbolic Interaction* 42(2):250–277. https://doi.org/10.1002/symb.383

5   Francis, Linda E. and Richard E. Adams. 2019. "Two faces of self and emotion in symbolic interactionism: From process to structure and culture—and back." *Symbolic Interaction* 42(2):250–277. https://doi.org/10.1002/symb.383

6   Turner, Jonathan H. and Jan E. Stets. 2005. *The Sociology of Emotions.* New York, NY: Cambridge University Press.

7   Osgood, Charles E., William H. May, and Murray S. Miron. 1975. *Cross-Cultural Universals of Affective Meaning.* Urbana, IL: University of Illinois Press.

8   Strang, Heather. 2002. *Repair or Revenge: Victims and Restorative Justice.* Oxford: Oxford University Press; Zehr, Howard. 2001. *Transcending: Reflections of Crime Victims.* Intercourse, PA: Good Books.

9   Currier, Joseph M., Jason M. Hollan, Rachel A. Coleman, and Robert A. Neimeyer. 2007. "Bereavement following violent death: An assault on life and meaning." pp. 177–202 in *Death, Value And Meaning Series. Perspectives on Violence and Violent Death*, edited by R. G. Stevenson and G. R. Cox. Amityville, NY: Baywood Publishing.

10 Lichtenhal, Wendy G., Dean G. Cruess, and Holly G. Prigerson. 2004. "A case for establishing complicated grief as a distinct mental disorder in *DSM-V.*" *Clinical Psychology Review* 24:637–662. https://doi.org/10.1016/j.cpr.2004.07.002.

11 Currier, Joseph M., Jason M. Holland, and Robert A. Neimeyer. 2006. "Sense-making, grief, and the experience of violent loss: Toward a mediational model." *Death Studies* 30:403–428. https://doi.org/10.1080/07481180600614351

12 Janoff-Bulman, Ronnie, and Cynthia McPherson Frantz. 1997. "The impact on meaning: From meaningless world to meaningful life." pp. 91–106 in *The Transformation of Meaning in Psychological Therapies,* edited by M. Power and C. R. Brewin. New York, NY: Wiley.

13 Ferrucci, Peiro. 2007. *The Power of Kindness: The Unexpected Benefits of Leading a Compassionate Life.* New York, NY: TarcherPerigee.

Postscript
Detailed Methodology

I have presented various aspects of this work at sociological and criminological conferences; discussed it at length with trusted colleagues and students; and attempted (with varying degrees of success) to get portions of the analyses published in academic journals. Time and again, I have been asked to share details of the specific strategies I employed, including those related to designing and developing the project; getting Institutional Review Board approval; recruiting participants and building rapport; collecting rich, nuanced data; and maintaining a healthy emotional space while doing so. When at the proposal stage of this book, it was suggested to me that I include a detailed postscript in order to provide details to these sorts of inquiries. Therefore, in this final section, I will detail the methodological strategies used in this study. I hope that such transparency will spark discussion about the best ways to approach topics of this sort. As a sociological social psychologist and a qualitative researcher, my inclination is to begin by positioning myself within my research process. Therefore, I will start with a statement of positionality, followed by a detailed description of the various methodological strategies employed here. I will conclude with a discussion of the limitations and strengths associated with such strategies.

Positionality

A great deal of reflexivity is necessary when undertaking research of this type. How participants related to me and what they chose to disclose about their feelings, perceptions, ideas, and experiences was undoubtedly influenced by how they saw me within each interaction, how they defined the roles I adopted, and how they felt they related, or did not relate, to me personally and/or professionally. For these reasons, I remained mindful and reflective as I engaged in observations and interactions with participants so that I could eliminate as many potential barriers as possible and establish research relationships that were trusting and forthright.

Inception

The inception of this project dates back to an experience I had while studying victim-related public policy in 2012 (which is described in some detail at the start of Chapter 7). I became interested in exploring the topic of forgiveness after loss to homicide after meeting two women with similar stories of loss but very different feelings about forgiveness, Barbara and Bev. Each had lost a daughter to homicide over 20 years prior to our initial interaction. These women were very close in age and were both white, currently unwed, lived in the same town, and considered themselves devout Roman Catholics. However, Barbara had forgiven the man who took her daughter's life and spent much of her time sharing her story of forgiveness with imprisoned offenders in order to help them to see the perspective of the parties they had injured. Bev was unforgiving and dedicated much of her time to leading a self-help group that took steps to block parole release for violent offenders like the man who killed her daughter.

In time, I came to learn that each of these women had attended the same two self-help groups in the past, Homicide Bereavement Circle (HBC) and Loved Ones Left Behind (LOLB), but each had a strong preference as to which group was a better "fit." Barbara was strongly inclined to attend LOLB whereas Bev was much more comfortable in HBC. The differences between the focus and emotions of these two individuals intrigued me, especially in light of their similar demographic characteristics and parallel experiences of loss. I began to wonder about their experiences and the causes of each of their feelings regarding (un)forgiveness. I decided to approach the leaders of each of the two self-help groups to ask for permission to attend a meeting as a guest.

Gaining entrée into these two co-victim self-help groups came easily after my initial introductions to the group leaders. By displaying their trust in me and their sponsorship of my work, other group members accepted me without reservation. Since that time, I have become very close to the leaders of each of these two groups and each has gone to great lengths to support my research. These connections led to opportunities to conduct participant observation of group meetings and other relevant events as well as to interview many current and past members of both groups. By developing a circle of strong community members who served as champions for my research, my social network of co-victims expanded exponentially.

Through my volunteer work on a commission focused on justice during my undergraduate studies, I also became well acquainted with several individuals who fostered my entrée into social circles of individuals who had lost loved ones to homicide beyond self-help groups. Through these networks, I was introduced to several individuals in the area's inner cities. In time, they also gave me their support and trusted my motivations and intentions.

These connections proved invaluable, especially in cases in which I was attempting to connect with individuals I had never met, who were not a part of any formalized support network, or who were from largely different demographic categories than those into which I fell. These connections allowed me to connect with several homebound elderly individuals and individuals who were previously incarcerated. Bonds formed through these networks allowed me to call upon individuals tightly connected to communities of color as well as communities in urban and impoverished areas into which I otherwise may have not been able to effectively gain entrée. For example, HBC is a chapter of a national organization supporting those who have lost loved ones to homicide, and this group consists of predominantly middle- to upper-middle-class white women. When I began searching for a self-help group with a more diverse membership, the established relationship I had with the membership of HBC fostered my entrée into another, more diverse group in another area of the state: Fellowship after Violent Loss (FVL). FVL is another chapter of the same national organization and, though the members of this third group had never interacted directly with the members of HBC, my involvement in the meetings of HBC allowed me to speak from a place of experience. Simply mentioning my attendance of monthly meetings of HBC gave me a sort of credibility and perceived trustworthiness among the members of FVL. Though they had never met, the co-victims in FVL felt a bond to those in HBC. I was therefore seen as a sort of "friend of a friend." Each of the groups I eventually became connected to may have been difficult to reach without having these strong ties to mutually trusted individuals who believed in the importance of my work.

Reflections

Throughout the data collection and analysis processes related to this study, I focused attention upon my own experiences before, during, and after interviews and observations. I spent a great deal of time reflecting upon my interactions with participants and group members. What follows are my reflections on the manner in which I related to participants.

I have never lost a loved one to homicide, and at times this fact emerged within interviews or when I was introduced to individuals at local events. Some participants assumed that I had experienced such a loss because of my research interests. When I answered their questions about this issue, there was often a moment of surprise, but I did not get the sense that this was bothersome to the participants; it just raised curiosity and eased our conversation into the welcomed topic of my research motivations. Often, this conversational topic allowed me to mention shared acquaintances and the positive experiences I had had in the past with these individuals. Responses from the participants were often very positive, including disclosure of their positive sentiments about that shared contact. This was often a welcomed divergence from our discussion of the participants' experiences, as it allowed for increased trust and a sense of having shared social networks.

Many of the individuals I interviewed were parents of victims of murder. As a mother, I was able to relate to these individuals on a very meaningful level. At events and before or during interviews, individuals often asked if I had children, and this question typically led into a positive exchange in which it seemed our bond was strengthened. Participants noted that they felt as if I could understand their losses, feelings, or struggles better than some because of my status as a parent. They felt that I understood the bond between a parent and child, and they believed that I could better imagine the loss of such a bond than someone who does not share the experience of the strength of the parental relationship.

Of 36 interviewees, only seven were younger than I was at the time of the interviews (five of those seven were male). In fact, I was substantially younger than most of the people I interviewed (16 participants were more than 20 years older than me). I successfully navigated this barrier by being very open about my academic position as an advanced doctoral student and my interest in learning from the experiences and wisdom of others. This quest for knowledge seemed to sit well with participants who perceived my youth as an asset expanding the knowledge base surrounding these issues, issues they felt were especially important, given their losses. Often, participants became nostalgic for the time when they were eager to learn and explore, or they spoke of their pride and support of my academic and career paths as if they were my mentors, offering me what knowledge they had accumulated over the years so that I could advance my own understanding and pass on my learning to a new audience through my work. In this way, my status as a student aided this exploration greatly.

Though I do have African heritage, I am invariably perceived by others as white. I was raised in a predominantly white, middle-class neighborhood where my family owned a home. I was not raised with any religious affiliation and attended public schools in the suburbs of Connecticut where the students were predominantly white and middle-class. During the time of this study, I was married with two school-aged children, living in an upper-middle-class area, and attending a state university where I had earned a Master's degree and was actively completing the final stages of my Ph.D. Though the educational level of my sample ranged from completing a GED while in prison to graduate-level degrees, most participants had substantially lower levels of education than I held (no participants in the current sample had higher levels of education than me, and only five interviewees had a Master's degree or were pursuing a Ph.D.).

Throughout data collection, I was cognizant of the risk of perceptions surrounding racial, religious, and socioeconomic differences becoming a barrier to engaging individuals within other demographic categories in meaningful and open conversations. I was concerned about inadvertently offending others or being perceived as having unscrupulous motivations. Mindful of these challenges, I entered into discussions with trusted individuals who self-identified as members of the categories into which I do not fall in order to learn how to best navigate these relationships. These individuals served as a conduit between myself and others with whom building trust may have become problematic, fostering connections between myself and participants outside my demographic categories. Several interviewees acted as ambassadors for my research and spoke of their support with potential interviewees, setting up telephone conversations or meetings on my behalf.

Though several of the individuals I interviewed or observed had upbringings and current living arrangements similar to my own, others had vastly different childhood experiences and currently lived in markedly different social environments. Participants did not ask about my social history, but the differences between my experiences and theirs offered a catalyst for my inquiry, especially when interviewees spoke of their religion, incarceration, gang involvement, or experiences of poverty or violence, none of which I had ever experienced. My lack of personal experience of such circumstances allowed for an ease of inquiry, as I was eager to learn of each participant's experiences and unlikely to assume my own history mirrored theirs. In this way, I believe the differences between my own social history and those of many of my participants was an asset to this research. It allowed me to engage with a naïve perspective on many topics directly or peripherally relevant to this study.

Personal Impact

There is no doubt that taking part in this research project impacted me personally and emotionally. Hearing so many stories of loss, trauma, and violence was often emotionally draining. Upon entering this project, I anticipated a negative impact upon my own emotional state, and I expected the process to necessitate self-care in order to remain motivated, focused, open, and as unbiased as possible. I did not, however, anticipate the positive emotions that would result.

In this section, I hope to offer a level of transparency with regard to the impact this project had upon me, both as it unfolded and in the long term, in order to offer readers a candid view of the qualitative research process. In order to do so, I begin by sharing an earlier version of the story that opens this book. When revising this manuscript, I received feedback pointing out that, at times, my writing within chapter introductions focused too directly upon my own emotional experience of the data-gathering process. I was told that this could distract from the focus of the book. Anticipating that this book may be used by some to better understand the process of qualitative research on sensitive topics, I did not want to simply delete from the manuscript all such references to my own emotional reactions. I therefore preserved one section of such writing for this postscript. Below, I offer the reader the unedited version of that opening story from Chapter 1, peppered with self-reflection and discussion of my own emotional reaction to the research experience. I hope that by doing so, budding sociologists who may be hesitant to engage in a project of this sort will be comforted by the level of transparency and the ultimate positive outcomes of what were, at times, very uncomfortable experiences.

Original Opening Story

As-salāmu ʿalaykum.

Wa ʿalaykumu s-salām.

Standing on the uneven sidewalk, sprinkled with broken glass, it is nearing 11 o'clock at night. Behind me is an abandoned lot, remnants of deteriorated concrete foundation visible through the overgrowth, littered with empty Keystone beer cans, wind-tattered plastic bags from the corner store, and crushed fast-food containers. Surrounded by strangers, I catch sideways glances as they take note of my pale skin and crisp-seamed slacks. These are people whose paths would likely never have crossed mine if it were not for Tanya inviting me to this site, the corner where her son Malik was gunned down by a rival gang-member eight years prior. The adjacent building, with boarded front door and broken window panes, had become the backdrop for the evening, with the occasional smell of marijuana wafting out of open windows, and the sounds of sirens as police rushed along the bordering street and loud bass shaking the ground as cars slowed in front of the ripped tent that served as a cover for two long folding tables, passengers peering out open windows to discern the meaning of the gathering.

This night, the anniversary of his death, also happens to be Malik's birthday, and Mother's Day. Tanya greets each arrival, with a long, purposeful hug, *"As-salāmu ʿalaykum."* *"Wa ʿalaykumu s-sal ān"* comes in response. My feeling of discomfort intensifies. It is not because of the area's reputation for violence, as I do not feel unsafe. It is not because of the nature of the event, as I have sat in mindful silence with countless others as they sob through the retelling of their stories of loss, showing me pictures of murdered children, trusting me to bare witness to their raw anguish. It is not because I was coming into contact with so many people with backgrounds so different from mine, as I had grown accustomed to building rapport and sparking friendships with people with all sorts of social histories. My ever-growing discomfort stems from my acute awareness of my lack of knowledge about the expectations of this social environment. I do not want to offend. I do not want to intrude. I do not want to cause any discomfort among my fellow gatherers. I knew that this would be an emotional night for which I had no frame of reference. I knew that Tanya would not be able to remain by my side. I knew that I would be viewed as an outsider, suspicious, and untrusted. I did not know that I would not be able to speak the language. It soon becomes evident that this exchange is a part of the Islamic tradition, a customary greeting and also an expression of solidarity in this context. As an outsider to the Islamic faith, I am not greeted in this manner and am therefore not expected to understand or respond in Arabic. This eases my discomfort only minimally.

Each new arrival adheres to the unwritten expectations of the event. They show respect and condolence for Tanya, then move through the ever-growing crowd, hugging and talking with some, fist-bumping others, greeting a few from a more formal distance. I receive a few cursory greetings, to which I reply with a smile, nod, and appropriate pleasantry. What does one say when meeting a new person at an event like this: a "birthday" for a murdered teen? I am certain my awkwardness is obvious. I remind myself that Tanya wants me to be there, that she finds some comfort in my presence and in her belief that I will find a way to generate something positive out of her loss. I am not intruding. I am not a voyeur. I am a student, a researcher, passionate about many of the things that mattered most to these gathering neighbors. I am here to learn and to bridge difference.

Soon, Tanya's other children begin to arrive. As they make their rounds, Tanya introduces each to me, saying, *"This is my friend Kristen."* Suddenly, I feel like an impostor. I only met Tanya recently, when she took part in an interview for my research. Did Tanya wish to keep the nature of our relationship private? If so, how was I to respond to the undoubtedly imminent questions of "How do you know Tanya?" Before I can fashion a response for that, as yet unasked, question, Tanya's youngest daughter, Aniyah, arrives. Aniyah had been home when I had been at Tanya's house the week prior, conducting Tanya's interview. Aniyah therefore has at least a cursory understanding of how I fit into her mother's life. I had also driven Aniyah to and from dance class earlier that day, as I helped Tanya prepare for the night's event, so I know that Aniyah regards me as someone her mother feels she can trust. As I think through the most prudent manner in which to answer that impending question, Tanya walks purposefully toward me, followed closely behind by a familiar face. Tanya introduces me to Sandra, who Tanya does not realize I recently met at another community event, and who Tanya intended to connect me to for the purposes of pursuing an interview for this research. Relief ensues, as this introduction assures me that Tanya is not intending to be secretive or intentionally vague about our relationship. And now I have another ally at the event, someone who is not expected to greet every newcomer, someone who is interested in my research as well as my educational path, as Sandra is currently pursuing a graduate degree as well. Viewed by the local community as a powerful, compassionate, committed community advocate, Sandra's immediate acceptance of me eases any tensions that may have surrounded my presence at this event. She also introduces me to J. R., who would become an advocate for my research in the coming weeks, helping me to diversify my sample by setting up several interviews with local men.

With Sandra's sponsorship, I am soon welcomed into the fold, most notably by the elder women in the space, as they insist upon my acceptance of large plates of food, homemade rice and beans, chicken wings, pasta salad, all the trappings of a backyard barbecue. In time, other young girls join Aniyah, laughing and singing as they begin "stepping" along the sidewalk. With the sound of the girls' rhythmic dance, as they stomp their feet and slap their thighs in unison, and the smell of the meat sizzling on the grill, the backyard-barbecue feel of the event intensifies, and the size of the gathering swells, as people spill off the sidewalk, up the steps and between the cars. Deion, who I had previously met and interviewed for this research, hangs a sign across the nearby stoop with the slogan of the anti-violence program he is a part of, which sponsors this event every year by providing food and paper-goods. On two separate occasions throughout the night, Deion waves over a wandering soul, drawn near by the smell of the burgers on the grill. He says to each, *"End violence, brother,"* and offers the passerby a plate of food. Later, Tanya approaches an elderly woman in threadbare garments and an overflowing pushcart, who was watching the event from a bit of a distance. Tanya asks her if she is hungry, to which the lady replies that she is. She says she had gone to the local church in search of food but the church was closed. Tanya reaches for a plate and piles it high with a large portion of every type of food lining the long folding tables. The stranger humbly takes the plate, nodding to show her gratitude, and edges toward the curbside, where she quickly consumes the offering, then shuffles off in the direction from which she emerged.

One would not have known this is a memorial for a teen, if not for the instant shift of emotional energy when the cake emerges and Tanya and her children gather in remembrance. Each child touches Tanya, putting their arms around her, gently squeezing her arm. The center of the cake is adorned with a picture of Malik, taken just weeks before his death, and Tanya says a short prayer in Arabic, attendees responding quietly in cadence. Tears well in Tanya's eyes, and she is encircled by all attendees, who now stand facing Tanya and her children, silent, somber, reflecting on the life lost, the pain persisting. After a few moments of silence, an elder woman in the group begins cutting the cake, careful not to disturb Malik's image, at the insistence of Malik's eldest sister. Others pass out slices, and everyone eats in silence. Tanya has again become the focus of all those present, as they quietly make their exits, taking plates of food and pausing by Tanya's side to acknowledge her pain, offer their condolences, and hold her momentarily while she cries.

I had offered to drive Tanya to this event, a small act of support that she had graciously accepted. Therefore, I am Tanya's ride home. After most people have dispersed, she and I pack the remaining items into my trunk and head back to her apartment. Tanya takes advantage of this time alone, expressing her feelings openly and venting about tensions that arose at the event between her youngest son and her fiance. She asks me if I saw her son "*puff up*" when her fiance had touched her arm. I had. She explains that she was worried that "*we were gonna have a real problem*" if her son called his older brother. Since she had shared details of the rift between these parties during her interview, which had lasted several hours, she feels that I am the only person she can discuss the issue with, as it is not an issue she shares with others. Therefore, as soon as the car door closes, she relaxes, and her emotions are unleashed, as she talks quickly and loudly about her thoughts and feelings as we drive ...

It is my hope that this original version of the opening story provides a deeper level of insight in terms of the interconnectedness of the researcher, the research participants, and the research context. As qualitative researchers, it is paramount that we remain mindful of our own reactions and experiences as we engage in the research process. We cannot remove ourselves, or our influence, from the research context, and we can only minimize our impact if we remain self-reflective.

Coping with the Emotional Intensity of Stories

Although ultimately rewarding and uplifting, experiences such as the one described above took an emotional toll as I immersed myself in countless stories of loss. I often shed tears driving home from particularly intense interviews or events, and I relied heavily upon my own emotional coping mechanisms in order to not allow the trauma participants shared to negatively affect my ability to function as a positive and upbeat student, teacher, mother, and wife. I had regular lunches with one participant who came to be one of my closest friends and biggest supporters. As someone who had assumed the role of a support person for those dealing with trauma, she was adept at asking the right questions, providing the space to reflect, and creating a sense of non-judgment and true acceptance. It is this type of social connection that proved vital to my own capacity to effectively cope with the emotional intensity of the stories within this work, coupled with the profound sense of caring and compassion I developed for my participants.

Vicarious Growth

Despite the raw, intense emotions I encountered and observed regularly throughout this project, the ultimate emotional consequence can best be described as upliftment. I was uplifted by the experiences of sitting in the presence of such resilient, strong, loving individuals who had endured such suffering yet always seemed to include in their stories the ways in which they were helping others, advocating for victims' rights, using their stories to educate, or creating altars, scrapbooks, charities, and events to memorialize the lives of those lost and remember the positive impact their loved ones had upon others. In the sense that I bore witness to the post-traumatic growth of many of my interviewees, I too benefitted from a sort of vicarious growth.[1] Being fully present as participants shared such poignant and raw stories of loss was undoubtedly heart-wrenching. But by subsequently spending countless hours emotionally engaged with these same individuals, in moments of calm, enjoyment, and even celebration, their growth and ability to persevere inspired within me a deeper appreciation for my own life, as well as my own potential for resilience. I have always been a grateful person, but this work increased my gratitude exponentially, driving me to appreciate every experience, and every life, more deeply and mindfully.

Overall, taking on the responsibility of these stories was not a burden, it was a gift. I felt honored to be entrusted with such powerful and personal tales and I continue to feel charged with using the experiences shared to bring about some positive result, whether it be through dissemination of my findings, advocacy for the rights of those who have experienced violence, or continued engagement with this population.

Connection to Participants

The strong connection I often came to feel toward participants made the emotional aspect of this research even more difficult, as these were no longer stories of strangers but of friends. I did not expect friendships to form so quickly and easily; in fact I did not expect friendships to arise at all. I (naïvely) expected to remain somewhat distant in the role of researcher, probing and analyzing in the most careful and respectful manner possible. Much to my surprise, more often than not, interviewees hugged me at the conclusion of our time together and asked that we remain in contact. They spoke of their gratitude for my attention and compassion. This often left me feeling both humbled and slightly awkward, as I felt that participants were doing me a service, not vice versa. Individuals expressed similar sentiments of gratitude as I became a regular participant in events and monthly self-help group meetings. Participants appeared genuinely happy to see me, often hugging me and inquiring about my family and work, and at times interviewees and group members would reach out to see if I was planning to attend specific events in hopes that we could reconnect or attend the event together. As time passed, I was invited to family gatherings, holiday celebrations, and personal memorials. Barbara, whose experiences became the inspiration for this book, even pulled me aside after a self-help group meeting to inquire as to whether or not I planned to attend a particular victim-focused holiday event, saying that she was going to attend if, and only if, I would be there. This was a moment I will never forget, as it stood out as a testament to the strength of the relationships formed and the positive impact my presence seemed to have upon many participants.

At times, and most notably while writing this book, this level of closeness I felt toward my participants made writing difficult, as I felt the responsibility of accurately and compassionately portraying and analyzing their words and experiences. At each stage of the writing process, I would ask myself how I believed the participants would react if they were reading over my shoulder. Would this be an accurate representation of their experiences? Would they agree with my analyses and conclusions? Would they feel I was being fair and true to their stories? These nagging questions helped me to construct the most valid and data-driven work as possible, as I remained aware of the potential reactions that awaited each piece. I aimed to develop the most relevant and accurate analyses possible while upholding the highest level of respect and compassion for all those involved in this research. In this way, I honor the stories shared, the lives lost, and the loved ones left behind.

Research Questions

As an inductive project, I was initially unsure where this exploration would lead. As my data collection process progressed, it became clear to me that the most valuable insights gathered from the emerging patterns surrounded two main topics: emotion (specifically the emotional transformation associated with forgiveness, or lack thereof) and identity. Therefore, for the final analysis, the guiding research questions became:

- *How do individuals who have lost loved ones to homicide understand and experience forgiveness, and how does this vary by cultural distance from the offender and social position (race, social class, age, religion, and gender)?*
- *How do forgiveness processes relate to identity?*

Conceptualizing and Designating Terms

In Chapters 1 and 4, I detail the main conceptualizations used in this book. Here, I will share the process by which I arrived at these conceptualizations as well as the process through which I designated new terms for such things as "benevolent forgiveness" and "speculative empathy."

Forgiveness (Benevolent versus Non-Benevolent) and Unforgiveness

Sensitive to the need to approach the topic of forgiveness from a somewhat naïve perspective, one of the questions I asked each interview participant early on in their interviews was, "Forgiveness means different things to different people; can you tell me what forgiveness means to you?" By including such a question early in the interview process, I was able to explore each individual's unique ideas about what is meant by this term. I did not anticipate how difficult the task of defining forgiveness would be for my participants.

When I asked interviewees this question, many struggled with the task of offering a coherent definition of forgiveness. They often stopped themselves mid-sentence to begin anew, at times becoming so flustered by their inability to define what they viewed as a common and known concept that they laughed uncomfortably or abandoned their attempts, saying things like, *"I give up! I guess I can't define forgiveness!"* Several interviewees had previously viewed a list of the main questions that would be asked during their interviews and had therefore been considering their definitions of forgiveness prior to our conversation. Even in these cases, participants often struggled with putting their ideas into words.

When asked in a more indirect manner, most interviewees were able to share their views on the concept. For example, some participants were able to define forgiveness by first describing what a lack of forgiveness, or unforgiveness, would *"look like."* Others came to clearly express their definitions by describing forgiveness that they had witnessed previously in others. However, in total, seven participants were unable, or unwilling, to offer a definition of the concept of forgiveness.

Three distinct definitions of forgiveness arose through analysis of interviews. I call these "extra-personal," "inter-personal," and "intra-personal" definitions of, or orientations toward, forgiveness. As described in detail in the first paper originating from this work,[2] the distinction between these three orientations lies within the focal point of the forgiver. Those who view forgiveness as extra-personal believe that forgiveness is in the hands of a higher power, and people, therefore, do not have the right, or power, to forgive one another. This type of forgiveness takes place after death. On the other hand, when individuals define forgiveness in an inter-personal manner, they explain that forgiveness is an interaction between the harmed party and the one who caused the harm. For them, forgiveness takes place in a moment in time, as it is a social interaction between two individuals. Finally, for those categorized as intra-personal, forgiveness takes place within oneself. It is a transformation of emotion in which the forgiver releases negative, other-directed emotion. It is therefore a dynamic construct and takes place entirely within the forgiving party.

Given the variation in participants' definitions, it became clear to me that it was necessary to choose a single, demarcated definition to utilize in my analyses. I returned to the literature and found that the conceptualizations used in research were just as varied as (if not more varied than) those voiced by my participants. This led me to reflect upon the patterns that were emerging in my data with regard to forgiveness after homicide. Given the ranging definitions I had now encountered in previous research and in my own discussions with participants, this was not an easy task. After a great deal of journaling, diagramming, and lengthy conversations with trusted others, I first realized that forgiveness itself is not an emotion. Rather, it is an emotional process. In order to decide the conceptualizations I would use for this book, I started by conceptualizing unforgiveness (as that process seemed to work well for my interviewees who struggled to define forgive-ness). Through this process, I determined that unforgiveness in this context was the continuation of strong, negative emotions felt toward the person who caused the harm, such as anger, hatred, or vengefulness. I therefore conceptualized unforgiveness as:

- *Unforgiveness: the persistence of negative, other-directed emotions that resulted from harm caused by prior actions of the other.*

I knew that unforgiveness would indicate the opposite of forgiveness, so I first conceptualized forgiveness as: *the release of negative, other-directed emotions that resulted from harm caused by prior actions of the other.* However, based on my experiences with co-victims and their reactions to the idea of forgiveness, I knew this would not suffice. For many, there was a significant difference between simply letting go of negative, other-directed emotion and not only letting go of these emotions but also replacing them with positive, other-directed emotions. That is to say, there is a meaningful dis-tinction that must be drawn between releasing one's anger or vengefulness and wishing the offender well. Therefore, the conceptualization of forgive-ness would need to be a bit more complex. Eventually, I constructed the following conceptualization:

- *Forgiveness: the release of negative, other-directed emotions that resulted from harm caused by prior actions of the other which may or may not be replaced by positive, other-directed emotion.*

This conceptualization allowed for further explication of the two distinct types of forgiveness discussed in this book, benevolent forgiveness and non-benevolent forgiveness:

- *Benevolent forgiveness: the release of negative, other-directed emotions that resulted from harm caused by prior actions of the other which are replaced by positive, other-directed emotion.*
- *Non-benevolent forgiveness: the release of negative, other-directed emotions that resulted from harm caused by prior actions of the other which are not replaced by positive, other-directed emotion.*

The establishment of the terms "benevolent" and "non-benevolent" was not taken lightly. I considered several alternatives, eventually balancing conno-tation with denotation by returning to the Latin roots of each word under consideration in order to decide which was best suited for this purpose. I wanted to choose terms that indicated the distinction in the inclusion or exclusion of the accompanying positive emotions without creating terms that would be perceived as value-laden. My initial musings surrounding use of the term "beneficent," eventually came to the conclusion that this term had connotations that were too value-laden. "Benevolent" has the same Latin roots as "beneficent," but its connotations are more directly connected to intention rather than action. That is to say, one is beneficent if his or her actions are good and produce positive outcomes for someone else, but one is benevolent if his or her intentions or motivations are good, despite his or her actions, or lack thereof. Therefore, forgiveness can be benevo-lent when it includes positive emotions and well-wishes for the other party. Benevolent forgiveness does not, however, necessitate acting upon these positive emotions.

I later considered dropping the term "benevolent forgiveness" in lieu of "compassionate forgiveness." Taken at its root, the word compassionate liter-ally means "to suffer together" and indicates a pairing of intense identifica-tion, an awareness of one's suffering, and a sincere motivation to help relieve that suffering. Given that this motivation to action is not a necessary compo-nent in order to enter a state of what I refer to as "benevolent forgiveness," I settled upon the more accurate term, making a note to include mention here of the possibility for compassionate forgiveness within, or beyond, this third category of forgiveness. That is to say, it may be meaningful to dif-ferentiate between benevolent forgiveness that does and does not include motivation to action. Alternatively, it may be useful to add a fourth category to the continuum of forgiveness, namely compassionate forgiveness. Such inclusion would lead to the following spectrum:

> *unforgiveness–non-benevolent forgiveness–benevolent forgiveness–compassionate forgiveness*

Incorporating this addition would allow us to recognize forgiveness that includes the (re)establishment of positive, other-directed emotion as well as that which includes a motivation to action, specifically to take steps to help relieve the other's suffering.

It is worth mentioning again here that it was my intention to remain as value-free as possible with regard to discussion of forgiveness in this book. In no way do I intend to evaluate forgiveness, or benevolent forgiveness, as superior or preferred to unforgiveness, or non-benevolent forgiveness. For example, the connection between benevolent forgiveness and positive emotion should not imply that this is a "better" type of forgiveness or that it is more virtuous, healthy, or advantageous than unforgiveness. Rather than implying value judgments, I hope to leave the reader in quiet wonder as to his or her own ideas about what is appropriate or best for the harmed party and for society at large.

Experiential versus Speculative Empathy

From the outset of my exploration of the connection between forgiveness and empathy, there seemed to be more nuance to the concept of empathy than previous researchers had outlined. Over a two-year period, I combed through countless journal articles on the topic, finding the majority within psychological literature but also locating some work in journals focused upon social work, criminal justice, law, management, and medicine. Various researchers and practitioners put forth definitions and distinctions that felt simplistic and/or underdeveloped. This could be due to the fact that I was approaching the topic from a sociological perspective and therefore was searching for a more holistic vantage point from which to investigate empathy as a social process related in some meaningful way to interaction and/or social position.

In 2015, I began constructing a journal publication on the main analyses presented in this book and, over the course of over three years, I received feedback, suggestions, and critique from countless reviewers as my work wriggled and transformed through over ten revisions. Despite the inherently disheartening nature of this process we voluntarily succumb to as academics, the feedback not only strengthened my writing but also bolstered my confidence in the value of the findings presented here. Never did reviewers disagree with the crux of my analyses; rather they pushed me to shorten my journal manuscript while simultaneously adding further explanation, detail, and theoretical connection. Given that the processes involved in shortening and lengthening a paper are mutually exclusive, I eventually determined that these analyses were bound for a manuscript of the current form, in which I would be free to add plenty of explanation, detail, and theoretical connection alongside longer and more situated quotes from participants whose stories deserved to be told without brevity and concern for strict (and frustratingly ambiguous) word counts.

Throughout this process, I was also encouraged by reviewers to seek out further work on empathy, specific studies that each had become aware of and felt were relevant to my analyses. Some of these works became citations in the current manuscript, but most added no further value, given that their perspectives upon empathy were lacking in that social element I was seeking or were very similar to those of other authors whose works I had already explored. The myriad perspectives that I absorbed while constructing (and reconstructing) my writing on the topic helped me to delineate what I was, and was not, seeing in my own analyses.

Eventually, I determined that the most effective and valid conceptualization of empathy for this manuscript would be constructed by setting aside the pre-formed definitions others had utilized before me and beginning with my data, a strategy commonly used by grounded theorists.[3] Through this process, I revisited my data countless times. I stared for long spells at the lists I had constructed of participants whose narratives fell within each of the categories I had established. I thought for what probably amounts to hundreds of hours about the differences between their cases, often rising late at night to write down my thoughts (so that I could return to sleep unpestered by my nagging brain), pulling my car over to seize the ideas formed during highway hypnosis (when notes on napkins and receipts became unreasonable, I positioned a notebook and pen alongside my passenger seat), or stopping unceremoniously along busy city sidewalks, dog leash in one hand, cell phone in the other, pecking out lengthy texts to myself to capture my ideas while my four-legged companion explored the scents of the area for a clue as to the meaning of our sudden halt.

After forming the skeleton of a definition of empathy based on what I was seeing within my data, I returned to what I felt were the most useful conceptualizations put forth by others in search of a definition that was clear and aligned with my analyses. Such a definition did not exist, so I synthesized the definition arising from my data with the language and specificity of definitions produced by researchers who preceded me. The resultant conceptualization became:

- *Empathy: the ability to recognize, or cognitively construct, the emotional experience of another, understand that emotional experience, and subsequently experience parallel or reactive emotions.*

After establishing this definition, I once again returned to my lists of stories demonstrating the various processes I had uncovered. This step assured me that the conceptualization I had landed on aligned well with my analyses. However, this step also made it clear to me that the processes through which participants were arriving at a state of empathy were distinct. Given this distinction, and the aims of this book, I decided to delineate these processes by labeling the two types of empathy.

The first term I chose came much more easily than the second. The term "experiential empathy" was well suited for the first pathway I discuss, and my data consistently confirmed the appropriateness of the term. As a dedicated teacher, my pedagogical training has led me to a firmly established definition of the term "experiential," indicating a grounding in first-hand experience. Given that the first empathic pathway I demonstrate in my work is based upon such direct, personal experience, the term "experiential empathy" was quickly established and never wavered, even as I considered alternatives and explored the various ways the term "experiential" is, and has been, used.

Arriving at the term "speculative empathy" was more of a challenge. After considering a variety of relevant terms, including "conjectural," "abstract," "conceptive," "conceptual," and "cognitive," I arrived at "speculative" and decided it was the most accurate term to use for the second empathic process. Both its denotation and connotation point toward the concept I am presenting. From the Latin *specere*, meaning "to look at," the process of speculation indicates intellectual contemplation, pondering, or consideration and does not necessitate a foundation of fact or experience. It implies a sort of curiosity or indeterminate wonderment. After returning to my data, I decided this term was well suited for what I was seeing in my participants' stories.

Methods

Gaining Entrée

The process of gaining entrée for this research spanned several years' time, although the rapport-building that took place early on was not in anticipation of the creation of such a project. When the project was born, I leaned on networks and communities that I had become a part of through volunteer work I completed during my undergraduate career and relationships I had formed as I planned activities, applications, and guest speakers for a class I developed in criminal victimology. Through these avenues, some of which are discussed in more detail in the "Inception" section of this chapter, I had become acquainted with several individuals in the two counties in which recruitment took place. This included co-victims, individuals who worked in organizations supporting co-victims, and restorative justice mediators and supporters. When the project was born, several of these individuals expressed interest in taking part in interviews or connecting me to others who had lost loved ones to homicide who they believed may be interested in being interviewed.

Interviews

The interviews that constitute the sample for this book include 36 in-depth, face-to-face interviews conducted between May 2013 and February 2015. Interviews took place in local restaurants or in respondents' homes or offices. At the conclusion of each interview, participants received $20 as compensation for their time.

The average interview lasted 1.5 hours. Two particularly long interviews lasted over four hours each, and the shortest interview concluded in only 16 minutes. In this case, the interviewee was a man who had returned to the community from prison less than two months prior to his interview. Having been incarcerated for 16 years, which constituted nearly half of his life, it was no surprise that this gentleman was hesitant to fully trust me and my intentions. His answers were typically concise and undetailed, and probe questions sparked very little elaboration.

All but one interview were audio-recorded, with participant permission, and then transcribed. Transcriptions included words and other relevant features of the conversation, such as laughing, crying, and very long pauses. I not only listened to what was said, but how it was said and how participants situated their stories within a longer life story. Many qualitative researchers[4] believe that negating such features of conversation removes subtle variations in speech patterns and participants' use of language which can become valuable aspects of the data, as such nuance can illuminate rich emotion, clarify intent, and add important layers of meaning to the words being stated.

My interview instrument was semi-structured, allowing respondents greater control to construct answers in ways they found meaningful as they shared their very personal and emotional accounts (a method used successfully by Mishler in 1986[5]). I utilized an interview guide with a broad opening question asking the participant to share his or her story with me, followed by supplementary probe questions used to elicit further clarification and elaboration as well as to gain insight into specific areas of interest.

I avoided a structured interview style, as the strict question–answer format can fragment the participant's responses into a form that is meaningful to the researcher but may be less so to the respondent.[6] By allowing interviewees to speak freely when relaying their stories, their answers remained within the context participants felt were most relevant and meaningful to their unique stories. As Catherine Riessman noted, "Precisely because they are essential meaning-making structures, narratives must be preserved, not fractured, by investigators, who must respect respondents' ways of constructing meaning."[7] This method of data collection minimizes researcher influence. Because researchers are not predetermining which questions are most important to ask or in which order topics will be raised, participants are allowed to begin by narrating their experiences as they see fit. In this way, responses are less influenced by the researcher's choices in regard to the order or structure of the interview as well as to the language used. These methods, used in narrative analysis, build on the insights of symbolic interactionism,[8] labeling theory,[9] neutralization research,[10] and discourse analysis[11] and have been used successfully to explore divorce,[12] chronic illness,[13] and violence.[14]

Self-narratives allow for identity expression and each has "an evaluative point to make about the self."[15] It is through the telling of one's story (to both self and others) that the self is created in that the speaker makes meaningful decisions about the way to construct the narrative in order to convey a certain identity or impression of oneself to the listener, selectively omitting or adding emphasis, for example. Therefore, storytelling can be viewed as a sort of performance.[16] Through narration of the story the speaker is essentially attempting to convince the listener of their description or interpretation of an event at which the listener was not present. "Narrativization tells not only about past actions but how individuals understand those actions," that is, how experience is structured and given meaning.[17] This selective reconstruction is especially relevant when individuals are recounting particularly complex, troubling, or traumatic life transitions or events,[18] as in the aftermath of losing a loved one to homicide. When trauma disrupts the routine, taken-for-granted structure and coherence of one's life, narrativization offers the opportunity "to 'reconfigure' a sense of order, meaningfulness and coherent identity."[19] Therefore, rather than looking to the narrative to understand the truth of what happened in an objective sense, we analyze narrative to uncover the meaning-making processes within the construction and delivery of one's story as well as its connections to the speaker's identity.

The connection between narrative and identity construction makes this form of analysis the ideal means to explore how forgiveness, or lack of forgiveness, affects the identities of those who have lost loved ones to homicide.

How individuals recount their histories … their stance as protagonists or victims, the relationship the story establishes between teller and audience—all shape what individuals can claim of their own lives. Personal stories are not merely a way of telling someone (or oneself) about one's life; they are the means by which identities may be fashioned.[20]

Narrativization is particularly likely when experiences have caused "a breach between ideal and real, self and society,"[21] both of particular relevance within this area of study. As Zehr eloquently noted, "[v]ictimization represents a profound crisis of identity and meaning, an attack on oneself as an autonomous but related individual in an orderly world … so we must recover a redeeming narrative which reconstructs a sense of meaning and identity."[22]

In order to consider multiple versions of participants' stories, several interviews were supplemented by various forms of communication following the interview itself. These included one formal and seven informal follow-up conversations regarding pertinent issues, often taking place while sharing a meal or transportation to a victim-centered event. Participants also regularly shared other forms of information with me, including offering further ideas and feelings via email and showing me scrapbooks, poetry, victim impact statements, videos, offender communications (both written to, and received from, the offender), newspaper clippings, and a self-published book related to the homicide and its aftermath. For many interviewees who shared such items, these were a part of their stories and held deep meaning, often being shared with others who had lost to homicide or with at-risk juveniles or offenders of similar crimes to those in which their loved ones' lives were taken.

Interview Questions

Below, I include the full interview script used for this project. It should be noted that, after the initial question, the order in which I posed questions changed from interview to interview. This tactic had two goals. First and foremost, it created a comfortable exchange. The interviews felt more like a conversation between friends than a formalized interview process. Secondarily, altering the order of the questions allowed me to elicit the most detailed and rich data possible. It allowed me to follow the direction of the narrative, thereby focusing upon topics the participant felt were most meaningful. After participants had detailed their stories, I probed into topics they raised within their narratives to elicit more nuance and depth from their initial thoughts before moving on to topics that had not organically risen from the narrative. This was followed by questions about demographic information.

These goals were accomplished while remaining mindful of context effects; the need to build trust throughout the interview process and ease the conversation into more sensitive topics; and the desire to end our time together in a positive and pleasant exchange. Therefore, though the order of questions would change, depending on the direction of the conversation, I ensured that questions such as, *"Do you feel as if you have forgiven* [the offender]*?"* were raised later in the conversation, after the participant had answered questions such as, *"Can you tell me what forgiveness means to you?"* and *"Is there anything that you feel is absolutely necessary in order for you to forgive?"* In doing so, I attempted to gather the participants' ideas and perspectives upon the concept and process of forgiveness prior to asking about specific cases of forgiveness or unforgiveness, so as to minimize the level of bias within participants' responses. Asking such questions early on also provided an opportunity to establish trust and build rapport with participants as well as ensure that we were using common meanings in our conversation surrounding what can be a very controversial topic in circles of co-victims.

Interview Script

- I'd like to start by asking you to tell me your story.
- Have you told your story often?
  - If yes: To whom?
- Do you think you are different now than you were before you lost (loved one)?
- Do you think that this event/loss has affected who you became over time or the path that you chose in life?
  - If yes: How so?
- Do you feel like this loss has become a part of who you are?
  - If yes: How so?
- Do you know anything about (the offender)?
- Do you feel as if the way you think about (the offender) has changed over time or has your thinking remained the same?
- Forgiveness means different things to different people; can you tell me what forgiveness means to you?
- Are there certain things that would make you more or less likely to forgive a person?
  - If yes: What sort of things would make you more likely to forgive? Less likely?
- Is there anything that you feel is absolutely necessary in order for you to forgive?
- Do you feel as if there is anything that is unforgivable?
  - If yes: What sorts of things do you consider unforgivable?

- Do you think that you've always seen forgiveness and unforgiveness the same way you do now?
- Where do you think your ideas about forgiveness come from?
- Has your experience losing (loved one) changed the way you think and feel about forgiveness and unforgiveness?
- Have you ever spoken with (the offender)?
  - If yes: What was that conversation like? What did s/he say/do? What was your reaction?
  - If no: Do you have any desire to?
    - If yes: What would you say?
- What do you think your reaction would be if you saw (the offender) (again)? How would you feel? What would you be thinking? What would you say/do?
- How do you feel about (the offender) now?
- Do you feel as if you have forgiven (the offender)?
- Who do you turn to when you need emotional support or someone to talk to? How do they help you? Do you think you are different now than before you turned to these individuals (or groups) for support or are you the same? Has forgiveness or unforgiveness come up when talking with these people (or groups)? Do you turn to the same people or to different people when you need support for other things?
- Before you lost (loved one), had you ever known anyone who'd lost a loved one to homicide?
  - If yes: Did they talk to you about their experience? Who did they turn to for support? Did they ever talk about forgiveness or unforgiveness?
- Have you ever attended any sort of victim groups or events?
  - If yes: How did you get connected to the group? When did you begin? What prompted you to go? How frequently did you attend? Do you feel as if it is beneficial to attend?
    - If yes: Why? Do you still attend?
    - If yes: Do you expect to continue attending in the future?
    - If no: Why did you stop attending? Do you think you'll ever go back? Why (not)?
- How do you see things as you move forward?

Recruitment Location

Recruitment for interviewees took place within two counties in the northeastern United States. According to the Uniform Crime/Incident-Based Reporting System, these counties rank high in index crimes overall, and violent crimes in particular, for counties in this area. Often these counties rank higher in violent crime than the majority of counties in large cities in the area, which are known for their high rates of violent crime. This offered meaningful recruitment locations, as individuals living within these areas are more likely than those living elsewhere to have lost a loved one to murder and to have meaningful social networks of significant others who have suffered similar losses. Recruiting in these two counties allowed for investigation of these issues within an area in which homicide is not so rare an occurrence as to limit the research potential. Research often focuses on large cities, especially when studying crime and its effects, but it is reasonable to believe that those who live in less highly populated areas may have experiences that are qualitatively different from those residing in very large cities.

Sampling

In order to establish a diverse sample of interviewees for this work, I utilized a combination of snowball and purposive sampling methods. Individuals were initially recruited from local co-victim self-help groups and victim support networks involved in the events I observed.

Six of my participants approached me to become interviewees when I spoke of my work in informal conversations during local events related to loss or crime. These conversations were usually fostered by the leader of LOLB, who consistently introduced me to members of the co-victim community, speaking to the value she saw in my work as well as my personal character. She routinely introduced me to others by saying, "*This wonderful lady is a student who is doing amazing work.*" By doing so, she piqued the interest of the individual while communicating her trust and confidence in me. Given her reputation within the community as a compassionate, inclusive, and thoughtful leader and mentor, her support of me and my work spoke volumes in terms of building within potential participants a sense of trust and comfort with regard to my motivations.

Three main contacts led to the majority of connections to participants through snowball sampling. The leaders of two of the co-victim self-help groups I observed (HBC and LOLB) each connected me to all of the active members of these groups. Almost all currently active members of these groups chose to participate in interviews. These interviews constituted the first ten interviews I conducted, and it quickly became clear to me that I needed to take steps to diversify my sample. Since certain types of individuals may be more or less likely to take part in victim self-help groups, I also felt it was necessary to ensure the sample included non-members in order to avoid a systematic exclusion of individuals who may have a different set of experiences from those who are drawn to, and remain within, co-victim self-help groups. I also sought to connect to individuals who were of generations, racial/ethnic groups, and religions different from those I was seen as falling within, as well as different from those that were most commonly seen in HBC and LOLB.

In order to begin this process of diversification, I sought guidance and support from the leaders of HBC and LOLB. One of the leaders of HBC immediately took out her address book in order to connect me to various former members of the group (individuals who maintained an identity as part of the group but no longer attended meetings regularly). This leader was viewed by the HBC membership, as well as the local community, as a well-respected and powerful community elder, so her sponsorship of my project was invaluable.

The leader of LOLB also went to great lengths to support the expansion of my sample beyond the LOLB community. She connected me to individuals she knew through community events but who were not involved in self-help groups. One of these contacts was heavily involved in a network of individuals in the inner city who advocate for anti-violence. This woman not only took part in an interview but also connected me to several individuals who had lost loved ones to violence, including an individual who runs an anti-violence program in the inner city. I spoke to this individual about the need to diversify my sample to include more individuals unaffiliated with co-victim self-help groups, men, and people of color. Since he fit these characteristics, he volunteered to take part in an interview and invited me to his office to discuss my work in more detail. This initial meeting led to my inclusion in a community outreach event outside his office that week. While there, several individuals who worked, volunteered, or utilized services of the program asked to become interviewees.

This snowball strategy was highly advantageous because it led to connections to folks who had different social experiences and upbringings than myself and who lived and worked in areas beyond the boundaries of those I had frequented. I connected to co-victims with whom I would have been unlikely to cross paths, had it not been for the relationships I had built over the years, including homebound elderly individuals.

The resultant diversity within my sample allowed me to not only include those who were seen by the world as blameless victims, but also those who were less likely to fit neatly into notions of "ideal" victimhood.[23] In order to best understand the effects of homicide on co-victims, I sought to include the stories of those who are likely to be perceived as "ideal" victims as well as those who are not. This was no easy feat, as building rapport with a wide array of storytellers can be difficult and time-consuming. Gaining trust can be especially challenging in cases in which the storyteller feels his or her story was previously misunderstood or misused and in instances in which the narrator has been outcast or attacked after the telling of his or her story. In my work, the process of building relationships over the course of several years fostered my reputation in the community as a person deserving of trust. This led me to connect to many individuals I would not have otherwise come into contact with and whose confidence I may not have been able to gain, including several participants who felt they were not perceived as an "ideal" victim. Particularly valuable were the stories of men of color who had had experience within gangs, had engaged in drug-trafficking, and/ or had been previously incarcerated for violent offenses. In many cases, once I had gained the trust of these storytellers and proved myself as genuine in my intent, I was viewed as a part of an inner circle. Participants connected me to friends and neighbors, offering their support as proof of my authenticity, and shared detailed stories that sometimes lasted several hours. A handful of participants told me that the stories they shared with me were ones they had never shared previously or had only shared with their most closely trusted others, such as spouses or siblings. Such narrations became mutually benefi- cial, as several participants shared how they felt unrestrained in their telling and therefore heard in ways they had not previously. The opportunity to share their stories in this fashion fostered within them a sense of the story having great importance and purpose.

It should be noted that my recruitment continued beyond the sample of 36 co-victims whose experiences are discussed in this book. Though I had reached saturation (discussed below) on the topics I initially set out to study, the complexity of these issues, coupled with the sociological focus of this work, motivated me to seek out deviant cases and cases with unique demo- graphic compositions. In particular, when I began analyses focused upon variation in emotion and identity by race and social class (which are discussed in Chapter 7), it became obvious that my sample of 36 was lacking. Because all but one of the co-victims in the current sample who resided in areas of concentrated disadvantage self-identified as people of color, questions remain as to whether cultural or structural explanations are most appropriate for understanding variation in experience.

In order to untangle the issues of culture and structure (race and social class), I purposively sought additional interviewees who were people of color who were raised and currently resided in areas of concentrated advan- tage and white co-victims who were raised in impoverished areas and were currently living in such environments. This was no easy feat, but, after many false starts, I succeeded in recruiting and interviewing nine co-victims fitting these specifications. These efforts also led me to form relationships with leaders of a third self-help group, FVL, whose membership consists of indi- viduals who self-identify as people of color and who have a range of social experiences and social histories. Through these connections, I was invited to attend a monthly meeting as a guest and was subsequently invited to return on three occasions. This also led to interviews of several members of this third self-help group. However, these interviews are not included in the current analysis. Analyses from these additional interviews will be forthcoming.

Response Rate

One of the challenges often faced by qualitative researchers is low response rates. This can be especially problematic if the research involves lengthy interviews; if the topic under investigation is sensitive or uncomfortable; and if the researcher is an outsider of the group under investigation, whether that be with regard to having experienced the phenomenon being explored or in terms of demographics or social history. For these reasons, I began this work with at least three strikes against me in terms of reaching a high response rate. Given the nature of my analyses and intentions with this work, I stood in solidarity with many other qualitative researchers before me in that forming generalizations from my findings was never my goal. Based upon my project title alone, I knew that my sample would be biased. The presence of the word "forgiveness" within my title would undoubtedly limit my work in terms of the variety of co-victims who would be interested in hearing about my project, willing to complete an interview, and openly discuss their experiences and perspectives.

Despite this awareness, the low response rate of this project was, at times, frustrating and disheartening. On several occasions, I connected with individuals who seemed quite interested in the project and in sharing their ideas and perspectives in interviews. I would pass along my contact information, excited to hear from them. But time would pass and contact was never made. In other cases, interviews were scheduled but, shortly before they were to take place, I would hear from the individual that they needed to reschedule. Being understanding to both sudden scheduling conflicts and anxieties that may cause potential interviewees to reschedule, I would wait a few days before attempting to make contact with these co-victims again. Unfortunately, on several occasions potential interviewees would not return my calls or emails. I established a sort of pattern of attempted contacts, in order to remain respectful of the person's need for space and time, maintain motivation and excitement regarding inclusion of the person's voice in the project, and strive to be as non-invasive as possible. This pattern began with the initial attempt to reschedule, a few days after the canceled interview, by phone or email, depending upon which the individual had provided and communicated a preference for. If I was not successful in connecting,

I would then wait one week before attempting to make contact again. The language I used in both of these attempts focused upon rescheduling the interview. After the second attempt, I waited another week, at which point my intention would shift. Rather than being a humble request for rescheduling an interview, this final call or email would be with the intention of communicating that I hoped all was well and that I would always be available to them if they wanted to reach out or make contact. In this way, I hoped to leave potential interviewees with a sense of acceptance and non-judgment. I wanted to ensure they knew that there were no hard feelings and that I would remain open to including their voices in my work, if and when they felt motivated to connect. The vast majority of such potential interviewees were never heard from again, but I felt comfortable in my process, communicating that their perspectives and voices are valued and sought after, but that the level of respect for their comfort and unique healing processes took precedence over this project. On a few occasions, potential interviewees did eventually make contact, usually after seeing me at subsequent victim-centered events. When reconnecting with such individuals at these events, I did not pursue an interview, rather I expressed delight at seeing them and inquired about their current situation (e.g., "How is your daughter? She must be out of school now, right?," "Did you get back up to the mountains this winter?"). This inevitably led these individuals to inquire about my work, asking politely about the state of the project or my degree. This provided me with the opportunity to mention that I was still recruiting people who wanted to share their stories. A few such conversations led to the individual asking if they could still take part by doing an interview, which, of course, I gladly scheduled.

It is interesting to note that the response rate for potential interviewees varied drastically between regular members of the self-help groups I attended monthly and all others. By far, the highest response rate for this project came from within LOLB and HBC. Nearly every regular attendee of each of these groups eventually took part in a one-on-one interview for this project, leading to a response rate over 90%. I believe this is a consequence of the strength of rapport I had built with these individuals by regularly attending monthly meetings and other events at which they were present. Although they knew of my research and this project, these regular members did not view me as a researcher. Instead, many viewed me as a friend, and others who I had not formed friendships with viewed me as a friend of a friend or, at the very least, as a part of their support community surrounding loss to homicide.

The second highest response rate was among those who considered themselves members of LOLB or HBC but did not regularly attend monthly meetings. Given my close relationships with the leaders of each of these groups, as well as the friendships formed with other members, this group of individuals also gave me the status of a friend of a friend. Though I did not keep detailed records of attempts made to recruit interviewees, I would estimate the response rate for this group to hover around 50%.

Without question, the lowest response rate in this project came from individuals who were not directly connected to the groups and events I observed and participated in. Such potential interviewees heard of my work through others who either took part or had a connection to me through avenues only peripherally relevant to this work. For example, colleagues and acquaintances who inquired about my research often attempted to connect me to individuals they knew from within their personal or professional circles who had experienced loss to homicide. Rarely did such connections lead to completed interviews, although many such leads resulted in phone conversations or emails, during which the individuals expressed intentions of taking part in an interview. I would conservatively estimate the response rate for this group of co-victims at 10–15%.

Saturation

Early on, I knew that it would not be possible to reach saturation on all of the topics I was interested in studying with this dataset, especially given that there are so many factors involved in a sociological exploration of this sort. Therefore, I aimed to reach saturation on the main topics I decided to investigate early in the project, namely definitions of forgiveness, emotion, and identity. By the time I concluded recruitment for this analysis, I had engaged in nearly three years of participant observation and had reached saturation on these main issues.

At each new interview, I was able to anticipate the way interviewees would answer various questions, based on the first clues I received. That is, once I had one piece of information that could place them within the identity matrix I was constructing, I could use the patterns uncovered with previous participants to effectively predict other pieces of data that I had not yet inquired about. For example, when J. R. suggested that I meet his friend, Deion, who was heavily involved in the anti-violence program J. R. directed (evidencing a transcender identity), I expected to meet someone who was future-focused, forgiving, and compassionate. When I later met Deion, he embodied the transcender identity perfectly. My field notes after our first conversation during a community outreach event demonstrate support of my prediction:

> *Deion certainly fits the transcender identity. He is very focused on helping kids and the community, on the future. He definitely sees* [the anti-violence

program] *as a platform to do wider good for those who may be "headed down a bad path," like he was. He says he has definitely forgiven. His focus is unquestionably outward.*

On the other hand, when Lorraine (a survivor) invited her son, Mark, to meet with us over breakfast, she said *"He's still very angry about the whole thing."* With that piece of information, I was able to anticipate that Mark would fit within a victim identity, maintaining a focus upon the past and the self; engaging in retributive acts or groups; and using language that indicated other negative sentiments toward the young men who killed his brother. Although Mark did not engage in any groups related to his co-victim experience, he demonstrated the key aspects of the victim identity, sharing details about his rage, vengefulness, and inability to *"move on."* He said:

> *I don't ever wanna graciously forgive these three kids and I don't ever wanna risk hating them less, and I don't ever wanna risk my justified rage ... I've sent one of the kids back to prison, because I have a lot of shady friends—not shady friends but cab drivers and bartenders, and people come and tell me things sometimes about the guy that's been released already, because they run into him late at night in a cab, and then I take that information and go to his parole officer, and he's back in jail, in prison for nine more months.*

By definition, when a qualitative researcher is able to correctly predict data before it is presented, he or she has reached saturation. At that point, I was collecting more stories, but I was not learning anything novel about the three co-victim identities and how they related to forgiveness. I therefore had reached saturation and began focusing more directly upon analysis.

Participant Observation

In order to supplement the data collected through interviews, I performed participant observation of local, relevant networks and events. Over the course of approximately three years, I attended monthly meetings of three co-victim self-help groups; local charity events and fundraisers surrounding issues of victimization or loss; private and public memorials; advocacy and community outreach events; and holiday and family gatherings. In total, my observation included 57 self-help group meetings, 36 public victim-centered events, and three private events.

During monthly meetings of HBC and LOLB, the two self-help groups at which I began observation, members begin by introducing themselves and sharing their stories. Each month I took this opportunity to introduce myself to anyone I had not yet met and explained my role as a researcher.

I mentioned the invitation I had received from the leader of the group and that I had interviewed several of the people in the room. Allowing for observation of meetings had become commonplace in both groups, and on a few occasions others in the room were also students from various schools and a range of departments studying issues such as grief and justice. During the meetings, I said very little but remained a part of the conversations when asked direct questions. Meetings were often followed by less formal conversations in hallways or parking lots, and members typically included me in such conversations, often inviting me to upcoming victim-centered events.

When invited to public victim events, I typically sought out the individual who invited me after noting details about the area, setting, people in attendance, and overall tone of the event. I then remained close to the individual who invited me, often entering into conversations between him or her and others at the event. When introduced to individuals I had not yet met, I told them briefly about my research and how I had met the individual making introductions. When attending a public event to which I was not directly invited, I assumed a position behind the other attendees and observed from a bit of a distance.

Pairing Participant Observation and Semi-Structured Interviews

The pairing of participant observation and semi-structured interviews is well suited for investigations of this sort because it allows for deep insight. Some participants spoke directly about the benefit of my presence within multiple interactions. For example, Letishia said she felt I could *"see"* her more clearly by hearing her story of loss. She said, *"I remember I met you at the barbecue, but* this *opportunity* [the research interview] *allows you to see me more."* She felt that our one-on-one conversation offered the opportunity to dive more deeply into issues she would not normally discuss in mixed company. Tanya shared a similar perspective. At the event described at the start of this book, and revisited in this chapter, Tanya introduced me as a *"friend"* despite the fact that we had only recently met. Having spent time together in multiple venues, she came to view me as a trusted confidant. This was most clearly demonstrated when she openly shared her concerns about the tension between her youngest son and her fiance. Tanya indicated that she felt that I was the only person she could discuss the issue with, and she told me that it was not an issue she disclosed to others. Both Letishia and Tanya felt that my presence in multiple moments of vulnerability and candor led to a depth of knowing that was unique and powerful. Having had this experience with several co-victims, I agree with these women wholeheartedly. The power of the bonds formed through this work allows for a degree of insight that would not otherwise have been possible.

This pairing of methods also allowed for broad consideration of the language chosen by participants in various social contexts. Analyzing the language participants used to describe offenders in a range of social circles allowed for insight into the speakers' attitudes toward the offenders as well as information about what groups the participants viewed the offenders and the self as falling within. Individuals may be averse to acknowledging commonality between the self and the individuals who took the lives of their loved ones. People are also not necessarily aware of the groups with which they identify, since identities function at both conscious and unconscious levels and people do not always deliberately control their identity processes.[24] When functioning at the unconscious level, people act automatically, out of habit or routine, based on previous experiences acting out aspects of their identities. Therefore, the current methods were chosen to allow participants to construct meaning and relay information without direct questions necessitating conscious awareness or acceptance of similarities. Having the opportunity to listen to the narration of participants' stories at multiple times, in varying contexts, and in different company, allowed me to note changes in the language used and the inclusion of certain aspects of the story, such as forgiveness. For some participants there were clear contextual differences, especially surrounding inclusion of stories of forgiveness and unforgiveness (discussed in the "Feelings of Group Rejection" section of Chapter 7).

Analysis

Throughout the data collection process, I used an inductive, grounded-theory[25] approach to allow themes to emerge from the data. Interview probe questions allowed for a deeper exploration of topics of interest, but only after participants had fully detailed their stories, deciding what aspects of their lives to share, how to describe both self and others, and what language to use. By beginning with observation and the participants' stories, narrated in their own voices and without influence from structured questions, I was able to await the emergence of meaningful themes. Analysis began with several themes that arose naturally from observations and respondents' stories. Inductively developed codes included empathy, understanding, and references to a shared humanity. Given the grounded nature of my work, I decided to use the individual as my unit of analysis, rather than the narrative, as I did not know where my research would lead and I therefore did not want to impose limitations upon my ability to expand my explorations beyond the narratives co-victims constructed and delivered.

As is common in grounded research, my analyses were an iterative process. As my research progressed, I checked novel explanations with new data in order to test theoretical robustness. At times, interview questions were rewritten and several questions were added to the original interview script in order to illuminate underlying processes and seek a deeper understanding of participants' experiences. As themes and patterns emerged within the data, I then took an abductive analysis approach,[26] immersing myself within relevant theories while collecting and revisiting data. I sought theories that explained patterns as well as any anomalies or variation. I organized cases in various manners, attempting to interpret the data in multiple ways in order to gain insight into possible patterns. Throughout the data collection process, I reconnected with several participants to ask follow-up questions and discuss topics that had emerged since their initial interviews. Such follow-up was often informal and took place via email, over lunch, or while sharing transportation or awaiting the start of an event.

I used QSR NVivo 10 to perform detailed analysis of the text using thematic coding.[27] Through use of this software, I was able to code sections of text as relevant for each emerging theme or concept. In doing so, the text remained linked to its original source so that the connection to the social context was readily available. Relevant codes included forgiveness/ unforgiveness, emotion, understanding, empathy, group membership, and group role.

After transcription, I read each interview thoroughly while listening to the audio recording and performed open coding. Where relevant, each interview was considered in reference to notes taken during events at which the participant was present. When new themes emerged, I revisited earlier interviews and observational notes to perform focused coding around relevant themes for the analyses presented in this book. Data was coded based on use of common language as well as contextual evidence. For example, several participants discussed *"anger"* or a lack of *"understanding"* but not every interviewee used this exact language. *"Anger"* was sometimes coded as such based on expressions that describe anger, such as, *"You feel the blood boiling in your veins,"* whereas a lack of understanding was coded as such based on the participant stating things like, *"How can anyone do that? I just don't know. I don't get it at all."*

Use of QSR NVivo 10 also allowed for ease in merging themes or creating sub-themes within larger areas of interest when relationships between concepts became relevant. Several parent and child nodes were produced, including child nodes surrounding direction of emotion (offender-directed, self-directed, other-directed, generalized), valence of language, and direction of focus within the parent node of identity. Codes were also examined across demographic attributes, such as race and gender.

The relationships between nodes were analyzed by creating tables to organize the data into categories. I also used diagrams to visually represent connections, especially as patterns surrounding empathy were fleshed out.

Throughout the data collection and analysis processes, these tables and diagrams were reconstructed several times as connections crystallized. Once final tables were constructed, I tested all analyses for statistical significance using Chi-square.

Ethics in Research with Human Subjects

I took many steps to protect my participants, including various means of maintaining their confidentiality and minimizing risk of harm. What follows is a detailing of several of the measures taken.

Protecting Confidentiality

The names used in this book, and other publications from this project, are pseudonyms and all identifying information was removed from transcripts and field notes prior to analysis. In order to protect confidentiality, I also changed any names that appear within quotes, such as the names of loved ones lost, offenders' names, or names of other co-victims of whom my participants spoke.

Pseudonyms were chosen in a relatively systematic manner. Each participant's name was located within a listing of names given to babies within the United States in the decade of the participant's birth. I then chose a pseudonym that was similar in terms of popularity during that time period. For example, if a 49-year-old female participant's name was within the top 20 names assigned to female babies in the 1960s, her pseudonym would also be within the top 20 names upon that list.

In some cases, I attempted to preserve characteristics of the name that were culturally meaningful. For example, if a name was a common shortened version of a longer, more formal name, I called the participant a similarly shortened name. For example, if a participant were named Matt, short for Mathew, I may rename him Jake, short for Jacob. Similarly, if a participant's name had an unusual spelling, his or her pseudonym would also be unusually spelled. If a name had ethnic or religious connotations, I attempted to preserve these characteristics as well. For example, if a participant's name was that of a Christian saint, his or her pseudonym would also be that of a Christian saint. Taking these measures created pseudonyms that served the purpose of concealing the interviewees' identities while maintaining the character of their names.

Confidentiality among Participants

It is inevitable that participants may recognize their own words or aspects of their stories or ideas within my work. This is inherent to many forms of qualitative research. It is especially likely in a publication like this due to the uniqueness of each case, the atypical nature of loss to homicide in some social circles, and the amount of detail included about each individual's story, experiences, and, in some cases, demographic categorizations.

In a few areas, the reader will notice quotes that are detached from any specific demographics or pseudonym. In these cases, I refer to the speaker as "a participant" or "one co-victim," for example. This is done to further protect the confidentiality of participants who shared their feelings or ideas about topics they preferred to keep private from other co-victims in their social circles. This study is somewhat unique in that many of my participants had such frequent, long-lasting, and candid relationships with one another that it is possible that a participant who reads this work may recognize the story or words of another interviewee. Before publishing, I brought this concern to a mentor of mine who also conducts semi-structured interviews and participant observation of individuals who are closely connected to one another, and she agreed that certain sections of participants' interviews may be best left unnamed for this reason. Detached sections of interviews involve discussion of topics that the participant may be unlikely to share with others in these closely knit social circles. For example, one forgiving participant felt that she was subtly rejected by specific unforgiving co-victims when the topic of forgiveness had arisen in conversation. In order to protect her friendships with other co-victims, her quotes remain unconnected to her story or demographic details. Aside from such sensitive, private topics, it is reasonable to believe that anyone who would recognize the story or words of another participant also knows the details of that person's story, ideas, feelings, and experience, given the frequency and type of interactions between such participants.

Reducing Risk of Emotional Harm

The amount of risk I anticipated for my participants varied depending on the manner of engagement each had with local co-victim events and groups. I did not anticipate any risk to the interview participants who were active members of victim self-help groups that was not present during the meetings that they chose to attend on a regular basis. During these meetings, difficult experiences are discussed openly and disclosure of personal stories can be emotionally challenging. Therefore, the emotionally charged nature of an interview would not be likely to cause unreasonable distress to those co-victims who regularly chose to take part in such meetings, openly discussing the same topics our interview touched upon. I also had no reason to believe that my participant observation of monthly meetings or other events increased the likelihood of such emotionally challenging moments, as my participation in the groups' conversations remained minimal.

I anticipated only minimal risk to interviewees who are not active members of victim self-help groups. Sharing their personal stories with me during interviews raised challenging emotions. Therefore, in initial contacts with potential participants, I took care to be very clear and explicit about the nature of the research and I provided written interview questions to all individuals who were considering participating, so that they were fully aware of the topics we would discuss if they chose to participate. All interviewees were also told that they could stop the interview at any time or skip any questions they were not comfortable answering.[28]

Providing Resources

Another safeguard that I put in place for all participants was providing a list of local support resources for the bereaved and co-victims of homicide in particular. The list included several options, some with monthly in-person group meetings, others with telephone hotlines, each with a different clientele, purpose, and/or philosophy. This list was attached to the consent forms given to all participants in case interviewees felt they needed further support coping with any emotions that arose during, or after, our time together. Each entry provided details about meeting days/locations, if applicable; names, telephone numbers, and email addresses of leaders or members charged with outreach or intake; websites; and a short description of the mission or focus of the group or program.

Choosing Interview Locations

Interviews were conducted at locations of the participants' choosing. The decision to allow this amount of choice was made for several reasons. First, allowing the participant to choose the interview location helped build trust and a solid rapport. It also gave the interviewee a bit of control. Given the feelings of uncertainty, vulnerability, and loss of control that accompany loss to criminal violence, allowing co-victims to make this choice was one small step in rebuilding their sense of empowerment and control over their lives and their stories. Finally, participants were allowed to choose the location of their interviews in order to ensure the level of privacy and intimacy each person felt comfortable within. For some, privacy was a priority, as they did not want to be overheard or seen overcome with emotion. These participants chose to be interviewed in their homes or offices. Others were unconcerned about privacy and preferred a less intimate environment, comforted by the buzz of passersby or diners nearby. These participants chose locations such as coffee shops, park benches, or cafeterias. In some cases, I assume the public location choice served as a sort of safeguard against the expression of raw emotion, as interviewees may have felt more in control of their emotional expressions when surrounded by strangers. Their grief was more easily held at bay in these locales than may have been the case if we had spoken in private.

Developing the Project

Before embarking upon the writing of this book, I analyzed participants' definitions of forgiveness in order to determine if such definitions are variable and to more fully flesh out my own conceptualization of forgiveness before moving forward. I sought to understand whether participants consider forgiveness an emotion, a state of mind, a religious experience, a speech act, a relational gesture, a behavior, or something else. Similarly, I wondered if forgiveness needed to be relational or if it was instead an internal proclamation or decision. Establishing a shared definition within the context of each interview was crucial to fully understanding each participant's perspective and experience. Considering participants' definitions, I also explored how individuals came to hold these definitions. Where do one's ideas about forgiveness come from? If definitions of forgiveness are learned, from whom are they likely to be learned? Are we more likely to adopt the definitions of those we are closest to (intimate partners and close family and friends) or do individuals who have also lived through the tragedy of losing a loved one to homicide become more influential due to a sense of shared experience? The findings related to these questions were published in *Violence and Victims*[29] in 2016.

I then undertook an analysis of the various factors that influence participants' forgiveness processes. I compared participants' answers to explicit questions about the factors that make forgiveness more or less likely to the lived experiences of forgiveness or unforgiveness they described at the outset of their interviews. The findings were published in *Humanity & Society* in 2018.[30] Building upon these foundational analyses, I focused upon the two most salient factors within participants' narratives of forgiveness (understanding and empathy) in order to analyze the social processes through which these forgiveness-fostering factors take root. In doing so, I found that the processes through which forgiveness occurs vary according to the cultural distance between forgiver and forgiven. I found there to be two distinct pathways to forgiveness that exist despite factors that make forgiveness unlikely. The first pathway depends upon the forgiver's ability to effectively assume the role of the offender based upon direct understanding of the social environment in which the homicide occurred. For those without such personal understanding, the second pathway involves a more abstract form of role-taking, which leads to the generation of empathy and compassion through redefinition of the offender as a victim. I determined that this redefinition is triggered by affect control processes, motivated by the incongruence between experienced emotion and the affective meanings individuals assign to their identities associated with the loss of a loved one to homicide. These analyses were first published in the *Journal of Ethnographic and Qualitative Research* in 2019.[31]

Finally, I examined the co-victim identity, including how it is constructed around one's victimization narrative and how it is connected to the emotional transformation of forgiveness. I found that three distinct identities emerge after violent loss. I termed these "victim," "survivor," and "transcender" narratives, and I demonstrate how each narrative type is distinct in terms of focus, tone, and purpose in a forthcoming article in the *Journal of Victimology and Victim Justice*.[32]

As I moved through these stages of analysis, it became clear to me that I was building toward a larger question than any one journal publication could answer. That is where this book was born. I decided to construct a single work that could lead the reader through the various questions that arise when we consider the process of forgiveness after loss to homicide, most poignant of which are "How do co-victims forgive those who take the lives of their loved ones?" and "Why?"

Limitations of Design

Despite its benefits, the methodology employed here limits the conclusions that can be drawn from this data. As previously discussed, the sample size, recruitment strategies, and sampling methods used in this work create limitations for the generalizability of findings.

A sample size of 36 interviewees is relatively large for a qualitative inquiry of this sort, but it removes the opportunity for use of advanced statistical techniques. Generally, sample sizes in qualitative studies are relatively small and are unrepresentative of larger populations, but as Catherine Riessman points out, "Although a limitation, eloquent and enduring theories have been developed on the basis of close observation of a few individuals."[33] Ideally, these lines of inquiry would be explored by multiple researchers, with a variety of both qualitative and quantitative strategies. I hope that this book spurs interest in others who may approach these topics with method-ologies complementary to those used here.

My recruitment strategies increased the likelihood that I have underrepresented those who work full-time, have young children, or are unable to travel, as these individuals may be less likely than others to attend monthly meetings or local events. Also, though the length of time since the murder ranged from four months to 48 years in my sample, I undoubtedly failed to accurately represent the feelings and perspectives of those who are still experiencing intense grief that is manifesting in such a way as to avoid contact with others or with events that trigger memories of the loved one lost. For those whose trauma is too fresh or who do not feel emotionally stable, attending such events or taking part in an interview surrounding the loss may be unthinkable.

My sampling methods created a sample that was disproportionate to the population of all residents in the recruitment areas who have lost loved ones to homicide in terms of race and level of participation in victim social networks. Snowball sampling also created bias in that individuals may have been likely to connect me to others who share similar attitudes toward forgiveness and held similar identities.

It is important to note that a substantial amount of overlap was present in the current sample between three categories of interest: black, Muslim, and having experienced living in areas of concentrated disadvantage. All of the Muslim participants self-identified as black, and all black participants had either directly experienced a violent lifestyle or lived within areas of concentrated disadvantage where such activities were relatively common as compared to their counterparts in more privileged areas. Therefore, further research is needed to untangle the variables of race, religion, and social environment in order to determine if the salience of various factors was culturally influenced, religiously based, or dependent upon one's previous or current social environment. For example, black interviewees were more likely than participants of other races to forgive; but these findings must be considered in light of religion and social environment before definitive conclusions can be drawn. The additional interviews I conducted after conducting the analyses discussed here will allow me to begin to more clearly tease out cultural versus structural factors influencing the forgiveness process, and it is my hope that others will join me in these efforts by creating complementary research projects.

It is also important to note that issues of cultural distance and social class are unavoidably confounded in this analysis. Within this sample, the majority of offenders were from lower socioeconomic classes. Therefore, most participants who stood at a distant cultural proximity from the offenders fell within higher social classes than those participants who personally identified with the offenders based on a shared environment. It is possible that individuals within areas of concentrated advantage are more likely to move to higher levels of generality when considering the identity of others (considering his or her humanity or suffering more generally rather than focusing upon a specific identity) than those within areas of concentrated disadvantage. That is to say, such higher-level abstraction could be a class-based phenomenon rather than triggered by the deflection resulting from the emotions associated with loss to homicide. Further work is needed to untangle these issues.

My sample is also disproportionate in terms of forgiveness. The vast majority of participants in this work had forgiven the individuals who took the lives of their loved ones. This is not to suggest that the majority of co-victims forgive the offenders in their cases. Due to the transparency with which I disclosed the focus of my research with potential participants, my sample was unlikely to include participants who felt strongly unforgiving. Though I always spoke of my work as a study of "forgiveness and unforgiveness,"[34] those who feel deeply angry or had strong motivations toward revenge may have been unlikely to take part in such a study. Also, those individuals who were most likely to attend victim-centered events or to be connected to other co-victims who had taken part in an interview (and therefore recruited through snowball sampling) may have also been more likely to be forgiving.

My findings may also be biased by my presence at the self-help group meetings and victim events. That is to say, my transparency as a researcher may have influenced the actions of those I was observing. This may have been especially true in regard to discussion of forgiveness, or lack thereof. Since participants were aware of this focus within my research, they may have been less likely, or more likely, to discuss such topics and there may have been a social desirability effect influencing their actions and language in this regard.

Though semi-structured interviews provided rich data and a freedom of expression that increases the validity of the findings, such methods may also hinder my ability to effectively uncover discrepancies and inconsistencies in individuals' stories and perspectives. When relying on respondents' own insights we must remain aware of the processes involved in self-presentation. If participants realized that their ideas, perspectives, or narratives were in any way inconsistent, they may have been likely to alter their language, omit aspects of their experiences, or make statements that were not accurate representations of their inner states or past experiences.

Strengths of Design

A qualitative approach is well suited for exploring new theoretical issues and clarifying social processes that we do not yet fully understand. It is ideal for gaining insight into complex, multifaceted processes, such as forgiveness after extreme offense, the generation of empathy, and identity construction. The greatest strength of this project is undoubtedly the wealth of complex, nuanced, and multilayered data accumulated for the cases involved. The use of qualitative methods, prolonged participant observation in particular, allowed for exploration of emotion and identity in context. Gathering data within participants' natural settings, especially observing group interactions, created an ideal setting for an in-depth investigation of these topics. Emotions associated with loss to homicide, as well as the co-victim identity, are most salient in such settings, as participants spend time sharing their stories, reflecting, learning from other co-victims, and both constructing and verifying their co-victim identities.

The pairing of methods utilized here allowed me to observe the narration of several participants' stories in multiple social contexts, which proved invaluable. For example, I witnessed Jeanne narrating her story in six separate contexts: her interview; annual homicide victim memorial events; a panel discussion for at-risk teens; and three different contexts of HBC meetings— those at which only regular members were in attendance, those with new attendees present, and those during which students had come to supplement their education in studies of grief or justice. The extent of my observations also allowed me to witness interactions between participants and a range of others. For example, I was present while Gloria interacted with a wide variety of individuals at meetings of both LOLB and HBC; homicide memorial events; holiday celebrations; fundraisers for victims of intimate-partner violence; and various Crime Victims' Rights Week programs. Witnessing these co-victims interacting in such a wide variety of social contexts allowed me insight into the way their narratives and identities were linked. In shaping and sharing their stories, participants in my sample were constructing and affirming their co-victim identities.

Another strength of this project is the extreme nature of the cases investigated. Other studies of forgiveness focus upon hypothetical and relatively minor transgressions. By investigating what could be classified as extreme forgiveness, this study expands the scope of our understanding of forgiveness and offers a springboard from which other inquiries can follow, investigating cases with varying levels of harm. This qualitative study of real-world, extreme harm may also remove the likelihood of ceiling effects common to quantitative analyses.[35] Participants in this study were allowed the opportunity to express themselves freely and without the constraint of pre-formed answer options, as are used with standardized surveys. These methods facilitate the investigation of wide variation in cases that other methods disallow.

Despite the limitations imposed by relatively small sample sizes and non-standardized research instruments used in qualitative research, there are several processes incorporated into work such as this in order to increase the validity of the results. What follows is a detailed discussion of the processes employed in this study. This section is meant to increase transparency and dependability as readers weigh the conclusions drawn here against various theories, previous findings, and future work.

Increasing Validity

Credibility

The greatest strength of qualitative research such as this is the richness of the data collected. Such data allows for several methods of maximizing internal validity, or credibility. Credibility refers to the truthfulness of the findings or the level of confidence in the accuracy of the conclusions drawn. In this project, I employed the processes of triangulation; member checking and critical review; and persistent observation and prolonged engagement in order to maximize the validity of my findings and interpretations.

Triangulation

The pairing of methods used in this study not only offered a unique and powerful vantage point to the research but also increased the trustworthiness of the findings by allowing for triangulation. Triangulation refers to the process of increasing understanding through consideration of multiple data methods and/or sources.

In this project, I employed triangulation of methods and of sources. The participant observation processes I utilized not only allowed me to triangulate between interviews and observations, but also provided opportunities to observe in a variety of settings and times. Events I observed were both private and public and occurred at different times of year. Some were regular events, happening monthly or annually; others were singular events. Each had its own composition of attendees, some solely consisting of co-victims (and myself), others incorporating other types of victims of crime, and some involving individuals who had never lost a loved one to homicide, such as advocates, governmental figures, social workers, law enforcement, local at-risk youth, and members of local religious institutions. The purpose of various events also differed. Some were memorials; others were meant to raise awareness or funds. Some were designed to support co-victims in particular; others had more broad goals. Some focused upon current or future offenders; others maintained a consistent focus upon those impacted by crime.

Observing and participating in such a wide variety of events related to the co-victim experience allowed me to engage with a wide range of people, both interviewees and those my interviewees interacted with, and to note change over time. It also allowed me to hear interviewees narrate their stories in multiple contexts, with numerous audiences, and under varying circumstances. Finally, since many of my interviewees were also regular participants in events and groups I observed, I was able to compare and cross-check participants' stories in multiple contexts. I observed 18 of the 36 participants interacting with others while taking part in victim-centered events *prior* to being interviewed and observed 22 in such interactions *after* being interviewed (14 were observed *both* before and after being interviewed). If I had only conducted interviews, I would not have had the opportunity to build such strong rapport with my participants (which also increases validity), nor to get a sense of each interviewee outside of the interview setting.

Participant observations also allowed me to address concerns surrounding independence when assessing interviewees' perceptions of the impact of significant others upon the self. An individual's perception of past events, of the influence of others, and of one's own inner thought processes is often less than accurate. By witnessing interactions between participants over time, I was better able to assess the impact others have upon individuals and to then couple this with the individual's perception of these influences, gathered through interviews.

Member Checking and Critical Review

On a few occasions, I shared my work with participants, seeking their corroboration or confirmation of my analyses and interpretations. This process of member checking often took place informally and sporadically. I regularly spoke with participants before, during, and after events, and I reached out to several participants via email who were particularly interested in my project based on their own educational and career backgrounds. I met with leaders of various groups and respected members of the community over lunch several times over the three years this project was in its data-gathering phase, chatting about the patterns I saw arising from my data. In some cases, I not only used these conversations to elicit feedback regarding my analyses, but I also sought advice regarding recruitment and trust-building, especially as it related to connecting to, and building rapport with, individuals who may have been difficult to reach or with whom it may have been a challenge to gain trust.

After this manuscript was fully formed (but still being revised), I shared it with a co-victim who was not a part of my sample and whom I had not met previously. She had never read any of my work nor studied the issues relevant here. She read the manuscript from the co-victim perspective and provided comments throughout, focusing on how my interpretations and findings resonated with her own experience. She said, *"This really made me reflect on my personal experience,"* and she noted that my interpretations were *"spot on."*

At several points, she noted that she agreed with how I *"described the process"* and commented, *"So far, I am reading and nodding, agreeing with everything."*

I also asked that this co-victim pay particular attention to the way the book elicited emotion within her. As someone who could not bring herself to utter the word "forgiveness" in relation to her lost loved one, she was well poised to use a critical eye to evaluate the language and tone of this book. She assured me that, despite the focus upon forgiveness, I had done *"a great job in discussing the various points of views that co-victims may have and didn't place too much favor on just one side."* She further noted, *"I did like that you often included paragraphs devoted to making sure that no offense was taken by the choice of words you used, and then you offered explanations for your use of terms."* She assured me that the section on "Avoiding Value Judgments" was well received:

> *I like that this is here. I think this addresses your concern about trying not to be offensive* [to varying perspectives]. *I think this section does tell the reader exactly that. This research is only focused on the process, not who is right or wrong.*

This co-victim's feedback was invaluable, as it assured me that the language I employed was unlikely to leave readers with varied experiences feeling judged or overlooked.

Finally, I shared this manuscript with a colleague who employs similar methodological strategies in her own research and regularly draws upon the same theories used here. She provided overarching as well as detailed critique as I completed final revisions. Her feedback was also invaluable, as she pushed me to take my analyses further and to bolster arguments through additional elaboration and clarification.

Persistent Observation and Prolonged Engagement

One of the greatest strengths of this work is the sheer amount of time spent in the company of each participant. The methods I employed allowed for deep levels of trust and strong rapport between myself and many of my participants, which facilitated understanding, appreciation for the uniqueness of each situation, and increased validity. I engaged with and observed many participants on multiple occasions, in a variety of settings, under varying circumstances, and in the company of fluctuating groups of people. The self-help group meetings and other victim events that I persistently observed allowed me the recurring opportunity to witness participants with varied experiences and social positions describing their ideas and experiences in their own words through the telling of their stories within a variety of meaningful social contexts. In many cases, these observations were then followed by interviews within which I was able to probe more deeply into topics of interest or inquire about situations or interactions I had observed.

Making myself present for the narration of participants' stories on multiple occasions and circumstances increased the validity of the resulting interpretations by providing the opportunity to build deeper levels of trust and a stronger rapport with participants than is possible in research relying solely upon single interviews. My methods also facilitated understanding and appreciation for the uniqueness of each narrative. For example, in many cases, through extended engagement, I became viewed as a member of the group or community in which my research took place. My presence was no longer questioned and co-victims became very comfortable with me. This increased the likelihood that their social interactions in my presence were truer to their typical behavior than would have been the case in the presence of someone viewed as a stranger or outsider.

Increasing Confirmability

Confirmability was also a goal of this work. Confirmability refers to the extent to which the findings of the research are shaped by the data, rather than being shaped by researcher biases. Triangulation, described above, helped achieve this goal, as did reflexivity and a grounded methodology.

Reflexivity

Throughout the data collection process, as well as the analysis and writing stages, I remained reflexive and attuned to my own biases and habits of thought. As Catherine Riessman points out, the researcher cannot avoid representational decisions that enter the research process at numerous points.[36] For this reason, she encourages researchers to strive for transparency and self-awareness, accepting that one cannot be fully neutral and objective. Knowing this, one must acknowledge and confront the inherent limitations and inevitable biases brought to the research process itself, especially as they relate to interpretation of the words of another. With this understanding, I strived for continued reflexivity, remaining aware of my biases, perspectives, and influence upon the construction of respondents' narratives, as well as my interpretation of these. I continually questioned my own patterns of thinking, with the help of trusted colleagues, and often stepped away from my work for lengthy periods in order to broaden my perspective. My memos from observations and those written prior to, as well as following, all interviews served as a sort of journaling process through which I was able to remain aware of my internal state, assumptions, budding ideas, and fluctuating levels of comfort or discomfort. This level of reflexivity increases confirmability, and therefore validity, by helping the researcher to remain continuously aware of his or her biases and limitations. Only through such awareness can we hope to minimize the effects of our inherent biases.

Grounded Methodology

The use of an inductive, grounded approach[37] in this work also increased the validity of findings. Rather than impose ideas or expectations upon participants through a structured interview script based on rigid research questions or predetermined hypotheses, participants were invited and encouraged to construct meaning in a very personal manner. Patterns and themes arose naturally from within narratives and interactions during victim-centered events. The grounded approach also kept me well connected to my data, as I revisited previous transcriptions or field notes as new connections or topics of interest emerged.

Questions for Further Discussion

1   Is consideration of positionality more important in qualitative research than in quantitative? Why (not)?
2   In what ways might research be biased by a variable response rate (a high response rate in one group or category and a low response rate in another, such as was the case in this work)?
3   Would another three years of participant observation have increased validity in a manner that would be worthwhile in terms of the value or usefulness of this research and its findings? Why (not)?
4   In what ways does trust built between the researcher and the participant influence the research process?
5   Can a researcher ever eliminate his or her biases? Why (not)?

Notes

1   Calhoun, Lawrence G. and Richard G. Tedeschi. 2001. "Posttraumatic growth: The positive lessons of loss." in *Meaning Reconstruction and the Experience of Loss*, edited by Robert A. Neimeyer. Washington, DC: American Psychological Association.
2   Hourigan, Kristen Lee. 2016. "Homicide survivors' definitions of forgiveness: Intrapersonal, interpersonal, and extrapersonal orientations." *Violence and Victims* (31)5:869–887. https://doi.org/10.1891/0886-6708.VV-D-15-00015
3   See Charmaz, Kathy. 1983. "The grounded theory method: An explication and interpretation." in *Contemporary Field Research: A Collection of Readings*, edited

by R. M. Emerson. Prospect Heights, IL: Waveland Press; Glaser, Barney, and Anselm Strauss. 1967. *The Discovery of Grounded Theory: Strategies for Qualitative Research.* Chicago, IL: Aldine.

4 See Riessman, Catherine Kohler. 2002. "Narrative analysis." pp. 217–270 in *The Qualitative Researcher's Companion,* edited by A. M. Huberman and M. B. Miles. Thousand Oaks, CA: Sage Publications; Presser, Lois. 2008. *Been a Heavy Life: Stories of Violent Men.* Chicago, IL: University of Illinois Press; Maruna, Shadd. 2001. *Making Good: How Ex-Convicts Reform and Rebuild Their Lives.* Washington, DC: American Psychological Association.

5 Mishler, Elliot G. 1986. *Research Interviewing: Context and Narrative.* Cambridge, MA: Harvard University Press.

6 Riessman, Catherine Kohler. 2002. "Narrative analysis." pp. 217–270 in *The Qualitative Researcher's Companion,* edited by A. M. Huberman and M. B. Miles. Thousand Oaks, CA: Sage Publications.

7 Riessman, Catherine Kohler. 2002. "Narrative analysis." pp. 217–270 in *The Qualitative Researcher's Companion,* edited by A. M. Huberman and M. B. Miles. Thousand Oaks, CA: Sage Publications (p. 220).

8 See Blumer, Herbert. 1969. *Symbolic Interactionism: Perspective and Methods.* Upper Saddle River, NJ: Prentice-Hall; Cooley, Charles Horton. 1902. *Human Nature and the Social Order.* New York, NY: Scribner; Mead, George H. 1934. *Mind, Self and Society.* Chicago, IL: University of Chicago Press; Stryker, Sheldon. 1980[2002]. *Symbolic Interactionism: A Social Structured Version.* Caldwell, NJ: Blackburn Press.

9 See Becker, Howard S. 1963. *Outsiders: Studies in the Sociology of Deviance.* New York, NY: Free Press; and Lemert, Edwin M. 1967. *Human Deviance, Social Problems, and Social Control.* Englewood Cliffs, NJ: Prentice-Hall.

10 See Maruna, Shadd and Heith Copes. 2005. "What have we learned from five decades of neutralization research?" *Crime and Justice: A Review of Research* 32:221–320. https://doi.org/10.1086/655355

11 See Holstein, James A. and Jaber F. Gubrium. 2000. *The Self We Live By: Narrative Identity in a Postmodern World.* New York, NY: Oxford University Press.

12 Riessman, Catherine Kohler. 1990. *Divorce Talk: Women and Men Make Sense of Personal Relationships.* New Brunswick, NJ: Rutgers University Press.

13 Bury, Michael. 1982. "Chronic illness as biographical disruption." *Sociology Health and Illness* 4(2):167–182. https://doi.org/10.1111/1467-9566.ep11339939; Riessman, Catherine Kohler. 1990. "Strategic uses of narrative in the presentation of self and illness." *Social Science and Medicine* 30(11):1195–1200. https://doi.org/10.1016/0277-9536(90)90259-U

14 Presser, Lois. 2008. *Been a Heavy Life: Stories of Violent Men.* Chicago, IL: University of Illinois Press.

15 Presser, Lois. 2008. *Been a Heavy Life: Stories of Violent Men.* Chicago, IL: University of Illinois Press.

16 See Goffman, Erving. 1974. *Frame Analysis.* New York, NY: Harper & Row.

17 Riessman, Catherine Kohler. 2002. "Narrative analysis." pp. 217–270 in *The Qualitative Researcher's Companion,* edited by A. M. Huberman and M. B. Miles. Thousand Oaks, CA: Sage Publications (p. 232).

18 Riessman, Catherine Kohler. 2002. "Narrative analysis." pp. 217–270 in *The Qualitative Researcher's Companion,* edited by A. M. Huberman and M. B. Miles. Thousand Oaks, CA: Sage Publications.

19 Crossley, Michele L. 2000. "Narrative psychology, trauma and the study of self/identity." *Theory & Psychology* 10(4):527–546 (p. 528). https://doi.org/10.1177/0959354300104005

20 Rosenwald, G. C. and Ochberg, R. L. 1992. "Introduction: Life stories, cultural politics, and self-understanding." pp. 1–18 in *Storied Lives: The Cultural Politics of Self-Understanding,* edited by G. C. Rosenwald and R. L. Ochberg. New Haven, CT: Yale University Press.

21 Riessman, Catherine Kohler. 2002. "Narrative analysis." pp. 217–270 in *The Qualitative Researcher's Companion,* edited by A. M. Huberman and M. B. Miles. Thousand Oaks, CA: Sage Publications (p. 219).

22 Zehr, Howard. 2001. *Transcending: Reflections of Crime Victims.* Intercourse, PA: Good Books (pp. 189–190).

23 Christie, Nils. 1986. "The Ideal victim." in *From Crime Policy to Victim Policy,* edited by E. A. Fattah. New York, NY: St. Martin's.

24 Burke, Peter and Jan Stets. 2009. *Identity Theory.* Oxford: Oxford University Press.

25 See Charmaz, Kathy. 1983. "The grounded theory method: An explication and interpretation." in *Contemporary Field Research: A Collection of Readings,* edited by R. M. Emerson. Prospect Heights, IL: Waveland Press; Glaser, Barney, and Anselm Strauss. 1967. *The Discovery of Grounded Theory: Strategies for Qualitative Research.* Chicago, IL: Aldine.

26 See Timmermans, Stefan and Iddo Tavory. 2012. "Theory construction in qualitative research: From grounded theory to abductive analysis." *Sociological Theory* 30(3):167–186. https://doi.org/10.1177/0735275112457914

27 See Weiss, Robert S. 1994. *Learning from Strangers.* New York, NY: Free Press.

28 No participants skipped questions or stopped the interview.

29 Hourigan, Kristen Lee. 2016. "Homicide survivors' definitions of forgiveness: Intrapersonal, interpersonal, and extrapersonal orientations." *Violence and Victims* (31)5:869–887. https://doi.org/10.1891/0886-6708.VV-D-15-00015

30 Hourigan, Kristen Lee. 2018. "Forgiving the unforgivable: An exploration of contradictions between forgiveness-related feeling rules and lived experience of forgiveness of extreme harm." *Humanity & Society.* 43(3):270–294. https://doi.org/10.1177/0160597618801049

31 Hourigan, Kristen Lee. 2019. "'The gentleman who killed my daughter': Exploring the effects of cultural proximity on forgiveness after an extreme offense." *Journal of Ethnographic and Qualitative Research* 13:212–230.

32 Hourigan, Kristen Lee. (forthcoming) "Emerging narratives in the wake of homicide: Victim, survivor, and transcender." *Journal of Victimology and Victim Justice*

33 Riessman, Catherine Kohler. 2002. "Narrative analysis." pp. 217–270 in *The Qualitative Researcher's Companion,* edited by A. M. Huberman and M. B. Miles. Thousand Oaks, CA: Sage Publications (p. 263).

34 "Non-forgiveness" was the term I used at the start of this research process. However, I soon came to use the term "unforgiveness" in conversations and

analyses, as this term is more consistently used (by both social scientists and lay-persons) to indicate the emotional state I was contrasting with forgiveness.

35 For one example of where ceiling effects may have impeded valid conclusions regarding forgiveness, see Jordan, Jennifer, Marijke C. Leliveld, and Ann E. Tenbrunsel. 2015. "The moral self-image scale: Measuring and understanding the malleability of the moral self." *Frontiers in Psychology* 6:1–16. https://doi.org/10.3389/fpsyg.2015.01878

36 Riessman, Catherine Kohler. 2002. "Narrative analysis." pp. 217–270 in *The Qualitative Researcher's Companion,* edited by A. M. Huberman and M. B. Miles. Thousand Oaks, CA: Sage Publications.

37 See Charmaz, Kathy. 1983. "The grounded theory method: An explication and interpretation." in *Contemporary Field Research: A Collection of Readings*, edited by R. M. Emerson. Prospect Heights, IL: Waveland Press; Glaser, Barney, and Anselm Strauss. 1967. *The Discovery of Grounded Theory: Strategies for Qualitative Research*. Chicago, IL: Aldine.

Appendix

Changing the Causal Direction

In Chapter 7, I argue that the co-victim identity can form independently from group participation. That is to say, though a co-victim identity is supported and verified within group settings, it does not emerge solely as a consequence of such group interactions. Below, I offer the reader the opportunity to view the crosstabulation of the identity and group participation variables in the opposite causal direction to that which was displayed in Chapter 7. Table A, therefore, takes each category of group participation and breaks it down by identity type. Therefore, the table indicates what percentage of all those falling into a certain group participation category displayed each type of identity. For example, in the first cell, the 57% indicates that 57% of all non-active interviewees displayed a victim identity. This table may become useful to a reader interested in exploring this topic with new methods and theoretical foundations. I look forward to such advances, as all conclusions drawn from the current project are open for reconsideration and reinterpretation as new knowledge arises and new methods are employed.

Table A Co-Victim Identities by Group Participation (*n* = 36)

Co-victim identity	Group participation		
	Not active	Past/present-focused	Future-focused
Victim identity	4	4	0
	(57%)	(50%)	(0%)
Survivor identity	2	4	2
	(29%)	(50%)	(10%)
Transcender identity	1	0	19
	(14%)	(0%)	(90%)
Total	7	8	21
	(100%)	(100%)	(100%)

Chi-square test's *p*-value < 0.001.

Index

actor, behavior, object (ABO) event 57–8, 69, 72, 77–80, 83, 86, 88, 90, 93, 95, 97, 176

abstract role taking *81*, 83, *89*, 92–5

actor, as used in Affect Control Theory *see* actor, behavior, object (ABO) event

Adams, Richard 80, 176

affect control 77–9, 95, 220; affect control theory 57–8, 77–8, 80, 86, 88, 92, 94–7, 176–7

affective commitment 106–7, 124–5, 132, 160–1, 166

affective meaning 78–9, 92, 97, 220; activity 78, 81, 95, 177; evaluation 78, 95, 177; potency 78, 95, 177

Anderson, Elijah 62, 72

Armour, Marilyn 123–4

attitudinal expectations 95, 109, 120–3, 126, 132, 154–5, 178

behavior, as used in Affect Control Theory *see* actor, behavior, object (ABO) event

behavioral expectations 109, 120–3, 126–7, 132, 154–5, 160, 178

benevolent forgiveness **11**, 14–17, 24–5, **25**, 31–2, 34, 68, **105**, 135, 141, 165, 171, 178, 195, 197–8

blameworthiness 5

Burke, Peter 109, 137n17

Clark, Candace 85

cognitive dissonance 44

commitment 106–7, 161; affective commitment 106–7, 124–5, 132, 160–1, 166; interactional commitment 106–7, 132, 161, 166

compassion 6, 14, 32–4, 47, 57, 73, 81–2, 88–9, 92, 95, **105**, 117–20, 148, 155, 158, 170, 178, 197–8, 220

conceptualization 13, 58, 175, 195–7, 199–200, 219

confidentiality, protecting 216–17

confirmability 227

credibility 224

Crenshaw, Kimberlé 169

cultural distance *see* cultural proximity

cultural proximity 60, *61*, 77, 95; close cultural proximity 60, 69, 72, 88–9; distant cultural proximity 60, 78, 80, 221

cultural scripts 77

definition of the situation 6–7, 48–9, 51–2, 65, 69–70, 78–80, 82, 85, 87–8, 94–6, 175

demographics, of sample 10–13, **11**

emotion norms 6, 20n17, 42, 44, 51–2, 79, 154, 157–8

emotional segue 148

empathy **40**, 44, 46–8, 58–60, 62–3, 68–72, 77, 80–1, 84–7, 90–1, 93–4, 115–17, 119, 170–1, 175–6, 181, 198–200, 214–15, 219; experiential empathy *61*, 61–2, 77, *89*, 91, 94, 200; speculative empathy 77, *81*, 86, 88–9, *89*, 91, 94, 200

empathy frames 85

entrée, gaining 185–6, 200

ethnicity *see* race/ethnicity

expectations 6, 44, 69, 86, 107, 110, 154, 157–8, 175, 179, 190, 228

extra-personal forgiveness 195

feeling rules 6, 25, 39, 42–4, 48–9, 51–3, 55n20, 174–6, 181
Ferrucci, Peiro 181
forgiveness fostering factors 39–40, **40**, 45, 219
forgiveness ideologies 39
forgiveness impeding factors 39–40, **40**, 42, 45, 49
Francis, Linda 80, 176

Govier, Trudy 41, 118
grounded theory 199, 214

Heise, David 78, 92
Hochschild, Arlie 52, 170
Hoffman, Martin 58, 62
Hughes, Everett 165
Hurvitz, Nathan 110

identity, person *see* person identity
identity, role *see* role identity
identity, social *see* social identity
identity standards 81–3
identity, survivor *see* survivor identity
identity theory 106–8, 132, 161, 176
identity, transcender *see* transcender identity
identity verification 106–7
identity, victim *see* victim identity
innocence, of victim **40**, 42, 45, 93
Institutional Review Board 184, 216–9
intent, of the act 42, 49, 51, 93
interactional commitment 106, 132, 161, 166
inter-personal forgiveness 195–6
interview script 7, 203–5, 228
intra-personal forgiveness 48, 195–6

loss, multiplicity of *see* multiplicity of losses

MacKinnon, Neil 92
master status 165
McCullough, Michael 62
meaning-making 6–8, 123–4, 181, 202
media 4, 6, 48
member checking 224–5
Mishler, Elliot G. 201
mitigating factors 50
motivation, toward forgiveness 15, 34, 177, 197–8
multiplicity of losses 4

narrative 7–8, 43–6, 49–50, 81, 88, 93, 97, 115, 127, 202–3, 214; narrative analysis 202
non-benevolent forgiveness **11**, 14–16, 24, **25, 105**, 119, 135, 178, 197–8
normative standards 4

object, as used in Affect Control Theory *see* actor, behavior, object (ABO) event
observation, participant *see* participant observation
offender-directed emotion 32, 92, 119–20, 178, 215

parallel emotion 46, 59, 84, 200
participant observation 7–9, 105, 113, 124, 151, 212–14, 217, 223–5
person identity 107, 109, 112–13, 131, 179
positionality 184
pro-social change **40**, 41–2, 45, 93

race/ethnicity 55n20, 60, 138n46, 164, 167–9, **168**, 208, 221
reactive emotion 46, 59, 81, 87, 200
recruitment 12, 205–6, 208, 220–1, 225
remorse 5, 39–45, **40**, 48–9, 93
response rate 209–11
responsibility, acceptance of *see* blameworthiness
restorative behavior 79
Riessman, Catherine 202, 220, 227
Rock, Paul 134
role expectations 59–60, 63, 69–71, 80, 82, **105**
role identity 107–9, 112, 120, 131, 179
role-taking 59–63, 68, 70–1, *81*, 86, 88–90, 94, 171, 175, 219

salience 106–7, 109
sampling 206, 220–2
saturation 211–12
selective affiliation 109, 132
self-concepts 88, 92, 110
self-efficacy 107
self-narratives 117, 202
self-sentiment 78–80, 82–4, 87, 92, 170, 180; fundamental 78–80, 82–3, 88–9, 91–2, 154, 157, 169, 175; situational 78; transient 79

self, theory of 92
seriousness, of an act 5, 68
Serpe, Richard 132
severity, of an offense 38, **40**, 42,
    45, 49, 93
Smith-Lovin, Lynn 171
social class 21n28, 55n20, 60, 138n46,
    166–7, **167**, 169, 171, 208, 221
social identity 80, 108–9, 112, 179
social networks 124, 133, 161, 187,
    206, 221
status characteristics 52
Stets, Jan 8, 59, 94, 109, 137n17
storytelling *see* narrative
Stryker, Sheldon 105, 132
survivor identity 104, **105**, 122–4, 148–9,
    149, 162–4, 166–8, 232
symbolic interactionism 6–7, 51, 59, 77,
    105, 107, 111, 202

tautology 150
thematic coding 215
Thoits, Peggy 7, 51, 108, 133, 137n17

transcender identity **105**, 115–16, 124,
    131, 134–5, 145, 149–50, **149**, 155, 158,
    162–4, **162–4, 166–8**, 169–71, **232**
transparency 188, 222, 227
triangulation 224, 227
Turner, Jonathan 8, 59, 94

understanding 36n4, **40**, 44–7, 58–63,
    69–71, 84, 86, 88–90, 93–5, 114–16,
    119, 154, 175–7, 214–15, 219
unforgiveness **11**, 14–15, 24–5, **25**, 45, 61,
    70, *81*, *89*, 90–1, **105**, 117–18, 195–6,
    198, 215, 230n34

validity 224–8
victim identity 82, 104, **105**, 113, 116,
    118, 121–2, 133–5, 145, 149, **149**, 162,
    162–4, 166–8, 178, **232**
Virshup, Lauren 108, 137n17

Walker, Margaret 118

Zehr, Howard 111, 203

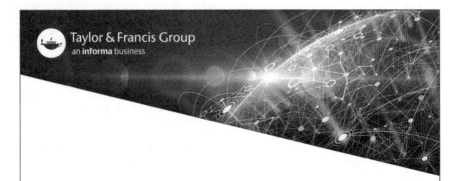